The Leading Rogue State

The Leading Rogue State

The United States and Human Rights

Edited by
JUDITH BLAU
DAVID L. BRUNSMA
ALBERTO MONCADA
CATHERINE ZIMMER

Paradigm Publishers
Boulder • London

Copyright © 2008 Paradigm Publishers

Published in the United States by Paradigm Publishers, 3360 Mitchell Lane Suite E, Boulder, CO 80301 USA.

Paradigm Publishers is the trade name of Birkenkamp & Company, LLC, Dean Birkenkamp, President and Publisher.

Library of Congress Cataloging-in-Publication Data has been applied for.

The leading rogue state : the U.S. and human rights / edited by: Judith Blau ... [et al.].
    p. cm.
  Includes index.
  ISBN 978-1-59451-588-0 (hardcover : alk. paper)
  1. Human rights—United States. 2. United States—Foreign relations. I. Blau, Judith R., 1942–
JC599.U5L39 2008
  323.0973—dc22

                  2008005902

Printed and bound in the United States of America on acid-free paper that meets the standards of the American National Standard for Permanence of Paper for Printed Library Materials.

Designed and Typeset by Straight Creek Bookmakers.

12 11 10 09 08   1 2 3 4 5

To Sociologists Without Borders

Contents

Tables and Figures

TABLES

FIGURES

Introduction
The Leading Rogue State

Frances Fox Piven

When World War II ended, Americans were proudly optimistic about their nation and their future. Americans believed that the United States had played the decisive role in defeating the fascist powers or, as was often said, in saving democracy. And most Americans were confident that the United States would now play a large role in the world guided by their moral commitment to a broad conception of democracy. In domestic politics, business had been chastened and tamed by the economic collapse of the 1930s, and the labor movement was vigorous and growing. The reigning Democratic Party was the party that had changed American society with its New Deal interventions. And the New Deal would become still a better deal, inspired by the principles Franklin Delano Roosevelt had enunciated when the war began, which became known as the four freedoms. In an address to Congress in January 1941, just after the United States entered the war, Roosevelt spoke of a world that honored these essential human freedoms for people everywhere: freedom of expression, freedom of worship, freedom from want, and freedom from fear of physical aggression. With the war's end, movement on that agenda could begin.

These promises did not seem mere rhetoric. The United States quickly took the lead in sponsoring the United Nations, which would bring the governments of all nations in the world together in the pursuit of peace and the human rights delineated by the four freedoms. Then, in 1948, the Universal Declaration of Human Rights was framed and made binding on all members of the United Nations. In 1949, as the split with the Soviet Union widened, two labor federations were established. The United States helped establish the International Confederation of Free Trade Unions. Over time, other human rights codes were elaborated, dealing with civil and political rights, racial and gender discrimination, and the rights of children, migrants, and others. And UN agencies to advise states on the implementation of these rights proliferated. Meanwhile, nongovernmental organizations dedicated to advocating the cause of diverse human rights also multiplied.

1

The moral optimism, even hubris, of the postwar years did not last. One reason was that the United States was soon to be reminded of its own flawed institutions by political movements that pointed the finger of blame at America itself. The civil rights movement began in the 1950s. American self-righteousness could not easily survive the boycotts, demonstrations, and marches by Southern blacks—or the fire hoses, police dogs, Klan murders, and enraged white mobs with which the protestors were greeted. Other shameful aspects of American life were exposed by protests and riots in Northern cities during the 1960s. American moral hubris was strained again by the war in Vietnam, which was depicted on television screens everywhere as a war against helpless villagers. And now there are the wars in Iraq and in Afghanistan. Where once the United States saw itself—and the world saw it—as the savior of oppressed peoples, the United States is now seen as the leading rogue state.

In fact, the grounds for American moral hubris were always shaky. How could the United States be a champion of human rights in the world when for two centuries the fundamental rights embedded in the U.S. Constitution, in U.S. political culture, and in U.S. laws had never been widely honored? Think of the right to vote, perhaps the foundational right in a democracy, and certainly the animating aspiration of the common people—the "people out of doors"—who fought the American Revolution. The right to vote was in fact gradually ceded to white men during the early decades of the nineteenth century and promised to black men by the Thirteenth Amendment in 1866, only to be chipped away again in the closing decades of the century by a convoluted system of voter registration, poll taxes, literacy tests, and organized trickery and intimidation by both political parties. Not surprisingly, the targets of vote suppression were minorities and the less well-off, those whose identities and demands were more likely to be troublesome. The consequence was to virtually purge blacks from the electorate in the Southern states, and to purge most poor whites as well. In the North, it was mainly the immigrant working classes whose votes were taken away. The lesson is simply that rights, even rights that are culturally embedded and backed by laws, are not self-implementing.

Or think about the Emancipation Proclamation, and the Thirteenth and Fourteenth amendments to the Constitution that followed. For over a hundred years the rights to personhood for the freed slaves and to due process under the law asserted by these declarations were deeply compromised, when they were not flatly denied by the system of legal apartheid and lynch-mob terror that returned Southern blacks to the status of deeply impoverished dependent laborers. These human rights, even rights seemingly firmly embedded in law, meant very little on the plantations of the rural South. Power meant more, and even during the heyday of the New Deal, Congress bent to Southern influence and excluded blacks from the labor and social program protections they inaugurated. One could go on to talk about other rights dishonored in practice, such as those of laborers, the poor, or the disabled, but the point is clear. The promulgation of rights as a moral credo or even as a legal code is insufficient in itself to ensure that those rights are realized in social life.

So, clearly human rights talk is rhetoric. But is it merely rhetoric? In fact, there are reasons to think it is not. Political elites have always been afraid of the human rights that practical politics sometimes forced them to rhetorically endorse. In the decades since the post–World War II enthusiasm for human rights, the United States has in fact refused to ratify most human rights protocols, sometimes to the considerable embarrassment of American political leaders.[1] What is it the nation's leaders are afraid of? Or, in other words, when do rights matter?

The answer I think is that the proclamations and declarations and laws and constitutions that pertain to the well-being of ordinary people matter when they become the inspiration of the protest movements that are sometimes the vehicle for popular influence. When the prospects for influence from below are snuffed out by the overwhelming power of the reigning constellation of political forces, constitutional rights do remain idle rhetoric. The Guatemalan constitution recognizes the rights of workers to organize and bargain collectively, and even provides for a judicial system to rule on violations of the labor code. But employers freely ignore decisions of the labor courts, and "illegal firings, plantation closures, temporary contracts, civil lawsuits, trumped up criminal charges, and violence targeting union leaders have all become commonplace."[2]

What is true in Guatemala is also true in the United States. Ideas about rights gain real traction in politics when they become the credo of great popular movements, and this is true despite our relatively developed electoral representative institutions. Think, for example, about the midterm election of 2006, when Democrats won a congressional majority because of the large shift in public opinion against the war in Iraq, and because of growing economic discontent. But the new Congress remained timid. It was reluctant to use its funding authority to end the war and even caved in to the lobbyists protecting the huge tax giveaways to hedge fund and private equity fund executives.

So, what are we to make of the familiar lists of demands for human rights that are part of the American political dialogue? You know the demands: Stop global warming, end imperial foreign policy, inaugurate health care for all, protect workers' rights, economic justice, clean elections, and so on? All such rallying cries are clearly derived from conceptions of human rights, and the peoples of the world, including Americans, should want and have all those things. They should also have the right to clean air and water, to arable land, to domestic markets shielded from floods of subsidized foreign goods, and the right not to be poor by the standards of their society. These rights are unlikely to be championed by the multinational corporations that are privatizing water, outsourcing the pollution and immiseration of globalized systems of production, and leveraging governments to accommodate them. They will gain traction only when they become the battle cries of movements of defiant people who refuse their cooperation on terms that ensure their misery. Just possibly, because it has happened before, those movements can change the world.

And it is in relation to such uprisings that human rights can come to actually matter. Rights talk can empower people, especially when rights are formulated in close communication with the angry and hopeful peoples of the world. The defiant movement of the British working class in the nineteenth century rallied to "the rights of free-born Englishmen." The rights were imaginary, but they were also inspirational because they tapped the myths and hopes of the brutalized workers of England. Our challenge, I think, is to listen very closely so that we can name the rights and evoke the images that will tap the myths and hopes of the ordinary people on whom we depend to stop the leading rogue nation of the world.

NOTES

1.   See Judith Blau and Alberto Moncada, 2007, "It Ought to be a Crime: Criminalizing Human Rights Violations," *Sociological Forum* 22, no. 3 (September): 368; and Judith Blau and Alberto Moncada, 2007, "Sociologizing Human Rights: Reply to Hagan and Levi," *Sociological Forum* 22, no. 3 (September): 382.

2.   See Kimberly Kern, 2007, "Guatemala: Banana Workers Union Leader Assassinated," *Upside Down World,* October 24, available at http://upsidedownworld.org/main/index2,php?option=com_content&task=view&id=971 ...

CHAPTER ONE

~

Human Vulnerabilities
ON INDIVIDUAL AND SOCIAL RIGHTS

BRYAN S. TURNER

The debate about the status and purpose of individual rights as against social rights depends a great deal on how we define these terms. Although it is difficult to come to a definitive philosophical or jurisprudential conclusion about social versus individual rights, textbooks on human rights recognize the difference between the two traditions (Gearon 2003). Furthermore, the difference between these two traditions is consequential in the real world. For example, the so-called twin covenants embrace this distinction. There is the International Covenant on Civil and Political Rights (ICCPR), which was promulgated on December 16, 1966, and came into effect on March 23, 1976. There is the parallel International Covenant on Economic Social and Cultural Rights (ICESCR), which was promulgated on December 16, 1966, and came into effect on January 3, 1976.

The ICCPR is often seen to embrace the classic liberal "negative freedoms," namely a set of rights that are "freedom-from rights," essentially freedom from oppression. By contrast, the ICESCR is regarded as embracing those rights and entitlements that have underpinned welfare systems in both liberal democracies and socialist regimes. They are the "positive freedoms" that provide people in need with resources to achieve certain desirable outcomes. These two covenants became somewhat entangled in cold war ideological conflicts between liberal capitalist democracies and socialist states. The controversial nature of the two covenants is illustrated by the fact that, while they were presented to the UN General Assembly in 1966, it took a further decade before they could be ratified in order for them to come into operation.

It is often said that, while the West has recognized the ICCPR because it is compatible with liberal ideology, socialist states have felt more comfortable with the ICESCR. For example, China has found it easier to support social and economic rights that are seen to be more consistent with its own emphasis on development.

The ICESCR came into force in China on June 27, 2001, but as of 2005, the ICCPR had not been ratified. If we take the view that economic development is a necessary precondition for the enjoyment of rights, then China has made great progress toward establishing a human rights regime.

Whereas somewhere around 22 million people had died of starvation during Mao's Great Leap Forward (1958–1960), China has subsequently managed to feed its own people, which represent 22 percent of the world's population on only 7 percent of the world's arable land. This economic growth is compatible with the notion of a right to development that was accepted by the Vienna Declaration in 1996 (Goldman 2005). Other authors have tried to conceptualize the distinction between authoritarian Asian regimes that often prefer to support social rights and liberal individualistic capitalism by recognizing that in Asia the responsibility of the state to its citizens can be understood in terms of "enforceable benevolence" or "patriarchal benefice" (Woodiwiss 1998). Therefore, attempts to conceptualize the difference between social and individual rights often implicitly or explicitly articulate ideological differences between socialism and capitalism, and hence the conceptual distinction is overburdened by history and ideology.

By contrast with China, the United States has championed the idea of personal liberty and individual rights, and it has therefore been reluctant to support social rights, remaining deeply suspicious of the human rights revolution (Ignatieff 2001). As a result, the United States has found itself isolated internationally, being often hostile to the United Nations and to specific UN institutions. For example, in 1997 the United States refused to join the international community in banning the use of antipersonnel land mines, and in 1998 the United States voted against the creation of the International Criminal Court. The dubious status of Guantanamo Bay in international law in the context of a war on terror has only reinforced this gap (Butler 2004). The situation has been summarized by Geoffrey Robertson (1999, 72) in his *Crimes Against Humanity* when he noted that "the nation with the most to offer the human rights movement in the twenty-first century will, it appears, do so only on the strict condition that other countries are the targets" of human rights legislation.

The United States has been specifically hostile to any formulation of social and economics rights that might limit the functioning its own version of capitalism or question its ideology of individualism. It has consequently opposed the ICESCR. The ideology of individualism is deeply suspicious of state involvement in social benefits and therefore often antagonistic to the development of social welfare rights. While individual rights such as freedom of conscience and freedom of religious belief have been defended, social rights—especially economic rights relating to unionism and labor laws—are regarded as aspects of international socialism. For example, in 1948, the American Bar Association's House of Delegates opposed the Declaration of Human Rights because it contained social and economic rights; the Eisenhower administration attempted to downplay the importance of the twin covenants on rights; and following action by Secretary of State Dulles, the United States did not ratify the Convention on Genocide (Galey 1998; Henkin 1998). The American political elite opposed the Declaration of Human Rights on the grounds that its social provisions smacked of communism, and with the fall of the Soviet Union in 1992, American conservatives were able to celebrate neoliberal economic policies as the only viable global strategy.

They proclaimed the "end of history," insisting that Western-style democracy was the only regime worth defending.

Although there has been much opposition to both covenants, it is necessary to provide a definition of social and individual rights, or at least to offer an analysis of the problems that are entailed by such a definition. Consequently, this chapter is concerned with understanding the differences between the social rights of citizens and individual human rights. Briefly, social rights are those entitlements that are enjoyed by citizens and are enforced by courts within the legal framework of a sovereign state. These social rights may be called "contributory rights," because effective claims are associated with contributions that citizens have made to society through work, war (or a similar public duty), or parenting (Turner 2001). In this model, rights and duties are closely connected.

A system of universal taxation is an obvious indication of the obligations of citizenship. In return for taxes, citizens expect certain benefits, such as security and welfare. By contrast, human rights are rights enjoyed by individuals by virtue of being human, and as a consequence of their shared vulnerability. Human rights are not necessarily connected to duties and they are not contributory. There is, for example, no corresponding system of taxation relating to the possession of human rights. There is as yet no formal declaration of human duties—although there has been much discussion of such obligations. The UN Educational, Scientific, and Cultural Organization (UNESCO) encouraged an initiative for a charter of the duties and responsibilities of states, but these initiatives have yet to have any practical consequence. While states enforce social rights, there is no sovereign power uniformly to enforce human rights. Social rights of citizens are national; human rights are universal, but it is often claimed that these are not "justiciable" and have no "correlativity" with duties.

This apparently neat division becomes blurred in practice, especially in the United States. Because Americans tend to regard the Constitution as a universal declaration of democratic rights, having universal implications for everybody, Americans have often resisted the idea that human rights treaties apply to them. The retention of the death penalty in the United States is in contravention of UN declarations, and the practice of "extraordinary rendition" is contrary to UN norms surrounding arbitrary arrest and unfair trial, as outlined in Article 8 of the Declaration of Human Rights. The U.S. government tends to resist such constraints, either from political expediency or because the Constitution trumps all competing international laws. In popular discourse in the United States, there is therefore a tendency to confuse the civil liberties of Americans (such as the right of black Americans to have the franchise) with human rights, partly because the Constitution is implicitly regarded as a universal legal code.

It is, however, important to retain the distinction. The bottom line is that the social rights of citizens are given (and taken away) by states, but human rights are not given by state legislatures and they cannot be taken away by states. Human rights are frequently the last line of defense against rapacious, arbitrary, and corrupt states.

Hannah Arendt presented an especially challenging criticism of "the rights of Man" in *The Origins of Totalitarianism* (1951) when she observed that these alleged inalienable rights were supposed to exist independently of any government, but once the rights of citizenship with the support of a government had been removed, there was no authority left to protect them as human beings. Human rights without the support of a sovereign state, she argued, are merely abstract claims that cannot be enforced. Critics argue that it is impossible to define what they are or to show how they add much to the specific rights of citizens of national states. The right to rights makes sense only for people who are already members of a political community. Against Arendt, it is important to protect the idea that there is a right to resist arbitrary governments and that the role of legitimate opposition (in a system of political parties) has to be protected. Human rights abuse is characteristically a product of state tyranny, dictatorship, and state failure as illustrated by civil wars and anarchy; a viable state is important as a guarantee of rights. There is a valid argument therefore that the liberties of citizens and their social rights are better protected by their own national institutions than by external legal or political intervention. The often chaotic outcome of human rights interventions in East Timor and Kosovo might force us to the conclusion that any government that can provide its citizens with security, but with weak democracy, is to be preferred over bad and ineffective government (Chandler 2002).

The history of social rights is essentially the history of citizenship. Historians have recognized the growth of citizenship in ancient Greece but also noted its restriction by birth to men, the exclusion of women, the presence of class divisions, and dependence on slavery (Finley 1983). Max Weber (1958) emphasized the importance of Christian universalism in the growth of citizenship in which faith rather than blood was recognized as the basis of community. He contrasted the autonomous city in Europe with the city in the East as a military camp. Although we can detect the ancestry of citizenship in the urban institutions of classical Greece and Rome, there is little evidence of *social* citizenship until the modern period. Because women were excluded from participation in public life, we should hesitate in assuming that citizenship was fully developed in ancient Athens and Rome. It is more accurate to argue that classical citizenship was limited in its scope, and therefore we might suitably call this classical form *political* citizenship, asserting that the revolutionary struggles that produced modernity also produced modern or *social* citizenship. Modern citizenship has two important characteristics: (1) It developed a notion of membership that is not in formal terms dependent on gender and ethnicity; and (2) it is closely connected with the rise of the welfare state.

Citizenship in the context of liberalism is also closely associated with the growth of individualism. However, the modern notion of individualism as subjectivity, the self, and privacy is more or less the opposite of the classical world. In classical Greece, private affairs were often negatively defined in opposition to the public sphere and public duty. The private arena was associated with deprivation (*privatus*), and the public sphere was one of freedom and reason, where citizens congregated for political debate, economic exchange, and entertainment. The autonomous individual could exist and develop only in the public domain. In the "quarrel between the ancients and moderns," Benjamin Constant compared respect for public institutions in the ancient city with the emphasis on conscience and individual subjectivity in modern society.

The liberty of the ancients, which arose from their active engagement in politics, required them to sacrifice their personal interests in their service to the polis. By contrast, the moderns are encouraged to pursue their personal pleasures, regarding politics as merely a means to protect and enhance their private lives. It was only when men left the privacy of the household that they emerged from these biological necessities to participate in politics as free individuals. This distinction was formulated in Aristotle in the contrast between *zoe* (biological life) and *bios* (the cultivated form of life). Men could rise to *bios* only through politics and the public sphere. In modern America, the great emphasis on the emotional integrity of the private individual is the exact opposite of the Aristotelian idea of politics and virtue (Brogan 2005). In modern society, human beings are bound together, but the common threads are paradoxically the private desires of consumption and a common mass culture.

NATIONAL CITIZENSHIP AND THE WELFARE STATE: T. H. MARSHALL

As we have seen, there is a common intellectual tradition that locates the origins of citizenship in the ancient *polis*. It is, however, sociologically more appropriate to treat citizenship as a product of three political revolutions—the English Civil War, the American War of Independence, and the French Revolution. These revolutions were the cradle of both modern nationalism and citizenship as the rights and duties of a person who is a member of a national community. The creation of European nation-states from the seventeenth century necessarily involved the creation of imaginary communities that assumed the existence of, and went a long way to create, homogenous populations. The Treaty of Westphalia in 1648 was the origin of the modern world system of nation-states, and state formation involved the creation of nationalist identities on the basis of a double colonization, both internal and external. This process was the cultural basis for the creation of national forms of citizenship.

National citizenship was politically important because it incorporated the working class into nascent capitalism through the creation of welfare institutions. In practice, welfare capitalism achieved the subordination of the working class with relatively little concession to the fundamental issue of inequalities in wealth and political power. Citizenship left the class structure of capitalism intact, and welfare states avoided the revolutionary conflicts of the class system that were fundamental to Karl Marx's vision of capitalist crises. However, there was great variation within different capitalist regimes. While in Germany Bismarck developed social rights through welfare legislation, political rights were underdeveloped. Neither fascism nor authoritarian socialism supported civil and political rights, although they did develop welfare institutions and social rights.

In the twentieth century, the understanding of citizenship was dominated by the sociological theory of T. H. Marshall (1950). Citizenship expanded through three stages: the growth of legal rights in the seventeenth century produced habeas corpus, the jury system, and the rule of law; political rights in the nineteenth century resulted in the parliamentary system, free elections, and the secret ballot box; and social rights in the twentieth century were associated with social security and the welfare state. Marshall argued that citizenship was a status position that ameliorated the class inequalities that arise from a capitalist market. The British welfare state can be regarded as the practical expression of the sociological theories of Marshall, the economic analysis of J. M. Keynes (1936), and the social policy of Richard Titmuss (1958).

In substantive terms, the mass mobilization of the population for warfare was an important condition for the growth of postwar social rights, but Titmuss also traced the origins of the National Health Service to the medical inspections of the South African Boer War, when the British working class was deemed unfit for combat. The expansion of social rights in the twentieth century was closely connected with military discipline and combat requirements, and subsequently with postwar social reconstruction.

Marshall's account of British social citizenship helps us to identify important differences between the development of citizenship institutions in Britain, the United States, and continental Europe. In British society, citizenship evolved through the nineteenth and twentieth centuries as an amelioration of the negative effects of social class and the capitalist market. Citizenship provided individuals and their families with some degree of social security. The tension in British citizenship is that it assumed significant state intervention in the regulation of the market, but also emphasized individualism, initiative, and personal responsibility. In the United States, citizenship is associated with political membership and assimilation in a society constituted by migration and race rather than with welfare rights and social class. The citizenship debate in the United States is still dominated by the legacy of Alexis de Tocqueville's *Democracy in America* of 1835 and 1840 and the theory of associational democracy. For Tocqueville (2003), the lack of centralized, bureaucratic government in America had encouraged individual initiative and voluntary associations rather than state intervention to solve local, community problems.

Contemporary sociological research has found that Americans were alienated from politics at a formal level, but their commitment to society was expressed through a multitude of local and informal associations (Bellah et al. 1985). Both British and American approaches are distinguished from continental European traditions, where historically citizenship is connected with culture and civility and the civilizing process. The bourgeois citizen was an educated and cultivated private person who depended on the state to guarantee freedoms and to sustain a moral public order against the threat of an uneducated and uncultured working class and peasantry.

The entitlements (or contributory rights) of Marshallian citizenship were conditional upon work, war, and reproduction. A person became an active citizen by contributions to the economy, wartime service, and parenthood. These social conditions have been eroded by the casualization of employment, the termination of conscription and compulsory military service, the transformation of family life through divorce, and the emergence of the lone-parent household. The economic foundations of traditional citizenship were based on a Fordist economy, which has been disrupted by the globalization of the economy. The neoliberal revolution of the late 1970s created a political environment in which European governments were no longer committed to the universalistic principles of the traditional welfare state. Thatcherism in Britain rolled back what she disparagingly had called "the Nanny State" and promoted private initiatives in an enterprise culture. In Tony Blair's government, New Labour policies adopted a "third way" strategy that encouraged joint ventures between public and private sectors in health care and education. Community enterprise was intended to replace the traditional voluntary associations in delivering services in the third sector. The economic results have been overshadowed by growing income inequality, the decline of the National Health Service, and an intractable pension crisis (Blackburn 2002).

THE FABRIC OF AMERICAN SOCIETY

The paradox is that human beings need to be protected from corrupt or failed states by human rights legislation, but they also need social rights to protect them from such conditions as old age, disability, and sickness. Because the United Nations is not a global government with unchallenged sovereign powers, citizens must rely on governments to provide them with a safety net of services: police, education, and health. Of course, the neoconservative criticism of this argument about the role of social rights is to argue that individuals should be expected and encouraged to provide for their own welfare through personal health insurance, installing security devices in their own homes, carrying a gun for personal protection, and so forth. This neoconservative position fails essentially to take notice of the vulnerability that is the common lot of humanity. The dominant U.S. liberal theme of the inviolable rights of (isolated) individuals does not take into account the inequalities and disadvantages that people inherit at birth—we don't start life with equal assets, either social or natural.

Furthermore, the aging of the U.S. population, the inevitable increase in disability and physical immobility, and the isolation and vulnerability of the elderly will produce a large cohort of U.S. citizens whose lives are highly precarious (Turner 2006). There is a tendency in neoconservative views of individual responsibility to "blame the victim" (Ryan 1971). This issue occurred in American public life with the infamous Moynihan report on the alleged inadequacies of the black family to cope with modern urban life (Katzmann 1998). While there may be a tendency to blame single black mothers for welfare problems, how can we blame the elderly for growing old or the disabled for their impairments? At present U.S. institutions are simply not geared up to cope with the consequences of aging populations, shrinking families, poor pension schemes, inadequate heath insurance, and the isolation of elderly men in particular in deprived inner-city areas (Klinenberg 2002). In international terms, the United States does not compare favorably with the Scandinavian countries, Japan, and much of northern Europe in terms of life expectancy, health care of children and the elderly, or death rates (from drugs, suicide, or car accidents) among young men (Kawachi and Kennedy 2002). Despite the liberal vision of an egalitarian society in the United States, income inequality remains the principal determinant of life chances: the more affluent live longer with healthier lives (Daniels, Kennedy, and Kawachi 1999).

The social rights that are installed in the Universal Declaration of Human Rights are intended to give protection to the vulnerable, the weak, and the dependent in order for them to live lives with some dignity. Human rights provisions relating to women are especially important, since without healthy mothers we cannot have healthy children. Article 25—Everyone has a right to a standard of living adequate for health and well-being—is one obvious illustration. Against such human rights, neoconservatives might claim that single mothers, dropouts, drug addicts, and the unemployed are just shiftless, feckless, hopeless people, but aging and attendant disabilities are the common destiny of us all, both rich and poor. Therefore, we need social rights and adequate support to enjoy a modicum of dignity (in old age, in sickness, and in isolation).

There is, by contrast, plenty of evidence to demonstrate that neoliberal global economics have resulted in many societies in increasing poverty, poor health, and declining life expectancy (Coburn 2000). Welfare regimes have been profoundly altered by the Anglo-American neoconservative revolution of the late 1970s, which created a political framework in which governments were no longer committed to such principles as a comprehensive welfare state and full employment. Neoconservative economic strategies were either emulated by or imposed on governments throughout the 1980s and 1990s. These global redistribution strategies that promoted welfare for work saw a reduction of state intervention, deregulation of the labor and financial markets, implementation of free trade, reduction in personal taxation, and fiscal regulation of state expenditure.

New Right theorists argued that judgments about human needs should be left to the operation of the market, not to governments. The historical period of Keynesian redistribution was replaced by more aggressive neoconservative regimes in which the enterprising, greedy, and self-regarding consumer became the driving force of the economy. The free market was claimed to be a necessary condition of personal freedom. Although these doctrines are called either neoliberal or neoconservative, they may well be thought of as a return to the doctrines of the eighteenth century, in which private vices such as greed were assumed to produce public goods such as wealth.

However, the problem facing contemporary American society is that, notwithstanding the claims made on behalf of American civil liberties, there are high levels of child poverty, inadequate medical and pension coverage, and massive income inequality. Given the ideals of the American Bill of Rights, Americans often have difficulty understanding why the rest of the world rejects or questions their democratic credentials and their generosity. One problem concerns the myth of U.S. international beneficence. Of the 0.10 percent of GDP that the United States spends on foreign aid, virtually all of it goes for direct military aid. Of course this leaves us with an even deeper sociological question: Why do Americans remain loyal to the liberal creed? One explanation is the effective manipulation of the media in the aftermath of 9/11. The Bush administration has been successful in using the media to exploit the terrorism threat, showing that there is no foreign policy alternative to the invasions of Afghanistan and Iraq. Only on rare occasions is the fragile nature of American civil society exposed, for example by traumatic events such as Hurricane Katrina (Blau and Moncada 2005).

CONCLUSION: LIBERTY AND EQUALITY

While the French Revolution promised to give us liberty, equality, and solidarity, many contemporary social and political theories tend to confront us with a choice: liberty (the individual rights of liberalism) or equality (the values behind ICESCR). American individualism often presents the dichotomy in even starker terms: Do you want communist authoritarianism or American liberties? In this conclusion, I want to suggest, albeit briefly, that this is a false dichotomy. Apart from anything else, the dichotomy is extreme. Of course, if I am faced with a choice, my rational response is to choose my freedom against welfare benefits, but individual and collective rationality do not always coincide. What is good for me and what is good for the collective often involve very different logics. However, this naive presentation of the choice merely reflects the ideological remains of the cold war.

The threat to liberty from authoritarian governments is nevertheless real, but communism does not have a monopoly over authoritarianism and arbitrary rule. Extraordinary rendition and imprisonment without trial are not the hallmarks of a democracy. We also have to recognize that liberal philosophies in Europe and in America have very different historical locations, accents, and significance. In Europe, twentieth-century liberalism was opposed to both fascism and communism as authoritarian states. Refugees from the catastrophe of fascism and genocide inevitably championed the rights that were inscribed in the ICCPR, namely the negative freedoms from oppression, and they were less interested in social rights.

Intellectuals such as Isaiah Berlin, Leszek Kolakowski, and Ernst Gellner supported individual rights opposing the determinism, reductionism, and social doctrines of both Marxism and sociology. They were concerned like Franz Neumann (1957) in *The Democratic and the Authoritarian State* to understand the roots of political violence, and in the process became suspicious and critical of mass society, the rights of man, and the classless society.

We need, however, to move beyond a cold war framework to think about how the individual rights of liberalism might be married to the social rights of the Universal Declaration. A comprehensive sociology of rights needs to find conceptual solutions to any separation of individual from social rights or to any elevation of one set of rights over another. In this commentary I have proposed that the concept of vulnerability can serve as a foundation for human rights and that analytically the integration of both types should rest on the resolution of the traditional sociological problem of agency and structure. We should not suppress the idea that human beings can be held responsible for their actions, but we need to recognize that social structures (of economic poverty, cultural deprivation, and political oppression) can also rob individuals of their dignity and autonomy. Combining individual liberties with social rights also requires the integration of rights and duties, since without the concept of human responsibility, social rights (indeed any rights) will remain partial and incomplete.

REFERENCES

Arendt, Hannah. 1951. *The Origins of Totalitarianism*. New York: Harcourt Brace.
Bellah, Robert, Richard Madsen, William M. Sullivan, Ann Swidler, and Stephen M. Tipton. 1985. *Habits of the Heart*. Berkeley: University of California Press.

Blackburn, Robin. 2002. *Banking on Death or Investing in Life: The History and Future of Pensions*. London: Verso.

Blau, Judith, and Alberto Moncada. 2005. *Human Rights: Beyond the Liberal Vision*. Lanham, MD: Rowman and Littlefield.

Brogan, Walter. 2005. *Aristotle and Heidegger: The Twofoldness of Being*. Albany: State University of New York Press.

Butler, Judith. 2004. *Precarious Life. The Powers of Mourning and Violence*. London: Verso.

Chandler, David. 2002. *From Kosovo to Kabul. Human Rights and International Intervention*. London: Pluto.

Coburn, David. 2000. "Income Inequality, Social Cohesion and the Health Status of Populations: The Role of Neo-Liberalism." *Social Science and Medicine* 51, no. 1: 62–82.

Daniels, Norman, Bruce P. Kennedy, and Ichiro Kawachi. 1999. "Why Justice Is Good for Our Health: The Social Determinants of Health Inequalities." *Daedalus* (Fall): 215–251.

Finley, Moses I. 1983. *Politics in the Ancient World*. Cambridge, UK: Cambridge University Press.

Galey, Margaret. E. 1998. "The Universal Declaration of Human Rights: The Role of Congress." *Political Science* 31, no. 3: 524–529.

Gearon, Liam, ed. 2003. *Learning to Teach Citizenship in the Secondary School*. London: Routledge/Falmer.

Goldman, Merle. 2005. *From Comrade to Citizen. The Struggle for Political Rights in China*. Cambridge, MA: Harvard University Press.

Henkin, Louis. 1998. "The Universal Declaration and the U.S. Constitution." *Political Science* 31, no. 3: 512–515.

Ignatieff, Michael. 2001. *Human Rights as Politics and Idolatry*. Princeton, NJ: Princeton University Press.

Katzmann, Robert A., ed. 1998. *Daniel Patrick Moynihan. The Intellectual in Public Life*. Washington, DC: Woodrow Wilson Center.

Kawachi, Ichiro, and Bruce P. Kennedy. 2002. *The Health of Nations: Why Inequality Is Harmful to Your Health*. New York: New Press.

Keynes, John M. 1936. *The General Theory of Employment Interest and Money*. London: Macmillan.

Klinenberg, Eric. 2002. *Heat Wave: A Social Autopsy of Disaster in Chicago*. Chicago and London: University of Chicago Press.

Marshall, T. H. 1950. *Citizenship and Social Class and Other Essays*. Cambridge, UK: Cambridge University Press.

Neumann, Franz. 1957. *The Democratic and the Authoritarian State: Essays in Political Theory*. Glencoe, IL: Free Press.

Robertson, Geoffrey 1999. *Crimes Against Humanity. The Struggle for Global Justice*. New York: New Press.

Ryan, William. 1971. *Blaming the Victim*. New York: Pantheon.

Titmuss, Richard. 1958. *Essays on the Welfare State*. London: Allen and Unwin.

Tocqueville, Alexis. de. 2003. *Democracy in America and Two Essays on America*. London: Penguin Books.

Turner, Bryan S. 2001. "The Erosion of Citizenship." *British Journal of Sociology* 52, no 2: 189–209.

———. 2006. *Vulnerability and Human Rights*. University Park: Pennsylvania State University Press.

Weber, Max. 1958. *The City*. New York: Free Press.

Woodiwiss, Anthony. 1998. *Globalisation, Human Rights and Labour Law in Pacific Asia*. Cambridge, UK: Cambridge University Press.

ADDITIONAL RESOURCES

Isin, Engin F., and Bryan S. Turner, eds. 2002. *Handbook of Citizenship Studies.* London: Sage.

Nussbaum, Martha. C. 2006. *Frontiers of Justice: Disability, Nationality, Species Membership.* Cambridge, MA: Belknap Press of Harvard University Press.

Wilkinson, Iain. 2005. *Suffering: A Sociological Introduction.* Oxford, UK: Polity.

CHAPTER TWO

~

Rights to Housing

DAVE OVERFELT AND DAVID L. BRUNSMA

The U.S. does not support the "right to adequate housing" or "housing rights," because such a right does not exist.
— Goli Ameri, U.S. delegate to 2005 UN Commission on Human Rights

Everyone needs a place where they can live with security, with dignity, and with effective protection against the elements. Everyone needs a place which is a home.
— Nelson Mandela (cited in Foscarinis et al. 2004)

Goli Ameri, though perhaps an "innocent" representative of the United States, arrogantly illustrates the consistent position of the American regime—the denial of humanity. Nelson Mandela, on the other hand, roots his understandings in an affirmation of humanity, not ideology, and recognizes housing, space, and place as humanity's epicenter. Herein lies the break between the United States and the majority of the rest of the world. Since the Universal Declaration of Human Rights (1948), the right to adequate housing has been a cornerstone of human rights, giving global moral, political, and social validation to housing as a basic human need. Most states that acknowledge international human rights covenants, treaties, and protocols through ratification recognize the centrality of human rights. These states also concede the real difficulties of achieving human rights via current social and economic structures; yet, despite this realization, states around the globe continue to see human rights as standards of achievement and continue to strive to implement them for their people.

If only some throughout the world or within a given state have palpable, concrete human rights, then none have them at all. However, the United States does not agree and remains an outlier in the worldwide human rights conversation both by arguing that neoliberal market capitalism provides sufficient opportunities for all and utilizing a rhetoric of "rights" that refers only to "individual rights" gained through political

16

endowment, the sole basis for those rights. A perspective such as this effectively denies worldwide consensus to be sure—a denial that forms the ideological roots for Ameri's statement that "such rights do not exist." International human rights doctrine, law, discourse, and struggles *do exist*; however, the United States not only fails to comprehend this, but, through its international policies and imperial aspirations, impedes progress at every turn—as a result, palatable human rights for all remain elusive.

This chapter discusses the collective notion of housing as a human right and the extent to which the United States flagrantly denies this fundamental right to the world's inhabitants, eschewing a discourse on human rights and disregarding the housing needs of its own people. First, we lay out the international language of housing via the prominent human rights documents and discuss the status of the United States within each. Second, we make the case that the U.S. avoidance of human rights laws has brutal results; that concurrently, the United States is taking regressive measures against the spirit of those treaties it has already signed; and that implicitly the United States is required to fulfill the requirements of many human rights treaties in the pursuit of equality. Finally, we consider what must be done to ensure adequate housing for all in the United States, as well as how to move the human rights movement to fruition.

HOUSING RIGHTS AS HUMAN RIGHTS

UN special rapporteur on adequate housing, Miloon Kothari, stated in 2001 that there were 1.6 billion urban and rural residents in the Global South living in overcrowded and poor-quality housing with inadequate access to safe food, water, and sanitation—a situation consistent with the U.S. experience. Yet, unlike the United States, most other nations of the world are making efforts to create and implement social, economic, and cultural structures that encourage human rights within their borders while simultaneously battling the forces of unrestrained economic globalization led by the United States and capitalism. Much of the U.S. roguishness and resistance regarding the right to housing as a human right, or human rights in general, serves to lightly veil (while simultaneously uncovering) the fact that these very same conditions exist within one of the wealthiest countries in the world.

So what does Ameri mean in the opening quote to this chapter? One could take her comments in two ways: (1) that the structural and ideological context of the United States makes such rights as "housing rights" and "human rights" an epistemological impossibility; or, (2) that such rights simply, in social and spatial reality, do not exist for citizens of the United States. Can these two rhetorically coexist? They can, and do, for they are tightly related—their rhetorical incoherence is by design. Looking at the record of the United States on ratifying or signing international human rights agreements, it is clear that the first is what she meant—or is it? In reality, in the United States, far too many live unemployed or underemployed and underhoused in cars, degenerating slums, staircases, cardboard boxes, basements, unsafe buildings, and improvised squatter settlements. The United States cannot agree to such rights to housing because extant structures do not offer such rights to everyone in their own borders. To agree to such rights would mean altering the fundamental structures producing this paradox. The extent to which the United States (read "capitalism") disregards human rights at home and abroad is startling. Internationally, diplomatically, through self-serving and dastardly policies of aid, relief, intervention, etc., as well as through its own Constitution and the institutions under the umbrella of "the state," the United States proposes equal opportunity while structurally denying it to the vast majority, thus denying humanity.

Housing Rights within Human Rights Protocols

The first and most central piece of international legislation in the development of the human rights dialogue is the 1948 Universal Declaration of Human Rights, which not only explicitly recognizes the human right to adequate housing but all of the rights discussed in this volume. In 1969, the Vienna Convention on the Law of Treaties clarified what it meant to be a signatory to an international treaty. In this, every signatory to an international treaty, ratified or not, should refrain from any retrogressive measures or actions that would violate the object and purpose of a treaty; in addition, no state may use internal law as a reason for not fulfilling this obligation of making good faith efforts to implement the provisions of said international treaty. In setting the stage for a structure of recognition and enforcement of human rights in this environment, housing was a central component of these movements.

The International Covenant on Economic, Social, and Cultural Rights (ICESCR) passed on December 16, 1966, went into force on January 3, 1976. It was signed by Jimmy Carter, but never brought to the Senate for ratification. Concerning this key housing covenant to which 148 states are party, 142 have ratified, while 6 other states have only signed—the United States, Belize, Laos, Liberia, Sao Tome/Principe, and South Africa. The ICESCR is a spectacular covenant, including five basic parts and thirty-one articles. This covenant includes the human rights to adequate housing; self-determination; nondiscrimination; work, including safe conditions, fair wages, equal opportunity, and holidays; leisure time and rest; unionization (national, international, strikes); social security; social insurance; family formation; care of children; motherhood; food production and security; physical, mental, and community health; human development; education; cultural life; benefits of science; creative activity, etc.—all positive human rights as dictated by the ICESCR. It also includes various negative human rights articulations (i.e., rights that the state or private entities cannot take action to remove), stating that all humans are due these rights free from state oppression, military or police intervention, exploitation, etc.

The human right to housing is also mentioned in the Convention Relating to the Status of Refugees (1959, Chapter IV, Article 21), the International Covenant on the Elimination of All Forms of Racial Discrimination (1965, Part I, Article 5, ratified in the United States, 1994), the Convention on the Elimination of All Forms of Discrimination Against Women (1979, Part III, Article 14), the Convention on the Rights of the Child (1989, Part I, Article 27), and the International Convention on the Protection of All Migrant Workers and Members of Their Families (1990, Part IV, Article 43). Apart from the International Covenant on the Elimination of All Forms of Racial Discrimination, the United States has only signed the others. The right to housing serves as a critical cornerstone upon which many other human rights can gain fruition. For example, access to proper sanitation (which, in itself, is key to maintaining gainful employment) and potable water is rather difficult without some sort of housing; the United States simply does not see the importance.

The centrally relevant articles of the ICESCR for an understanding of housing as a human right are Articles 10 and 11. Article 10 assists families as the fundamental unit of society, protecting mothers and children from exploitation—it specifies the right to safe physical spaces—that is, housing. Article 11 is more direct, stating that "the States Parties to the present Covenant recognize the right of everyone to an adequate standard of living for himself and his family, including adequate food, clothing and *housing,* and to the continuous improvement of living conditions" (Center for the Study of Human Rights 1994, 12, emphasis ours) and that states will take appropriate steps to ensure the realization of this human right. The plethora of human rights safeguarded by the ICESCR is deeply tied to the rights to housing, yet people are put in the position of having to choose between one fundamental human right (housing) and others (health, food, safety) while not guaranteed any.

Housing Rights within Human Rights Organizations

There are several other impressive human rights organizations that highlight housing as a human right: the UN Human Settlements Programme (UN-Habitat) and the Organization of American States (OAS). The UN-Habitat is direct in its mission: "to promote socially and environmentally sustainable towns and cities with the goal of providing adequate shelter for all." Mandated by the UN General Assembly, their mission is outlined and supported by the Vancouver Declaration on Human Settlements, the Habitat Agenda, the Istanbul Declaration on Human Settlements (in which the United States was the only dissenting voice), and the Declaration on Cities and Other Human Settlements in the New Millennium. However, surprisingly, the least known, yet highly relevant organization is the Organization of American States (OAS) with membership stretching from Canada to Chile.

The founding documents of the OAS, the American Declaration on the Rights and Duties of Man and the American Convention on Human Rights, both require member states to respect the right to housing (among many other human rights) regardless of ratification status. The United States is a member of the OAS and, as such, is subject to the obligations inherent in OAS membership. Having signed the OAS charter, the United States is required to take constructive steps toward the establishment of equality among all in its territory and to do nothing to impinge upon the securing of these rights in other member states. The U.S. position in this organization, as an imperial power, is to pollute these treaties with watered-down language to make sure not only that they are toothless but that the United States will not get into hot water over not doing anything about implementing them.

THE LEADING ROGUE STATE ON HOUSING ABUSES

Since the United States has thus far refused to ratify the pertinent human rights treaties, there is technically no legal obligation that requires progress in housing rights. However, as we have already mentioned, there are a number of important documents that have strong implications and, in this sense, the United States is doing very poorly from an international perspective. As a wide variety of organizations review housing indicators in the United States, the following is a brief review. However, before we discuss the failure to provide adequate housing, we must first make the nature of adequate housing understood.

According to a developing international consensus, "adequate" housing requires that housing fills all of the following requirements: It must be affordable, habitable, and accessible, with a security of tenure, cultural adequacy, and a location sufficient for employment possibilities and necessary services. It is important to emphasize here that the right to adequate housing has never been interpreted internationally to mean that the government must supply housing to all those who request it without charge; instead, it requires that all those nations that are party to the treaty will work, by all appropriate means possible, to progressively ensure that everyone has access to such housing.

Having refused to ratify most of the treaties on human rights, the United States has been quite resistant to the growing international and domestic consensus on the centrality of the right to housing. On the other hand, having ratified both the Convention on the Elimination of All Forms of Racial Discrimination and the International Covenant for Civil and Political Rights, the United States has committed itself to offering all peoples equal access to housing and the creation of conditions in which everyone can enjoy full access to political, social, and cultural rights. Since the United States is internationally committed to ensuring and creating equality, there has been great international concern over the growing inequalities in the United States as women, children, racial and ethnic minorities, the disabled, and the elderly are all disproportionately affected by these conditions. Furthermore, with adequate housing deeply intertwined with possibilities for adequate employment (and many other important, everyday facts of living, e.g., hygiene and health), the nature of the commitment to equality requires greater attention to equality in housing. In other words, housing is essential to the everyday existence of humans.

Despite the fact that most of these treaties are not currently enforceable by U.S. law, U.S. courts have recognized that the interpretation of domestic law must not conflict with international treaties. Thus, while federal law often overrides conflicting international law, the international law has the status of common law when the federal statute is ambiguous or absent; furthermore, international law overrides conflicting national laws. Recently, many federal courts have made reference to international laws and treaties in developing their decisions. It is particularly important to note this emphatically: *Courts are already paying attention to international laws whether or not these treaties have been ratified!* In fact, there are some constitutional scholars (e.g., Charles Black and Akhil Amar) who see the Constitution, in the Ninth and Thirteenth amendments, as having already created the right to minimum sustenance, including housing.

Thus we can find that, in the federal Constitution and many state constitutions, the United States is responsible for the well-being of its people. The people of the United States have a right to be well, and housing is a cornerstone of achieving these rights.

Abuses

The difficulties of attaining, maintaining, and affording adequate housing in the United States are widespread and systemic. According to COHRE, there are only four counties in the United States in which a full-time minimum-wage worker can afford one bedroom. Nationwide, an increasing percentage of wages is being spent on housing. In 1991, 38 percent of minimum-wage workers' wages were spent on housing; by 2001 this had increased to 45 percent, leaving, for example, single mothers spending as much as half of their income on housing (COHRE 2005). Importantly, the shift toward service jobs in the labor market continues to increase the difficulty of attaining and maintaining gainful employment, let alone finding the kinds of blue-collar jobs of the post–World War II era that offered a lifetime career with benefits. The lifetime increase of these workers' wages remains small in this era, and these trends have continued to worsen during the days of the Bush administration, as welfare programs of all sorts have been under attack.

The compounding, gendered, and racialized nature of all this leaves the minimum-wage worker in a precarious position that, with even the slightest absence from work, could result in a disastrous fall into poverty and, in the worst-case scenario to which 3.5 million people have fallen victim, homelessness. If the latter becomes the case, the possibilities for an adequate living situation grow even thinner as the criminalization of homelessness becomes widespread. Police departments increasingly pursue and arrest the homeless while destroying what little property they may have, making already difficult lives more so. Despite a nationwide lack of shelters and beds for those without, a crackdown continues, leaving the homeless with fewer and fewer places to go.

The widespread and growing poverty throughout our nation increases the already difficult and expensive process of attaining and maintaining adequate housing. In order for housing to be considered "adequate" the United Nations states, in General Comment 4, that the following must be present: legal security of tenure, availability of services, materials, facilities, infrastructure, affordability, habitability, accessibility, location, and cultural adequacy. In fact, 3.8 percent of U.S. whites, 13 percent of Hispanics, and 22 percent of blacks live in housing that is severely to moderately deficient (Foscarinis et. al 2004). Without access to adequate housing facilities, the possibilities for living the life our culture tells us to live grow increasingly slim—the possibility of individually fully engaging in political and economic rights becomes a ruse in the midst of structured and systemic denial of adequate housing—making human rights a much needed discourse and reality in the United States.

Even if one is able to gain access to adequate housing, increasingly frequent forced evictions add a level of difficulty in maintaining this housing. The primary cause for an increase in forced evictions in the United States has been the growing gap between housing costs and the incomes of minimum- and low-wage workers;

furthermore, public housing cannot begin to meet the needs of the poor. Importantly, current policy trends are working to exacerbate this problem through decreasing the amount of public housing available in general. Finally, while mixed-use policies (the new gentrification) sound better on the surface and have been positive in a purely economic sense, there has not been a one-to-one replacement of public housing. As the poor are told to leave public housing and neighborhoods are "rehabilitated" in an effort to break up concentrations of poverty, the promises of helping the poor out of poverty go unfulfilled as public housing is unevenly replaced with far less-affordable housing, single-family dwellings and loft apartments. Indirectly then, these mixed-use policies create forced evictions.

Finally, the possession of adequate housing also plays a role in the development of rights for self-determination, nondiscrimination, employment (including safe conditions, fair wages, equal opportunity, holidays), leisure and rest, unionization (national, international, strikes), social security, social insurance, family formation, care of children, motherhood, food production and security (in 2002, the U.S. Census found that 12.1 million households containing 35 million people were "food insecure"), physical, mental, and community health and safety, human development, education, cultural life, benefits of science, and creative activity, among others. Adequate housing is the grounded and rooted space wherein these things humanly develop. The point of this list is essentially to emphasize the fact that all of these rights are tightly connected; without all of these rights, it is hard to establish any of these rights.

WHAT MUST BE DONE? WHAT COULD BE DONE?

While it may be "painful" for citizens of the United States to consider housing as a human right—they must begin to do so—the pain of the enduring structural and systemic inequality in the access and affordability of adequate housing and its intimate linkages to other basic human rights is much greater for the majority of its citizens. There is a gulf of difference between individually based civil rights and collectively rooted human rights! The average citizen of this, the United States of America, not to mention the heads of government, business, the military, education, and science, must tackle these collective questions head on. To do that requires an epistemological shift, a shift in the grounds for knowledge about the world and its concomitant future. As there is a difference between individual and collective rights, there is a correlate difference between individual civil rights law and collective, international, human rights law. Many countries are realizing the ineffectiveness and logistical nonconstitutionality of the former framework that works well for capital and a few vested individuals and turning instead to the latter, a more inclusive and expansive framework that provides the possibility of working for all.

In the United States, there currently appear to exist two basic strategies for pursuing the human rights of its citizens: nonjudicial and judicial. The nonjudicial route has been a consistent, grounded struggle of the people working with NGOs through community organizing and through activists mobilizing and educating others on the abuses of human rights by the current structure. For example, Neubeck (2006) describes the Poor People's Economic Human Rights Campaign, which gathered testimonies to document human rights violations in the United States. Its principal strategy has been to petition the Inter-American Commission on Human Rights, leading to a historic housing hearing in 2005; such work should continue and build bridges between other peoples' movements. Groups and movements such as these monitor and report on local, state, and federal levels of government with particular attention to their compliance with international treaties. We must organize and write reports to the United Nations on the U.S. status regarding housing. This leads to an idea of local implementation of human rights doctrine, treaties, protocol, etc. (e.g., Pennsylvania Campaign, Massachusetts Human Rights Bill, California Statewide Economic Human Rights Campaign, Urban Justice Center, etc.). Like the Kyoto protocols, which the United States turned its capitalistic back to, many communities throughout the United States have signed the Kyoto Protocol. Why not locally sign ECOSOC and hold the United States accountable to what the rest of the world is awakening to?

Judicial strategies in a society founded upon individual, capitalist, patriarchal, white supremacist structures and ideologies will continue to be highly problematic for the pursuit of human rights. While federal laws in the United States provide little support for rights to housing, there are many international treaties to which the nation is obligated. Through careful attention to these treaties in conjunction with already existing legal structures, an argument for housing rights is not difficult to make, as we have briefly demonstrated. As Dr. Seuss has put it, there are "thinks we have not thunk yet"—there remain a wide variety of untapped legal possibilities to pursue. Yet, such "thinks" would still, eventually come up against an antiquated and anti–human rights constitution such as that of the United States. The U.S. Constitution will have to be rewritten, like those of so many other nation-states around the globe, to incorporate human rights—such a convention has never been called. This is imperative, for it forms the foundation from which the institutions and structures of the society operate. Seeing a constitutional convention as a human convention, rewriting the U.S. Constitution, politicians like Charles Rangel (D-NY) and Jesse Jackson, Jr. (D-IL), have introduced legislation to amend the U.S. Constitution to establish, in these cases, a right to housing (much like in South Africa).

The time *has* come—it has not passed. The local, national, and global impacts of doing nothing (or doing the same thing and expecting different results—the definition of insanity) are disastrous! While there is a lot of catching up to do, it is essential that Americans understand their entitlement to collective human rights, and that the ruse of individual rights coupled with state-sanctioned inequalities based on false notions of meritocracy, etc., in an increasingly interdependent world leads nowhere. We must raise the status of human rights discourse in the press, national politics, in our communities, writing, and lives. We must organize and write reports to the United Nations on the U.S. status regarding human rights in the United States. We must demand human rights in our particular corners of this country, and if this country will not respect them, take it to the international community. The manner in which the United States enters this epistemological revolution, this discussion of human rights, this discourse and praxis of human rights, is crucial: Our old models of seeing the world will not work, our cognitive capitalism will not work, the ideological contours within which we operate and interpret the world (via civic and political rights, individual rights frameworks) will not work. There are other models that should be given attention, models developed (and being developed) by peoples across the globe for millennia.

The wealthiest nation in the world was made so on the backs of exploited peoples for centuries. At a time long after the worldwide recognition of this history, the litany of U.S. abuses regarding housing remains as atrocious as it has ever been. Given the Vienna Convention, what should be done to the United States for its gross violations regarding this matter? This chapter has started making some suggestions for housing as a human right and for the U.S. role in the human rights revolution more generally. This revolution will be even bigger than the civil rights and anticolonial movements, but for now, the United States remains the leading rogue nation.

REFERENCES

Center for the Study of Human Rights. 1994. *Twenty-Five Human Rights Documents.* New York: Columbia University.

Center on Housing Rights and Evictions and the National Law Center on Homelessness and Poverty. 2005. "Housing Rights for All: Promoting and Defending Housing Rights in the U.S.," in *A Resource Manual on International Law and the Human Right to Housing,* available at http://www.nlchp.org/content/pubs/2007%20Forum%20Human% 20Rights%20Manual%20FINAL1.pdf.

Foscarinis, Maria, Brad Paul, Bruce Porter, and Andrew Scherer. 2004. "The Human Right to Housing: Making the Case in U.S. Advocacy." *Clearinghouse Review Journal of Poverty Law and Policy* (July): 97–114.

Gomez, Mayra, and Bret Thiele. 2005. "Housing Rights Are Human Rights." *American Bar Association, Human Rights,* 32, no. 3: 2–4.

Kalin, Walter, Lars Muller, and Judith Wyttenbach. 2004. *The Face of Human Rights.* Baden, Switzerland: Lars Muller Publishers.

Neubeck, Kenneth J. 2006. *When Welfare Disappears: The Case for Economic Human Rights.* New York: Routledge.

ADDITIONAL RESOURCES

Association for Community Organizations for Reform Now:
      http://acorn.org.
Centre on Housing Rights and Evictions:
      http://www.cohre.org.
Harvard University's Joint Center for Housing Studies:
      http://www.jchs.harvard.edu.
UN Human Settlement Programme:
      http://ww2.unhabitat.org/programmes/guo/statistics.asp.
UN Statistics Division—Housing:
      http://unstats.un.org/unsd/demographic/sconcerns/housing/default.htm.
U.S. Census Bureau, Housing Statistics:
      http://www.census.gov/hhes/www/housing.html.

CHAPTER THREE

~

Health as a Human Right

ANTONIO UGALDE AND NÚRIA HOMEDES

In the first part of this chapter we present the international covenants and declarations that constitute the foundations for the right to health, and we discuss the complexities of establishing systems to protect this right and the potential conflicts between exercising the right to health and other civil and political rights. The second part discusses the performance of the United States in implementing the right to health.

THE RIGHT TO HEALTH IN INTERNATIONAL COVENANTS

One of the first references to health as a right appears in Article 25 (1) of the Universal Declaration of Human Rights: "Everyone has the right to a standard of living adequate for the health and well-being of himself [sic] and his family, including food, clothing, housing and medical care." A more specific recognition to the right to health is enunciated in the International Covenant on Economic, Social and Cultural Rights (Article 12.1): "The States Parties to the present Covenant recognize the right of everyone to the enjoyment of the highest attainable standard of physical and mental health." The constitutions of more than 100 countries include the right to health, and several regional charters affirm the same right, including the African Charter on Human Rights and People's Rights (Article 16) (June 1981) and the European Union Charter of Fundamental Rights (Article 3: Right to the Integrity of the Person, and Article 35: Health Care) (2000).

It has to be recognized that many countries have failed to implement their commitment to health as a fundamental right, and several organizations have been demanding greater compliance (Pogge 2007). Nevertheless, the signing of the covenants and conventions is important, has legal implications, and pressure groups can

25

use them to advance their causes. For example, the acceptance of the international documents and the constitutional mandate to health began to have tangible effects in some countries with the HIV/AIDS epidemic and the availability of antiretroviral drugs. In several countries organized groups of patients took their governments to court, claiming their constitutional right to health and to the expensive antiretroviral treatment. To the dismay of the governments, they were successful. Patients with other treatable and expensive diseases have followed suit, and the right to health is no longer merely symbolic.

HEALTH AS A CONCEPT AND CONTRASTING VIEWS OF HEALTH AS A RIGHT

It has been suggested that social rights have not been embraced by some countries with the same conviction as civil and political rights. The following are possible reasons invoked by these countries for the lukewarm regard to health as a human right: There is no universally acceptable definition of health, and we do not know how to measure the level of health attained by an individual or a community, therefore, we have difficulties in determining to what we are entitled. In the case of mental health, the complexity is even greater. Very often, health is a relative and subjective concept, to the point that two persons enjoying or suffering the same health conditions might have opposite responses when asked about their health status.

It is understood that the right to health does not mean the right to be healthy. Health determinants are multiple, and several of them—such as genetic makeup and a few environmental factors—are at present out of anybody's reach. Furthermore, health status also responds to individual choices, and, as it will be discussed, forcing people to adopt healthy lifestyles might be considered an infringement of civil rights. Forcing citizens to exercise, to eat organic foods, to lower their intake of trans fats, and to adopt other healthy lifestyles or to avoid behaviors that have harmful health consequences would be unacceptable in many societies and beyond the powers of the government.

Promoters of health as a right have retorted that even if the government cannot impose certain changes, it has the obligation to establish the conditions that would enable people to make healthy choices, through promotional activities and providing incentives for positive changes and disincentives to those who promote unhealthy lifestyles. The regulatory power of the state is undeniable, as is its power to protect and promote the health of its citizens. Yet, few states have used this power and responsibility as exemplified by the long battle to control tobacco, traffic accidents, harmful chemicals, or dangerous products.

Public health experts struggle to balance the conflicts between civil and health rights when they need to control the spread of communicable diseases, which often requires the imposition of legal restrictions to the freedom of movement and quarantines. Segregation and isolation have been imposed on those suffering certain communicable diseases such as leprosy, bubonic plague, tuberculosis, and even HIV/AIDS.

Some have even suggested that a right to health is not compatible with some civil rights. Discussing this conflict, Gruskin (2006, 6) affirms that greater clarity about the relationship between health and human rights "is essential to make our work more effective, as well as to enable us [who support health as a right] to make counterarguments that will be persuasive not only to the skeptics but for the public health community at large." The degree of coercion that a government can exercise in the name of the right to health has to be carefully monitored and can be accepted only under exceptional circumstances.

Other authors question the feasibility of implementing the right to health if citizens do not have sufficient food, potable water, basic education, or adequate housing and suggest that attempting to make health a fundamental right could delay economic growth and as a result postpone health improvements. The two sides of the argument, health as a right and the reasons to postpone it until other rights are fulfilled, are well presented in Braveman and Gruskin (2003).

According to other authors, the U.S. refusal to ratify the International Covenant on Social, Economic and Cultural Rights was partly based on two issues: (1) the fact that accepting health as a right could delay and even deny civil and political rights (Lie 2000); and (2) a reaction against socialist nations that place health as a right above civil and political rights, as exemplified by the following pronouncement (Steiner and Alston 1996, 268): "The urgency and moral seriousness of the need to eliminate starvation and poverty from the world are unquestionable ... the idea of economic and social rights is easily abused by repressive governments which claim they promote human rights even though they deny their citizens the basic ... civil and political rights." In sum, the hesitation to include health as a fundamental right has been based on the difficulty of defining health and the ideologically perceived conflict between social and civil and political rights.

GENERAL COMMENT 14 OF THE COMMITTEE ON ECONOMIC, SOCIAL, AND CULTURAL RIGHTS

From the perspective of many human rights experts, health is a fundamental right and essential for all other human rights. General Comment 14 (GC 14), issued by the Committee on Economic, Social, and Cultural Rights (United Nations 2000), details how the right to the highest attainable standard of health (Article 12 of the International Covenant on Economic, Social and Cultural Rights [ICESCR]) can be exercised. The committee recognized that the right to health depends on the realization of other rights contained in the International Bill of Rights, including the rights to life, food, human dignity, housing, work, education, equality, privacy, and freedom from torture, as well as access to information, and the freedoms of association, assembly, and movement. Paragraph 8 of GC 14 says:

> The right to health contains both freedoms and entitlements. The freedoms include the right to control one's health and body, including sexual and reproductive freedom, and the right to be free from interference, such as the right to be free from torture,

nonconsensual medical treatment and experimentation. By contrast, the entitlements include the right to a system of health protection which provides equality of opportunity for people to enjoy the highest attainable level of health.

The ICESCR understands the right to health as the right to attain the highest possible standard of health, recognizing that not all individuals can achieve the same health status due to genetic and socioeconomic differences. Among nations differences will also exist based on the national income and the social environment, such as the presence of violence and armed conflicts. The limitations of the government are also taken into account, and it is accepted that governments cannot resolve all health problems or protect each citizen "against every possible cause of human ill health" (United Nations 2000, Paragraph 9).

According to GC 14, public health and medical care services (i.e., preventive, promotional, curative, and mental and physical rehabilitation) need to be available, physically accessible, economically affordable, culturally appropriate, and of quality. All residents should have equal access to services, including prisoners, undocumented migrants, asylum seekers, and minorities. Of particular relevance for the United States is the legal obligation to ensure that "the privatization of the health sector does not constitute a threat to the availability, accessibility, acceptability and quality of health facilities, goods and services" (GC 14, Paragraph 35).

General Comment 14 establishes clearly what constitutes a violation of the covenant: "A State which is unwilling to use the maximum of its available resources for the realization of the right to health is in violation of its obligations" (Paragraph 47). Violations occur also by acts of omission, for example, the state's failure to regulate organizations and corporations to ensure that their actions do not violate the right to health of those who are in the state's jurisdiction (Paragraph 48).

An additional important detail is that the ICESCR acknowledges that the achievement of such comprehensive goals has to be progressive, taking into account the availability of resources and other social needs. Paragraphs 38 to 42 of GC 14 address the international obligations of the states to provide assistance and cooperation, particularly economic and technical, to help less affluent nations to achieve the same health goal. Because of the influence that the United States has in international affairs, it is important to quote parts of Paragraph 39: "To comply with their international obligations ... States parties which are members of international financial institutions, notably the International Monetary Fund, the World Bank, and regional development banks, should pay greater attention to the protection of the right to health in influencing the lending policies, credit agreements and international measures of these institutions."

THE UNITED STATES AND THE RIGHT TO HEALTH

The problems affecting the U.S. health care system are not new and are worsening. In the words of Alan Sager, codirector of the Health Reform Project at Boston University: "Our health care is in a car that is accelerating toward a cliff" (cited in Appel 2007). Even though the United States has not ratified the ICESCR, it has signed it, and Americans could expect that the government would pay more than lip service to its articles. To verify the U.S. commitment to Articles 11 and 12—that is, to health as a right—we briefly analyze the status of the U.S. health care system along the four basic principles of accessibility, affordability, equity, and quality enunciated by the ICESCR.

Accessibility

Health services are not available in several parts of the country because private health care organizations are reluctant to work in certain locations—for example, in rural areas. Many undocumented immigrants would not approach a health provider because of fear of deportation. Some hospitals and health centers, including charitable religious hospitals, deny services to undocumented immigrants simply because they do not have papers. General Comment 14 states that "health facilities, goods and services must be accessible to all" (Paragraph 12.b), and this includes immigrants regardless of their legal status. The obligation of health workers to offer care to everybody in need is as old as the Hippocratic oath.

Affordability

The number of persons who cannot access health services because of economic con-straints is huge. It is estimated that in 2007 about 47 million people (compared to 40 million in 2000) were uninsured, and one in three residents, or over 100 million, could not afford all the services they needed. The annual cost of health insurance for a family of four was estimated to be about $11,500, an amount unaffordable to many (Conyers, n.d.). But even those with insurance often did not have comprehensive coverage due to preconditions, service exclusions (for example, for drugs, mental health services, physical therapy, hospital care, and health devices), or hefty copayments.

While no health system is perfect and all countries need to make strong efforts to improve affordability of some health services, the United States compares poorly with other Western nations. In surveys conducted in recent years in six industrial nations (see Table 3.1), the Commonwealth Fund found that the United States had the worst affordability scores (Davis et al. 2007).

One of the most sensitive indicators of health is infant mortality. In 2002, the U.S. infant mortality rate was 7.0 per 1,000 live births while the average for seventeen Western European countries and Japan, Canada, and New Zealand was 4.3, and overall, the United States ranks twenty-eighth in the world (U.S. DHHS 2005).

Equity

We can define equity as care that does not vary in quality and accessibility because of personal characteristics such as age, gender, ethnicity, religion, geographical location, and socioeconomic status. Splitting Table 3.1 into two groups (below- and above-average income) we find that in the United States, the poor had significantly more access difficulties than the poor of the other five countries. It is easy to understand

Table 3.1 Comparing Access Measures of Sicker Adults, 2005 (in %)[a]

Cost-related access problems[b]	Australia	Canada	Germany	New Zealand	UK	U.S.
Had a medical problem but did not visit doctor or clinic in the past year because of cost[c]	18	10	20	32	5	44
Did not get a medical test, treatment, or follow-up because of cost the past year[c]	23	15	17	24	5	44
Did not fill a prescription or skipped dose because of cost last year[c]	22	26	15	22	9	51
Last time needed medical attention had to wait six or more days for an appointment[c]	15	35	14	4	17	27
Out-of-pocket expenses for medical bills more than $1,000 (U.S. equivalent) in the past year[c]	14	14	8	8	4	34
Physicians think their patients often have difficulty paying out-of-pocket costs (2006)[d]	27	25	35	39	14	42

Notes:

[a]Sicker adults are defined as persons ages eighteen and older who rated their health status as fair or poor; reported having a serious illness, injury, or disability that required intensive medical care in the previous two years; reported that in the past two years they had undergone major surgery; or reported that they had been hospitalized for something other than a normal delivery.

[b]For reasons of space we have selected only a handful of measures. Using all measures the U.S. score continues to be the worst compared to the other five countries.

[c]*Source:* Commonwealth Fund International Health Policy Survey of Sicker Adults, 2005.

[d]*Source:* Commonwealth Fund International Health Policy Survey of Primary Care Physicians, 2006.

why this is the case. The U.S. health care system is based on an expensive network of private insurance and providers and a limited and decreasing safety net system, while the other countries provide universal health services through national health systems or social security schemes.

Within the United States there are significant equity and access variations by states that are related to differences in income and in state health policies. The proportion of uninsured children varies from a low of 5 percent in Vermont to a high of 20 percent in Texas; the U.S. average is 10 percent (Cantor et al. 2007). When looking at ethnic disparities within the United States, the infant mortality rate among blacks in 2005 was 14.1 per 1,000 live births, almost 2.5 times the rate among non-Hispanic white infants (5.8). Those differences may also reflect disparities in the health status of women before and during pregnancy (U.S. DHHS 2005).

Quality

Compared to the other five industrial nations, the United States also ranks last in many quality indicators, including coordination among professionals, medical and medication errors, persons lacking a regular physician, provision of counter-referral information (containing information on the diagnosis and treatment) to primary care physicians, and physician-patient communication (Shea et al. 2007). The United States scores poorly in the rate of deaths due to surgical or medical mishaps, 0.7 per 100,000 in the United States versus 0.4 in the thirty countries that are members of the Organization for Economic Cooperation and Development (OECD), which includes Korea, Mexico, and Turkey.

Costs

The problems of access, affordability, and quality are not due to lack of resources allocated to health. The ICESCR states: "Each State Party ... undertakes to take steps ... to the maximum of its available resources, with a view to achieving progressively the realization of the rights recognized in the present Covenant" (Article 3.2) [in our case the right to health]. The United States is spending an enormous amount of resources on health, but, as discussed above, is not achieving progressively the realization of the right to health; in fact, the opposite is occurring. The begging question is: What has gone wrong? The United States spends on health care 4.3 times more than on national defense (California Health Care Foundation 2005) and considerably more than any other country in the world (Catlin et al. 2007). In 2005 the country spent $2 trillion or 16 percent of its GNP, and health expenditures continue to escalate well above inflation. It is estimated that by 2015, the figure will double to $4 trillion (20 percent of the GNP). In contrast, other advanced nations with universal coverage spend less of their GDP on health (Switzerland 10.7, Germany 9.7, Canada and France 9.5) (Pear 2004).

Health experts have identified a variety of reasons that explain the waste of health resources, including inadequate use of the infrastructure; poor management, planning, and coordination; and the fragmentation of the system—all of which create inefficiencies. If we try to understand the reasons behind these inefficiencies, we find that one of the most important ones is the ideological approach to health. For U.S. decisionmakers, health is a commodity that can be better supplied by the market. The private health sector has to generate profits and compete. Competition requires large expenditures in advertising and promotion. Competing hospitals purchase expensive equipment that frequently lies idle because there is not sufficient demand, or—even worse—physicians generate unneeded demand for the use of technology, raising the cost of health care and potentially increasing iatrogeniatry. The price of medicines in the United States is the highest in the world because of the government's refusal to accept price controls as do other Western nations. In sum, the driving force of capitalism is the maximization of profit, a principle that is not conducive to the realization of the right to health.

Corruption is another source of wastefulness, and the private health sector is prone to rampant corruption. Health Maintenance Organizations (HMOs), health insurance companies, drug companies, hospital chains, and solo practitioners all overcharge and deceive clients and the government. Box 3.1 includes a good example of abuses by health corporations.

Box 3.1 The Tale of a Hysterectomy in a Tenet Healthcare Hospital

Jenny had a hysterectomy at a Tenet hospital and received a bill of $34,681.26 for a three-day hospital stay, exclusive of medical services and pathology tests, and was billed $5,202 as her co-payment. She was shocked because she had a good insurance package through her employer, and the co-payment was higher than her monthly take-home pay. Jenny was even more surprised when she found out that the insurance company, Blue Cross Blue Shield, had accepted just about 11 percent of the charges or $4,168. After much investigation, her insurance company stated that based on its contract with the hospital the co-payment should be $625.23. A few days later, the patient received a second bill from the hospital in the amount of $29,387.83 ($34,681.26 minus the $3,543.43 paid by Blue Cross Blue Shield and minus her deposit of $1,750 made at the hospital before the surgery). In other words, the hospital was transferring to the patient the amount of the bill that the insurance company did not pay. Jenny, still in recovery at home, was extremely upset since she had been required to sign a statement accepting the right of Tenet Healthcare to confiscate her assets if she failed to pay the charges. After consulting with the legal office of her employer and the insurance company, she found that what the hospital had done was illegal; co-payments were to be based on the payments agreed upon between the insurance carrier and Tenet Healthcare.

To make matters worse, there was a problem with the surgery that could be attributed to low quality of care, and the patient had to have a second surgery. The billing problem repeated itself. If Jenny, a health professional, would have been one of the 100 millions of North Americans without health insurance or without complete insurance, she would have been obligated to pay a total of $63,158.34 for the two operations and a total of six hospital days, an amount above her yearly take-home income from her job as a university professor. In addition to this figure, there were bills from the physician and the pathology lab.

After full recovery Jenny made an appointment with the nurse auditor because she wanted to understand the billing system. She learned, among other things, that the hospital charged $167 for four disposable surgery gowns, $154.50 for six surgical gloves, $186.75 for wire sutures, $57.86 for one Toradol pill (a painkiller), $33.55 for a 500 mg acetaminophen pill, and $170.86 for 30 mg of morphine. She also learned that she was billed for the rent of each piece of equipment used during the surgery, and that her stay in the recovery room was charged by the minute ($16 per minute). Of course, Jenny did not know why she had been kept in the recovery room for such an extended period of time, whether it was because a hospital room was not available or because she had been given more anesthesia than needed. The 196 minutes that she was charged for were well over the normal recovery time, and no explanation had been given by the physician indicating that there had been any complications.

While reviewing the bill with the audit nurse Jenny discovered that she had been double-charged on one occasion and that during the second stay she had been billed at the rate of an intensive care bed instead of a regular room. After just 45 minutes of reviewing the charges, the hospital reduced her bill by $3,926.25. Jenny's case suggests that patients cannot know if invoices reflect services rendered, and most patients without Jenny's training, an internal medicine physician and Ph.D., can be easily robbed by health corporations or, more disturbingly, cannot be certain whether recommended procedures benefit the patient or are prescribed to increase the economic health of the corporations and care providers.

This is not an isolated case. It is estimated that 90 percent of hospitals bills for charges are incorrect and that the errors cost patients an average of $1,350. In some cases, as we have seen, the overcharges can amount to tens of thousand of dollars, and audits have found charges of $129 for a box of tissues.

Source: Interview by first author, January 2003

Overcharging is not limited to hospital corporations. In 2001, Tap Pharmaceuticals paid $875 million to settle a case of fraud against the U.S. government. In 2005, GlaxoSmithKline was fined $150 million for the fraudulent price increase of two drugs (Ugalde and Homedes 2006), and the IRS has asked GlaxoSmithKline for $7.8 billion in back taxes. Recently Pfizer, the world's largest pharmaceutical company, was fined $430 million for attempting to defraud a federal program, and in June 2007 AstraZenaca, Bristol-Myers Squibb, and Shering Plough were asked to pay damages for overcharging Medicare, pension funds, insurers, and patients (*Bloomberg News* 2007). Other health services suffer similar problems; in 2007, the New York State attorney general commented, "We're finding increasingly that home health care seems to offer crooks many opportunities to exploit loopholes and oversights in the regulations" (Confessore 2007). Rare is the month that fines are not imposed on health corporations, the costs of which they simply pass on to the consumer in higher prices.

Executives of health corporations receive high compensation for running inefficient corporations and accumulating profits for the shareholders. For example, United Health CEO William McGuire received $1.6 billion worth of share options in addition to his salary (*United Health Group v. McGuire* 2006). According to the *Investors Business Daily* (Britt 2004) the pay of the five top executives of the top health insurance companies almost doubled over the last four years (2000–2003), to $3 million a year, perhaps as a reward for implementing the 59 percent increase in the price of premiums or for the doubling of annual profits and margins during the same period (ibid.). Families USA (2002) reported that in 2001 the executives of ten big pharmaceutical firms received an average compensation of $48 million. When in 2006 Pfizer's CEO left the company, he received in pension, stock, and other benefits a package worth $180 million (Appel 2007).

Solo practitioners, small groups of practitioners, hospitals, physical therapy chains, HMOs, pharmaceutical firms, and lab companies all compete for a piece of the immense pie of health resources. According to economist Karen Davis (2007), the fragmentation of the U.S. health insurance system leads to very high administrative costs. In 2005, the United States spent $143 billion on administrative expenses. If in 2004, Davis argues, the overhead expenses of insurance companies could have been lowered to the level of industrial nations with low administration costs, such as Japan, France, or Finland, the United States could have saved $97 billion a year (Appel 2007). As Harris (2007) succinctly put it: "Health care [in the United States] often seems to operate by a unique set of economic rules that result in huge inefficiencies."

Blocking the Change from Business to a Human Right

Meizhu Lui, the executive director of United for a Fair Economy, referring to the health sector remarked: "Our government, instead of helping péople, is being held hostage by these profit-making companies" (cited in Appel 2007). Like other industries and interest groups, associations of physicians and other health workers and health care corporations make sizeable political contributions and spend considerable resources lobbying to maintain and increase their profits and privileges. If we put together all the expenses for lobbying by the health care industry, the amount for 2007 is around $444 million (Center for Responsive Politics 2007). According to the Center for Responsive Politics, during the 2005–2006 election cycle (not a presidential cycle), health associations and corporations donated a total of $99 million to political candidates (63 percent to Republicans).

DISCUSSION

The United States has not accepted health as a human right. The contradiction of spending more health resources per capita than any other country in the world and at the same time having lower coverage and more inequitable services than other industrial nations requires an explanation. For U.S. policymakers health is a product like any other, and market forces are the best means to promote competition, lower prices, improve quality, and satisfy consumers. The information that we have presented shows that this is not the case. It does not take a rocket scientist to know that health cannot be grouped in the same basket with other consumer products. The preservation of the myth that health should be treated like any other product has one purpose: capital accumulation. The beneficiaries of the U.S. system are not the majority of the population. Corporations spend an inordinate amount of resources in lobbying and in political campaigns. Elected officials return the favor by promoting the myth and legislation that keeps the system in place. When all the above practices and poor decisions occur in health-providing corporations, the results are very troubling. We are not just discussing low-quality, high-priced products and services; we confront life-threatening situations and unaffordable needed services—in short, the violation of health as a human right.

Presently, the United States is the most influential player in the international arena. The United States has not been satisfied with denying health care to millions of its citizens, residents, and undocumented workers, but has attempted, with more or less success, to export the privatization of health services to other countries under its economic and political dominance. Reasons of space do not allow us to discuss how the U.S. government, regardless of the party in power and in contradiction to Paragraph 39 of GC 14 (cited above), has utilized its dominant position in the International Monetary Fund, the World Bank, and other international and bilateral organizations to replace the solidarity principles upon which the health care systems of other countries were based by those of the market. Bilateral free trade agreements have also been used to open the health care systems of many nations to transnational corporations, to extend the life of drug patents that assure high drug prices, and to weaken public health measures for the benefit of the corporations.

REFERENCES

Appel, Adrianne. 2007. "Profits Soar, along with U.S. Uninsured." Unpublished report. Inter Press Service, available at http://www.commonwealthfund.org/publications/publications_show.htm?doc_id=441618. (Accessed March 31, 2008.)

Bloomberg News. 2007. "3 Drug Makers Are Convicted in Reimbursement Overcharges," June 22, available at http://www.nytimes.com/2007/06/22/business/22Drug.html. (Accessed March 29, 2008.)

Braveman, Paula, and Sofia Gruskin. 2003. "Poverty, Equity, Human Rights and Health." *Bulletin of the World Health Organization* 81, no. 7: 539–545.

Britt, Russ. 2004. "Health Insurers Getting Bigger Cut of Medical Dollars." *Investors Business Daily,* October 14, available at http://www.investors.com/breakingnews.asp?journalid=23544168&brk=1. (Accessed March 29, 2008.)

California Health Care Foundation. 2005. *Health Care Costs 101—2005.* March 2, http://www.chcf.org. (Accessed March 31, 2008.)

Cantor, Joel C., Dina Bellof, Cathy Schoen et al. 2007. *Aiming Higher: Results from a State Scorecard on Health System Performance.* New York: Commonwealth Fund.

Catlin, Aaron, Cathy Cowan, Stephen Heffler et al. 2007. "National Health Spending in 2005." *Health Affairs* 26, no. 1: 142–153.

Center for Responsive Politics. No date. Available at http://www.opensecrets.org/lobbyists/indus.asp?ind=H&year=2007. (Accessed March 31, 2008.)

Confessore, Nicholas. 2007. "Cuomo, Investigating Medicaid Fraud, Issues Subpoenas to 59 Home Care Agencies." *New York Times,* August 21, available at http://www.nytimes.com/2007/08/21/nyregion/21cuomo.html?ref=nyregion (Accessed March 29, 2008.)

Conyers, John, Jr. (no date). H.R. 676 Fact Sheet. Business Will Pay Less. http://www.house.gov/conyers/news_hr676_1.htm. (Accessed March 31, 2008.)

Davis, Karen. 2007. "Learning from High-Performance Health Systems around the Globe." Invited testimony. Senate Health, Education, Labor, and Pensions Committee Hearing. Health Care for All Americans: Challenges and Opportunities. January 10.

Davis, Karen, Cathy Schoen, Stephen C. Schoenbaum et al. 2007. *Mirror, Mirror on the Wall: An International Update on the Comparative Performance of American Health Care.* New York: Commonwealth Fund.

Families USA. 2002. *Profiting from Pain: Where Prescription Drug Dollars Go.* Publication 02-105. Washington, DC: Families USA. http://ipsnews.net/news.asp?idnews=37237. (Accessed March 31, 2008.)

Gruskin, Sofia. 2006. "Rights-based Approaches to Health: Something for Everyone." *Health and Human Rights* 9(2): 5–9.

Harris, Gardiner. 2007. "Report Rates Hospitals on Their Heart Treatment." *New York Times,* June 22, available at http://www.nytimes.com/2007/06/22/us/22hospital.html?ex=1 340164800&en=a0b5b83418c33261&ei=5088&partner=rssnyt&emc=rss. (Accessed March 29, 2008.)

Lie, Reidar K. 2000. "Human Rights, Equity and Health Sector Reform." Unpublished report, available at http://www.ethica.uib.no/rights22.pdf. (Accessed March 29, 2008.)

Pear, Robert. 2004. "U.S. Health Care Spending Reaches All-Time High: 15% of GDP." *New York Times,* January 9, 3.

Pogge, Thomas. 2007. "Montreal Statement on the Human Right to Essential Medicines." *Cambridge Quarterly of Healthcare Ethics* 16: 97–108.

Shea, Katherine K., Alyssa L. Holmgren, Robin Osborn, and Cathy Schoen. 2007. "Health System Performance in Selected Nations: A Chartpack." Unpublished report. New York: Commonwealth Fund.

Steiner, Henry J., and Phillip Alston. 1996. *International Human Rights in Context: Law, Politics and Morals.* London: Oxford University Press.

Ugalde, Antonio, and Núria Homedes. 2006. "From Scientists to Merchants: The Transformation of the Pharmaceutical Industry and Its Impact on Health." *Societies Without Borders* 1: 21–40.

UN Economic and Social Council. Committee on Economic, Social, and Cultural Rights. 2000. Substantive Issues Arising in the Implementation of the International Covenant on Economic, Social and Cultural Rights. General Comment 14. E/C.12/2000/4. New York: United Nations. Available at: http://www.unhchr.ch/tbs/doc.nsf/(symbol)/ E.C.12.2000.4.En. (Accessed March 29, 2008.)

United Health Group, Inc. v. McGuire, (2006). U.S. District Court Case No. 06-CV-1216-JMR-FLN.

U.S. Department of Health and Human Services. HRSA. 2005. Child Care USA. Available at http://mchb.hrsa.gov/mchirc/chusa_05/pages/pdf/c05hsi.pdf. (Accessed March 29, 2008.)

ADDITIONAL RESOURCES

Doctors without Borders/Médecins Sans Frontières (MSF):
    http://www.doctorswithoutborders.org/home.cfm.
Joint UNAIDS Programme:
    http://www.unaids.org/en/default.asp.
World Health Organization:
    http://www.who.int/en.

The two conventions pertaining to *worker organization and union rights* (written in 1948 and 1949) call for countries to allow workers to freely join organizations of their choosing and allow them to exercise their right to organize. This includes protections from antiunion practices and/or interference on the part of employers. Conventions pertaining to *forced labor* (written in 1930 and 1957) call upon ratifying nations to "suppress the use of forced or compulsory labor in all of its forms within the shortest possible period." Forced labor is, in essence, work extracted from individuals involuntarily, often under the threat of penalty.

Child labor is dealt with in two conventions: one dealing with minimum age (1973) and another extended to the worst forms of child labor (1999). The former calls for governments to establish national policies to abolish child labor and minimum ages for employment. The second acknowledges the contemporary realities of child slavery and prostitution worldwide and calls on ratifying members to take immediate and effective measures to eliminate them. The final set of conventions, finalized in 1951 and 1957, call for *equal remuneration and nondiscrimination in employment* by race, sex, religion, political opinion, national extraction, and social origin.

In formulating these conventions and encouraging ratification by member states, the ILO is aiming to set global standards for human rights and worker dignity. Moreover, mechanisms are in place to try to ensure that countries follow through on their ratification. This includes ILO supervision of how a given country is doing in the aforementioned regards, including requiring reports by ratifiers, and publicizing quite explicitly (on its website and via publications) both successes and violations of conventions. The ILO also offers technical assistance to countries that wish to implement conventions, especially those that have weak internal bureaucratic structures. Finally, the ILO attempts to enforce the conventions, where appropriate, by receiving complaints from workers, citizens, and organizations within ratifying countries and moderating efforts to resolve the problem. The ILO's actual enforcement power, however, is relatively weak at best.

Despite a limited ability to ensure compliance with its major conventions, the degree to which countries worldwide have adopted the core or "fundamental" conventions noted above is quite remarkable. Of the thirty-five countries included in the Americas, for instance, twenty-seven have ratified each of the eight conventions. All eight conventions have been ratified by forty-nine of fifty-one European countries. And, worldwide, 71 percent of countries have ratified all eight.

What is surprising in the midst of more general and positive acceptance of these workers' rights standards internationally is the conspicuous resistance of the United States. The United States has passed only two of the eight conventions. One, pertaining to forced labor, was ratified by the Reagan administration during the 1980s in an effort to put pressure on communist countries. The second, on the worst forms of child labor, was ratified under the Clinton administration, which saw engagement with and increased funding to the ILO as a way to address mounting labor tensions in the United States in the face of administration efforts to push through "free trade" agreements (Elliot and Freeman 2003).

The fact that the United States has not ratified conventions pertaining to workers' rights to organize or protection from discrimination in employment is especially troublesome in several regards. First, the United States as a large, powerful, and wealthy country has disparate impact culturally and internationally on what other countries tend to do. Second, U.S. reluctance to ratify existing and quite basic worker protections and, indeed, fundamental rights on the international scene speaks to its priorities both internationally and domestically. As we describe in greater detail below, the United States has become increasingly hostile to the interests of working citizens. It is a notable outlier in these regards and the only major industrialized nation to ratify fewer than half of the eight ILO conventions. In fact, the United States has ratified a lower number of conventions than each and every one of the fifty-one countries of Europe.

Some of the U.S reluctance to be accountable on the international scene can be traced to its history with the ILO, which has waxed and waned considerably with administrations since 1934, when the United States became a member. Fear of signing on to a convention that might conflict with national policy or states' rights has also played a significant role, as has the disparate power of U.S. business leaders in discussions pertaining to the ILO and the stance the United States might take. And, finally, the general reluctance of U.S. labor leaders to pursue a broader, international agenda or, in some instances, push against ILO conventions in favor of more nationalist policies has most assuredly also been a critical reason for the lack of broader support (Elliot and Freeman 2003).

Importantly, the lack of attention and accountability to the ILO conventions has had important implications for U.S. workers and their capacity to collectively organize in the United States. Indeed, combined with significant union legal defeats, the undermining of more radical unionism historically, and now globalization, the status of U.S. workers is tenuous at best. What is especially intriguing about the U.S. case, in the face of what appears to a problematic contemporary scenario, is that historically speaking, workplace justice and worker protections were initially part and parcel of what many viewed as basic U.S. citizenship rights. This has changed over time, however, with the rise of corporate power, legal restrictions on working-class activism, and bureaucratic union politics—all of which, when explored historically, help explain the U.S. status as a rogue nation on the international human rights and workers' rights front. Below we outline the current weakness of organized labor in America and the important historical trends that have led to this present state of affairs.

THE PECULIAR CASE OF THE UNITED STATES

By all accounts, the labor movement in the United States is at perhaps one of the lowest points in the past 100 years. Whether measured by participation in organizing efforts (Figure 4.1), or, more important, the percentage of the American workforce represented by unions (Figure 4.2), there has been a steady decline of organized labor's influence in America. These trends and the weakening of the labor movement that they represent have allowed the federal government to oppose or ignore international pressure on important labor issues. The political and economic landscape today, in fact, is dominated by employers: Time and again corporations in core manufacturing and extractive industries have used the strike to break unions, with little or no political or legal backlash (Bandzak 1992; Rosenblum 1995). Corporations have also been generally successful in avoiding new unionization efforts (Clawson and Clawson 1999; Kleiner 2001), and have been more than willing to move beyond the U.S. borders to secure cheap labor (Cowie 1999).

This assault on organized labor has been facilitated by an increasingly probusiness political and legal climate, beginning particularly with the presidency of Ronald Reagan. It was, after all, President Reagan who legitimized the use of the strike as

Figure 4.1 Percentage of employed nonunion population participating in NLRB-sanctioned organizing drives

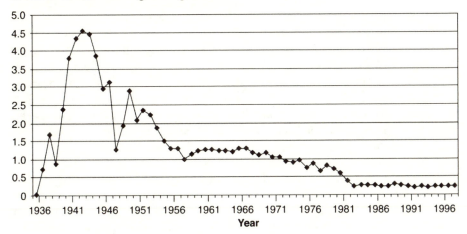

Figure 4.2 Union membership rate

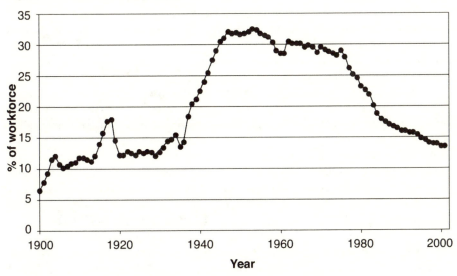

Source: Bureau of Labor Statistics (Hirsch and Addison 1986).

an antiunion tactic when he fired striking air traffic controllers in 1981. Moreover, Reagan's influence extended to the legal dimension of class struggle; he broke with the tradition of appointing both labor and management advocates to the National Labor Relations Board (the federal agency that regulates private-sector labor law) by nominating voracious probusiness candidates, who in turn created a more unsympathetic legal environment for labor unions (Gould 2001). And, while organized labor has adopted more aggressive social movement–style tactics to overcome these hostilities (Fantasia and Voss 2004), there have been a number of restrictions on the behavior of unions, such as limiting the time and manner of picketing (McCammon 1994).

To assume that the United States has always privileged the interests of capital over labor, however, would be to ignore much of this country's political and economic history. Perhaps the most notable high-water mark for organized labor was the New Deal of the 1930s, which instituted many of the protections outlined in the international treaties and conventions described above (particularly the right to organize, codified by the National Labor Relations Act of 1935). As a political figure, President Franklin D. Roosevelt was quite successful articulating the demands of the average working man and woman, effectively building a populist movement that had labor rights at the forefront (Roscigno and Danaher 2001). Moreover, it was under Roosevelt that the United States joined the ILO, sending an important signal about this country's commitment to the importance of dignity at work around the globe.

Importantly, the progressive support of labor rights also predated FDR and the New Deal. In 1912 Socialist presidential candidate Eugene Debs received 6 percent of the popular vote, and, when he ran again while in prison in 1920 (for his opposition to the World War I), he garnered 3.4 percent of the vote. As these and other historical examples illustrate, America has often been a place for more progressive voices when it comes to issues of employment and labor rights. What, then, has led to such a discrepancy between contemporary U.S. policy and that of the rest of the world?

There has been considerable debate among sociologists, political scientists, and historians on this question, and over the validity of "American exceptionalism." Regardless of why socialism could not and did not take hold in the United States, scholars on various sides have identified important historical moments that have pushed the United States in a more probusiness direction.

Perhaps the most thorough and compelling discussion of this shift is outlined in Josiah Lambert's (2005) *If the Workers Took a Notion.* In his analysis, Lambert notes how labor rights, particularly the right to strike, were at one point in American history largely identified by workers and even political leaders as a citizenship right—a citizenship right that was seen as a mechanism whereby corporate political influence could be held in check and basic rights of citizenship and dignity preserved. As Lambert suggests, this right has been eroded by a number of factors, most notably efforts by the executive branch of the federal government to recast workers' organization as strictly an economic right. By doing so, broader legal discussions and ideological connections to human rights were stripped away. Other scholars have come to a similar conclusion; Fantasia (1988) describes how the state was able to legally restrict many union activities (sympathy strikes, refusing to handle hot cargo) that dramatically limited the tactical arsenal of aggrieved workers.

As important as top-down pressure was—a top-down pressure that created an uneven playing field upon which labor confronted corporate power—the dynamics of the labor movement itself have been likewise influential. The history of the labor movement is replete with unions exploiting rightward shifts in the state to advance their own interests and reduce the influence of rival unions. Perhaps the most notable example of this has been the American Federation of Labor and its struggles with other labor organizations, including the Knights of Labor, the International Workers of the World, and the Congress of Industrial Organizations (originally a splinter of the AFL).

Formed in the late nineteenth century, the Knights of Labor represented perhaps the first serious effort to radically reform American society based on the interests of the working class. What stands out about this organization, which was able to unite workers from various backgrounds, both skilled and unskilled, was that it was wholly opposed to overt expressions of class conflict, particularly the strike, instead preferring to establish cooperative ownership of industry. Not surprisingly, however, this proved difficult to achieve, and contentious strikes in places like New Jersey led to significant conflict between the union and employers. As Kim Voss (1993) argues in her book, *The Making of American Exceptionalism,* the hands-off approach of the state and the militant antiunion tactics of employers eventually broke the union, creating an opportunity for the more conservative AFL to grow.

Yet the demand for a more militant approach to unionism did not die along with the Knights of Labor. Only a few years after its death, the International Workers of the World (IWW) was formed, a more militant, vocally anticapitalist organization based on the industrial syndicalism model that eschewed long-term contracts and political campaigns (Dubofsky 1969). Instead, the IWW preferred to win its benefits at the point of production, striking often (or turning up at companies with existing labor tensions) to achieve victories for its constituents. While the AFL was opposed to the IWW, often aligning with employers to break strikes by Wobblies, according to Howard Kimeldorf (1999), the AFL actually borrowed the point-of-production tactics to win members who were otherwise drawn to the IWW. The AFL, however, never embraced the international vision of the IWW and, in some cases, has stood with American industrialists against ILO conventions.

The final, and perhaps most far-reaching, important conflict within the labor movement took place during the Great Depression. It was at this time that the demands for unionization by the growing ranks of industrial workers could no longer be ignored by the craft-oriented AFL. Initially the AFL attempted to address these concerns by forming the Committee on Industrial Organizations, spearheaded by John Lewis and his United Mine Workers of America. When it became apparent that the AFL was not really committed to this new project, witnessed by its failures to organize steelworkers, a number of unions broke away to form the Congress of Industrial Organizations (CIO).

The conflict, while often between craft and industrial interests, was complicated by the growing influence of communist leaders, particularly in many of the CIO unions. Once again, more conservative elements within the movement used broader political and legal shifts to win greater control of the movement. Specifically, the Taft-Hartley Act of 1947, which rolled back some of the union victories of the New Deal, also entailed and reflected the red scare of the day by requiring all union elected officials to sign a noncommunist affidavit. As many have argued (Stepan-Norris and Zeitlin 2003), these leaders tended to be the most militant and successful, and by forcing them out, the labor movement lost a substantial asset. In the process, it also lost momentum and leverage that would have quite likely been used to push U.S. ratification and compliance with ILO conventions.

This purge, the AFL-CIO merger of 1955 that eliminated competition among unions, and a booming postwar economy gave way to a much more docile movement, less interested in international labor law than in protecting the narrow economic benefits of its members. Indeed, some have argued that this period was marked by a labor-management "accord," a tacit agreement that ensured union members access to steady wage increases while restricting their ability to question management's rights on the shop floor (Nissen 1990). This institutionalization of industrial conflict allowed union leaders to achieve new levels of legitimacy in American politics (Mills 1948). Yet such actions also alienated much of the rank and file, witnessed by the growth of wildcat strikes during and after World War II (Zetka 1992).

It is not particularly surprising that the growth of a bureaucratic movement, increasingly disconnected from its base, would be particularly vulnerable to the frontal assault on labor that we have witnessed during the past twenty-five years or so. Moreover, the leaders that came to power during the red scare of the 1940s and 1950s were indifferent and even hostile to international labor concerns (Elliot and Freeman 2003), removing an important pressure point on lawmakers otherwise unwilling to ratify progressive international treaties.

CONCLUSION

If the United States has failed to support the basic mission of the ILO, then the question becomes, what are the implications, if any, of the lack of U.S. leadership on international labor rights? Internationally, U.S. unwillingness to take a stand on these issues has significant ramifications for how global capitalism is implemented around the world. By refusing to sign on to the ILO's conventions, the United States has given domestic corporations the freedom to act with impunity when doing business in other countries (corporations based in a nonratifying country are not subject to the ILO's conventions when doing business in a foreign country, even one that has ratified them). The use of child labor, resistance to unionization efforts, and indifference to poor working conditions are persistent practices that have given rise to considerable anti-U.S. sentiment and opposition to globalization.

Domestically, workers have also been harmed by the willingness of firms to shift production offshore, where companies face few ramifications for violating workers' rights. While the loss of jobs is the most commonly cited consequence of foreign trade, the last quarter century has also witnessed a steady decline in the living standards of American workers; wages are no longer tied to productively, health care has become increasingly expensive, and other aspects of the social safety net, such as pension programs for average citizens and workers, are becoming rare as well. Making a stronger commitment to the ILO would not only send a message to U.S. companies about their labor practices in other countries (and bring at least some measure of enforcement), it would also create new pressures on companies in the United States to implement decent labor standards (many of which are already codified under U.S. law), including workers' right to organize and protection from discriminatory employment practices—discriminatory practices by race and gender, for instance, that continue to pervade U.S. workplaces despite supposed protections embodied in federal law (Roscigno 2007).

Given our earlier discussion of the current state of the U.S. political and economic climate, such a goal may not be easily obtained. There is, however, some room for optimism, particularly the possibility that organized labor in the United States may exert more influence and leverage on the international front. First, after years of ignoring declines in union membership, in 1995 the reformer John Sweeney was elected president of the AFL-CIO on the platform of making organizing a major priority for this organization. The shift toward membership recruitment has picked up so much momentum that some militant unions, including Sweeney's own SEIU, have left the AFL-CIO to establish their own federation, Change to Win.

Importantly, this new shift has a distinctively international flair. First, organized labor strongly opposed U.S. ratification of free trade agreements like NAFTA. While part of this concern was motivated by the fear of job losses, there has been a growing recognition among unionists that recent immigrant communities from Central America and Asia hold the key to labor's future. Ruth Milkman (2006) describes how the recent revitalization of Los Angeles's labor movement, for instance, has been driven heavily by the influx of immigrant workers into key unions. To the extent that these workers bring a greater awareness to labor issues in other countries, then it seems that organized labor in America may become increasingly concerned with broader, international protections of workers' rights offered by the ILO. Indeed, perhaps the coupling of workers' rights with basic human and citizenship rights—once a cornerstone in American political and economic philosophy—will be resurrected. We certainly hope so.

REFERENCES

Bandzak, Ruth A. 1992. "The Strike as Management Strategy." *Journal of Economic Issues* 26: 645–659.

Clawson, Dan, and Mary Ann Clawson. 1999. "What Has Happened to the U.S. Labor Movement? Union Decline and Renewal." *Annual Review of Sociology* 25: 95–119.

Cowie, Jefferson. 1999. *Capital Moves.* Ithaca, NY: Cornell University Press.

Dubofsky, Melvyn. 1969. *We Shall Be All: A History of the IWW.* Chicago: Quadrangle Books.

Elliot, Kimberly Ann, and Richard B. Freeman. 2003. *Can Labor Standards Improve Under Globalization?* Washington DC: Peter G. Peterson Institute for International Economics.

Fantasia, Rick. 1988. *Cultures of Solidarity.* Berkeley: University of California Press.

Fantasia, Rick, and Kim Voss. 2004. *Hard Work.* Berkeley: University of California Press.

Gould, William B. 2001. *Labored Relations.* Cambridge, MA: MIT Press.

International Labor Organization. 2007. "About the ILO." Available at: http://www.ilo.org/global/About_the_ILO/lang—en/index.htm. (Accessed February 11, 2008.)

Kimeldorf, Howard. 1999. *Battling for American Labor: Wobblies, Craft Workers, and the Making of the Union Movement.* Berkeley: University of California Press.

Kleiner, Morris M. 2001. "Intensity of Management Resistance: Understanding the Decline of Unionization in the Private Sector." *Journal of Labor Research* 22: 519–540.

Lambert, Josiah Bartlett. 2005. *If the Workers Took a Notion.* Ithaca, NY: ILR Press.

McCammon, Holly J. 1994. "Disorganizing and Reorganizing Conflict: Outcomes of the State's Legal Regulation of the Strike Since the Wagner Act." *Social Forces* 72: 1011–1049.

Milkman, Ruth. 2006. *L.A. Story.* New York: Russell Sage Foundation.

Mills, C. Wright. 1948. *The New Men of Power: America's Labor Leaders.* New York: A.M. Kelley.

Nissen, Bruce. 1990. "A Post–World War II 'Social Accord'?" Pp. 173–208 in *U.S. Labor Relations, 1945–1989,* edited by Bruce Nissen. New York: Garland.

Roscigno, Vincent J. 2007. *The Face of Discrimination: How Race and Gender Impact Work and Home Lives.* Lanham, MD: Rowman and Littlefield.

Roscigno, Vincent J., and William F. Danaher. 2001. "Media and Mobilization: The Case of Radio and Southern Textile Worker Insurgency, 1929 to 1934." *American Sociological Review* 66: 21–48.

Rosenblum, Jonathan D. 1995. *The Copper Crucible.* Ithaca, NY: ILR Press.

Stepan-Norris, Judith, and Maurice Zeitlin. 2003. *Left Out.* Cambridge: Cambridge University Press.

Voss, Kim. 1993. *The Making of American Exceptionalism.* Ithaca, NY: Cornell University Press.

Zetka, James R., Jr. 1992. "Work Organization and Wildcat Strikes in the U.S. Automobile Industry, 1946 to 1963." *American Sociological Review* 57: 214–226.

ADDITIONAL RESOURCES

Change to Win:
    http://www.changetowin.org.
Coalition of Labor Union Women:
    http://www.cluw.org.
International Labor Organization (ILO):
    http://www.ilo.org/global/lang—en/index.htm.
ILO Fundamental Conventions:
    http://www.ilo.org/public/english/standards/norm/introduction/what.htm.
ILO History:
    http://www.ilo.org/public/english/about/history.htm.
International Trade Union Confederation:
    http://www.ituc-csi.org/spip.php?rubrique1&lang=en.
Service Employees International Union:
    http://www.seiu.org
Unite Here:
    http://www.unitehere.org.

CHAPTER FIVE

~

Rights of the Child

BRIAN GRAN

The United States indeed is *the* leading rogue state when it comes to children's rights. In the nation perhaps most oriented to rights, a startling irony is that this large group of U.S. citizens—its children—do not possess the full range of rights that their peers in other countries enjoy, and U.S. leaders prefer it that way. In this wealthy, democratically oriented society, many U.S. leaders have serious misgivings when it comes to whether or not children possess the rights that adults do, let alone whether to enforce them.

When it comes to children's rights, the designation of the United States as the leading rogue state is underscored by how its children fare. Compared to children living in other wealthy democracies, young people living in the United States experience higher levels of poverty, worse health outcomes, more severe educational inequalities, and greater vulnerabilities to incarceration. Of the Organization for Economic Cooperation and Development (OECD) countries, for the year 2000, the United States had the second-highest level of children living in poverty (Whiteford 2007). Infant mortality levels in the United States are higher than in most other OECD countries (Shi, Macinko, Starfield, Xu, Regan, Politzer, and Wulu 2004). Given that U.S. public education is often financed by local property taxes, across the U.S. children living only miles apart experience vastly different opportunities and resources during their schooling. Only recently has the U.S. Supreme Court abolished capital punishment for young people. State governments within the United States are willing to incarcerate their citizens at much younger ages than in most other affluent democracies, as young as age six, with two states not setting minimum ages. In contrast, the government of the nation of Georgia received international criticism when it recently lowered its age of criminal responsibility to age twelve, in contravention of a General Comment issued by the UN Committee on the Rights of the Child.

The U.S. rogue status when it comes to children's rights is further illustrated through its notoriety as only one of two countries whose national governments have not ratified the UN Convention on the Rights of the Child (hereinafter "Convention"; Detrick 1999, 719). This convention is the paramount international agreement on children's rights. Have U.S. leaders identified weaknesses and concerns for this UN convention that leaders of other countries have overlooked?

The United States is the leading rogue state because, to the extent U.S. laws conflict with the Convention, these laws raise questions for the legitimacy of U.S. laws, not the Convention.

The United States is the leading rogue state because it has a wealth of resources available to implement the Convention. In addition to its economic resources, the United States has a stable government whose legal system is designed to protect rights of its citizens. While concerns persist about its civil society, the United States enjoys a wealth of nonprofit organizations that advocate on behalf of children.

The Convention is the contemporary agreement that advances children's rights at the international level. In this chapter, we examine treaties and conventions that led to the Convention, studying how these documents were different from each other and the Convention. After examining comments made on the Convention by the UN Committee on the Rights of the Child, an international committee of experts that monitors member states' implementation of the Convention, we examine documents devised following the Convention, studying the changes they have made. This chapter concludes by examining whether children living in the United States enjoy rights announced in the Convention and, if they do not, which rights are absent. It considers whether critical reasons exist for the U.S. government to withhold ratification of the Convention. This chapter seeks to demonstrate that the United States is the leading rogue state when it comes to children's rights.

RIGHTS OF CHILDREN

When conceptualizing rights, two dominant ideas are typically considered: citizenship and human rights. A dominant conceptualization of citizenship rights is T. H. Marshall's idea that citizenship is based on civil, political, and social rights. In a lecture he gave at Cambridge University in 1949, Marshall said that for England civil rights are typically employed in the legal system and include the right to a trial; political rights are used in the political system and include the rights to vote and assemble; and social rights are based in the welfare state, including the rights to education and health care. Citizenship rights consist of all three rights and all three rights are interdependent. For a citizen to vote effectively, a political right, she must be able to read newspapers and other news media as a critical consumer.

Other scholars have extended Marshall's conception of citizenship rights to include additional rights. An important addition is economic rights. Economic rights are typically considered to be rights to control the workplace, which may include freedom from hazardous work. A more recent extension is the right to participation. Janoski (1998) conceptualizes this right as the right to participate in workplace government, but others conceive of this right as broadly extending to other parts of society, such as participation in community.

Human rights are distinct from citizenship rights primarily in two ways. As Bryan Turner (1993) has noted, human rights are effective tools against governments when those governments do not acknowledge or even seek to prevent enforcement of citizenship rights. Blau and Moncada (2007, 10) define rights as "moral entitlements that humans have by virtue of being human." They (2006, 46) stress that human rights "can be *doctrine, practices, attitudes,* and *laws.*" Like Marshall's conception of the interdependency of citizenship rights, Blau and Moncada (2006, 14) argue that individuals need freedoms to exercise their human rights and, in turn, need human rights to exercise their freedoms.

Children's rights have bases in citizenship and human rights, but are considered distinct because of the unique interests of young people. Young people are less powerful and more reliant on others to advance their interests. Situations of economic exploitation of children typically arise because of a young person's reliance on an adult. Due to their chronological age, young people are understood to possess rights that are important to their growth and development, such as education. To enjoy their freedoms as young people and later as adults, young people must possess rights they can enforce (Blau and Moncada 2007, 34).

TREATIES PRIOR TO THE CONVENTION

Children's rights were enshrined in major international treaties in the last century. The first major international treaty espousing children's rights was the Declaration of the Rights of the Child, sometimes called the Geneva Declaration. This treaty was adopted in 1924 by the League of Nations. The United States never joined the League of Nations; consequently it was not part of the league when this declaration was adopted. This declaration was short, making five declarations that a child must be given resources to ensure his or her material and spiritual well-being, must be provided aid when in need, and must be prepared to earn a living without exploitation. This declaration has two interesting components relevant to this chapter. The declaration dictated that a child must be raised so that she learns she is obligated to share her abilities with others. Second, except for the declaration's title, the word "right" is absent. Nowhere else in this declaration is the language of "rights" used. Therefore, despite the lack of "rights," this declaration required members of the League of Nations to ensure that resources were distributed to children and that adults, especially parents, do a good job of ensuring a child's material and spiritual well-being.

Following World War II, an important institution for children's rights was established and a notable declaration was adopted. In 1946, the UN International Children's Emergency Fund, better known as UNICEF, was established by the UN General Assembly. In 1953, when it became a permanent component of the United Nations, UNICEF's name was changed to the UN Children's Fund. Its initial focus was on the welfare of children, with its first work delivering food and other goods to

European and Chinese children following World War II. Over its lifetime, UNICEF has come to incorporate a focus on the rights of children.

In 1948, the Universal Declaration of Human Rights was adopted by the United Nations. The United States supported this declaration, as well as its Article 25 (2), which states, "Motherhood and Childhood are entitled to special care and assistance." This article was important because of its stated concern for children's well-being, which would serve as reference points to the Convention.

In 1959, the Declaration on the Rights of the Child was unanimously adopted by the UN General Assembly. Containing ten principles, this Declaration acknowledges that children need support and protection due to their age and vulnerabilities. It pronounces various rights of children that are found in the Convention, including the civil right of identity; social rights of health, social security, and education; and protection from discrimination, among other entitlements.

Between the 1959 declaration and the 1989 UN Convention on the Rights of the Child, other provisions were made to expand and enforce rights of children. The Convention Against Discrimination in Education obligates member parties to ensure that young people do not encounter discrimination in education. Bearing in mind when this convention entered into force, 1962, it is a powerful document that challenged and continues to challenge education policies for many countries. This convention has only ninety ratifications; the United States has not ratified it.

THE UN CONVENTION ON THE RIGHTS OF THE CHILD

The UN Convention on the Rights of the Child is among the most ratified UN conventions of all human rights treaties. Only the national governments of Somalia and the United States have not ratified the Convention, although both have signed it, Somalia in 2002 and the United States in 1995. By ratifying the Convention, a government acknowledges its obligation to implement the Convention and that it will account for this implementation. Signing the Convention indicates a willingness to pursue government ratification of it. In 1995, then–U.S. ambassador to the United Nations Madeleine Albright signed the Convention on behalf of the U.S. government, but then-president Bill Clinton did not submit it to the U.S. Senate for its advice and consent, a necessary step to U.S. ratification.

The Convention is organized into four separate components. The first component is the preamble. The second component presents definitions and what non-UN institutions are important to implementing the Convention. The third component discusses the formation and work of the UN Committee on the Rights of the Child (hereinafter "Committee"). The fourth component identifies specific rights of children.

The preamble refers to earlier declarations and covenants, emphasizing principles arising from these statements relevant to the Convention. In addition to the Geneva Declaration and the Declaration of the Rights of the Child, the Convention refers to the Declaration on Social and Legal Principles related to the Protection and Welfare of Children, which is concerned with the welfare of all children, particularly the well-being of children who are adopted or placed in foster care. The Convention mentions the UN Standard Minimum Rules for the Administration of Juvenile Justice, which sets out procedural due process guidelines for young people. The Convention directs attention to the Declaration on the Protection of Women and Children in Emergency and Armed Conflict, which reminds national governments to prevent harm to women and children during military conflicts. The Convention refers to documents containing general principles that apply to children, including the charter of the United Nations, the UN Declaration of Human Rights, and two international covenants, the International Covenant on Civil and Political Rights and the International Covenant on Economic, Social and Cultural Rights.

The second component defines important concepts to the Convention and proceeds to identify key social institutions. An essential definition of the Convention is that of the word "child": a person under age eighteen or younger than legal majority as determined by the member party (Article 1). The second component identifies government as a principal actor in implementing the Convention, but emphasizes that member parties must consider the rights of a child's parents or guardians (Article 5). The Convention obligates member parties to implement rights without discrimination and to protect a child from discrimination (Article 2). The primary consideration of all actors who affect a child is that child's best interests (Article 3).

The third component proscribes steps for signing and ratifying the Convention by member parties (Articles 46 through 49). The Convention permits member parties to amend the Convention. Individual member parties can reserve portions of the Convention, by which the member party indicates its unwillingness to implement that article, unless the reservation is incompatible with the Convention (Article 51). A member party may also denounce the Convention (Article 52). Articles 46 to 54 present details of finalizing the Convention.

The most significant part of the third component is the establishment of the UN Committee on the Rights of the Child (Article 43). The primary objective of this committee is to monitor whether member parties have implemented the Convention. The Committee has ten members whose terms last four years, although they may be reelected. In addition to the Convention's obligation of member statements to publicize the Convention's "principles and provisions" (Article 42), the Convention obligates each member state to report to the Committee two years after ratifying the Convention and then every five years (Article 44). Among other objectives, a member party is to identify challenges in implementing the Convention. The Committee may request expert advice from UNICEF and other professionals in implementing the Convention (Article 45).

The fourth component is the heart of the Convention and is the presentation of children's rights. Rights articulated in the Convention can be categorized into seven broad categories. The first is the right to life (Article 6); the second category comprises rights to identity and nationality (Articles 7 and 8, respectively). The Convention indicates a child is entitled to a name, nationality, and to parental care (Article 7). It obligates member states to respect these identity rights (Article 8).

The third category embraces rights to live with parents and family (Articles 9 and 10). The Convention instructs member states that a child should not be separated from his parents unless the separation is in the child's best interests. If a child is separated from his parents, the Convention obligates member states both to respect and support the child's right to maintain relations and direct contact with parents. The Convention obligates member parties to provide appropriate protection and assistance to refugee children and to work together to help refugee children reunite with their parents (Article 22).

The fourth category is civil rights, including freedoms from bodily harm and punishment, as well as a prohibition of capital punishment and life imprisonment for offenders younger than age eighteen (Article 37). Articles 37 and 40 articulate rights to procedural due process within a legal system, for instance, a right to legal assistance. The Convention does not articulate a right to be free from military service to young people, but obligates member parties to refrain from military recruitment of people younger than age fifteen (not age eighteen).

The fifth category comprises rights to beliefs, expression, and access to information. Articles 13 and 17 of the Convention indicate that a child has a right to free expression, which necessitates "freedom to seek, receive and impart information" from a variety of news and information sources. The Convention also indicates a right to free thought, conscience, and religion while acknowledging a parent's right to direct a child in these rights (Article 14). A child, according to the Convention, enjoys freedom to associate and assemble with others (Article 15), but at the same time has the right to expect that her privacy will not be interfered with. A child has the right to participate culturally and artistically and to enjoy her cultural background and practices (Articles 31 and 30, respectively).

The sixth category deals with the social rights of children. A child possesses the right to an adequate living standard (Article 27) and to a compulsory and free education (Article 28). Besides a right to rest and leisure (Article 31), a child possesses the right to the highest standards of health and related kinds of care. Article 23 states that disabled children have rights to special care without cost, and Article 25 indicates that a child who is placed in care has the right to regular review of his treatment.

The seventh category encompasses the economic rights of children. The Convention states that a child has the right to be free from economic exploitation and hazardous work (Article 32). It obligates member states to battle the illicit transfer of children (Articles 11 and 35), exploitation in general (Article 36) and in particular sexual exploitation and abuse (Article 34), as well as forced participation in the illicit drug trade (Article 33).

Optional Protocols

Since the Convention became effective, two optional protocols (OPs) to the Convention on the Rights of the Child have been made. According to UNICEF, these two OPs develop relevant aspects and expand obligations of the Convention.

The OP on "The Involvement of Children in Armed Conflict" became effective in 2002. This OP has more than 110 members, including the United States. It requires member states to prevent an individual under age eighteen from directly participating in armed hostilities. This OP also obligates member parties not to compel into military service an individual younger than age eighteen. This OP obligates states to increase their minimum age of military recruitment to age eighteen, in contrast to Article 1 of the Convention, which stated age fifteen.

The other OP, "On the Sale of Children, Child Prostitution, and Child Pornography," also became effective in 2002. Nearly 120 national governments are parties to this OP, including the United States. As its name indicates, this OP prohibits the sale of children, child prostitution for money or other consideration, and child pornography.

General Comments of the UN Committee on the Rights of the Child

Important extensions to the Convention are the General Comments made by the UN Committee on the Rights of the Child. These comments are the Committee's interpretation of the Convention as they pertain to areas of children's rights. Since 2001, the Committee has issued ten comments (see Table 5.1).

"Children's Rights in Juvenile Justice" is a comment from the Committee that takes member parties to task for not enforcing procedural due process rights of children and for not collecting information on how children fare in their juvenile justice systems. The comment on children who have disabilities recognizes the large number of children who have disabilities, while acknowledging the difficulties for some member states in enforcing rights of these children due to resource constraints. The Committee emphasizes that children who have disabilities should not experience discrimination in general and in enforcing their rights in particular.

Noting that it has addressed 130 member parties to state that corporal punishment is contradictory to children's rights, through its comment on corporal punishment the Committee places the problem of corporal punishment within a broad framework of convention articles and other international documents on children's rights. Through

Table 5.1 General Comments of the UN Committee

General comment	Year
Children's rights in juvenile justice	2007
The rights of children with disabilities	2006
The rights of children to protection from corporal punishment and other cruel or degrading forms of punishment	2006
Implementing children's rights in early childhood	2006
Treatment of unaccompanied and separated children outside their country of origin	2005
General measures of implementation for the Convention on the Rights of the Child	2003
Adolescent health	2003
HIV/AIDS and the rights of children	2003
The role of independent human rights institutions	2002
The aims of education	2001

the "early childhood" comment, the committee emphasizes to member states that young children also possess rights, which member parties are expected to enforce.

The "unaccompanied children" comment faces questions of rights of children who are separated from their parents and guardians, potentially because they have been ensnared in child trafficking and the sex trade. The longest comment, it squares with important challenges to implementing the Convention when children's rights cross national borders, which raises critical questions for implementing the Convention and enforcing rights of extremely vulnerable children in globalizing economies.

The comment on "General Measures of Implementation" clarifies Article 4 of the Convention, which requires member parties to pursue "all appropriate legislative, administrative and other measures" to implement the Convention. This comment reminds member parties that a strict focus on the Convention, rather than the spirit of the Convention, can result in failure to reach the Convention's overall objectives.

The "Adolescent Health" comment encourages member parties to expand their notion of a young person's health to consider the challenges young people face as they become adolescents, as well as ensuring their privacy—an important right for adolescents. The comment on "HIV/AIDS" seeks to ensure that the rights and well-being of children whose lives are affected by HIV/AIDS are promoted by member parties. "The role of independent human rights institutions" encourages member parties to establish national independent institutions, such as children's ombudspersons, that will monitor implementation of children's rights. "The Aims of Education" expands on Article 29 of the convention, emphasizing the importance not only of access to education, but quality of content.

These comments have generally clarified issues of children's rights and, in some cases, clarified the tasks of member parties in implementing the Convention and enforcing children's rights.

THE LEADING ROGUE STATE

This chapter argues that the United States is the leading rogue state when it comes to children's rights. Although the U.S. government played an important role in the Convention's development, including signing the Convention, the United States is one of two nations that have yet to ratify the Convention. Despite consistency between U.S. laws and children's rights articulated in the Convention, the U.S. national government has not ratified the convention. What differences that do exist can be overcome to benefit children living in the United States. Resources do not stand in the way of U.S. ratification of the Convention. The United States should ratify the Convention for the good of its children and for children living elsewhere.

U.S. Investment in the Convention

As various scholars have noted, the U.S. government was heavily involved in drafting various Convention articles (Todres, Wojcik, and Revaz 2006, 3). Indeed, some articles are derived from U.S. legal doctrines (Todres, Wojcik, and Revaz 2006, 5), including antidiscrimination (Skoler 2006) and the notion of the best interests of the child, a 100-year-old concept in American law (Ellis 1990, 3; Mason 2006). Articles dealing with freedom of expression (Matthews 2006) and freedom of thought and conscience arise from American conceptions. Furthermore, the U.S. government has ratified two optional protocols to the convention (Revaz and Todres 2006), steps that indicate an awareness of children's human rights and a willingness to implement them.

The Gulf between U.S. Laws and the Convention

Scholars have undertaken analyses of the gulf between U.S. legal doctrine and the Convention, with the overarching, fundamental question of whether differences are so vast that ratifying the Convention would produce significant changes in U.S. laws (see Table 5.2).

An important book, *The UN Convention on the Rights of the Child: An Analysis of Treaty Provisions and Implications of U.S. Ratification,* was published in 2006. Edited by Jonathan Todres, Mark Wojcik, and Cris Revaz, among this book's different objectives is a discussion of the distance between the Convention and U.S. laws implementing children's rights. This volume builds on *Children's Rights in America: UN Convention on the Rights of the Child Compared with U.S. Law,* a volume Price Cohen and Davidson (1990) edited shortly after the Convention entered into force that examines differences between the Convention and U.S. laws.

Gulfs between U.S. laws and the Convention are generally found in social rights and rights involving bodily control and privacy (Tosado 2006). Enforcing social rights is often considered expensive; ensuring that children maintain an adequate living standard, for instance, is expected to raise tax levels. This perspective ignores the costs of enforcing other kinds of rights. Fulfillment of rights based in the legal system requires resources for functioning court, legal, and prison systems. Rights involving bodily control, such as freedom from corporal punishment, are sometimes viewed as contrary to parents' rights to discipline their children. This reasoning is faulty, however, for it treats children as less than human. The criminal justice system does not tolerate assaults; why should it tolerate assaults on children?

Distances between the Convention and U.S. laws for other rights are shorter. Regarding rights to association and assembly, Tosado (2006) contends that U.S. laws are generally consistent. The best interests of the child, as described, have a basis in U.S. legal doctrine, which also regards the right to life as fundamental. Although important concerns exist, children in the United States do possess rights to identity and nationality, freedom of beliefs and freedom to express themselves, and rights to assemble and associate. Substantial differences exist across its fifty states, yet children in the United States generally are entitled to be free from economic and other forms of exploitation, as well as military service until age eighteen, which the United States has confirmed through ratifying the two OPs.

The United States is the leading rogue state because, to the extent U.S. laws conflict with the Convention, these laws raise questions of *their* legitimacy, not the legitimacy of the Convention. In addition to ratifying the OPs, other evidence exists

Table 5.2 Comparison of Convention Articles and U.S. Laws

Rights	Convention Articles	U.S. Laws	Notes
Best interests	3	Consistent (Mason 2006)	
Life	6	Consistent (Johnson and McNulty 1990)	
Identity, nationality	7, 8	Consistent (Skoler 1990)	
Receive parental care and live with parents and family	7, 9, and 10	Consistent (Myers 1990)	
Freedom from bodily harm and punishment, procedural due process, and military conscription before age fifteen		Conflicts with freedom from bodily harm (Pates 2006), punishment (Remple and Wojcik 2006), procedural due process (Szaj 2006 but see Myers 1990, Davidson 1990, Sobie 1990, and Johnson 1990), but consistent regarding military conscription	U.S. ratified the Optional Protocol on the Involvement of Children in Armed Conflict
Beliefs, expression, and access to information	12, 13, 14, and 17	Beliefs (Lantier 2006) and access to information are generally consistent (Lee 2006), but conflicts with expression (Szaj 2006, but see Matthews 2006 and Shepherd 1990)	
Association, assembly, privacy, participate culturally	15, 16, 30, and 31	Consistent, except privacy rights are weaker (Tosado 2006, Guggenheim 1990)	
Social rights (education, health care, adequate living standards, socioeconomic security, rest and leisure, and appropriate care)	23, 25, 27, 28, and 31	Education (Dolinsky 2006, Bitensky 1990) generally is consistent, but important concerns exist regarding health care (Todres 2006), adequate living standards (Taylor 2006, Weill 1990, and Johnson and McNulty 1990), socioeconomic security, rest and leisure (Armstrong 2006), and appropriate care	
Economic rights (economic exploitation, hazardous work, sexual exploitation, illicit drug trade)	11, 32, 33, 34, 35, and 36	Economic exploitation, hazardous work, sexual exploitation, and illicit drug trade are generally consistent, but conflicts do exist (Mason 2006 and Boskey 1990)	U.S. did ratify Optional Protocol on the Sale of Children, Child Prostitution, and Child Pornography

that the United States is "changing its mind" when it comes to the Convention and children's rights. The U.S. Supreme Court, not only resistant to domestic but international pressures, referenced the Convention in 2004 when deciding *Roper v. Simmons,* a case in which the Court declared that the Eighth and Fourteenth amendments prohibit execution of an offender if she was under age eighteen when she committed the crime.

The United States Has the Resources

Among the wealthiest of all nations, the United States enjoys a strong economy that produces immense resources. Although the electoral system on which it is based requires significant repairs, the U.S. national government is stable and its system of making laws is predictable and calculable. The U.S. legal system also is far from perfect, but it is extensive and to some degree has already established the objective of serving the best interests of children living in the United States. Civil societies of the United States are healthy when it comes to children. The United States is blessed with many nonprofit organizations that advocate for and serve the interests and rights of its children.

Of course, governments of many countries without these rich resources not only have managed to ratify the Convention, they have taken significant steps to implement children's rights. It is impossible to claim that the United States is incapable of ratifying the Convention because of material, governmental, legal, or other kinds of constraints.

Why the United States Should Change Its Rogue Identity

The United States should ratify the Convention for the good of its children and for children living elsewhere. Ratifying the Convention would not significantly change federal or state laws (Price Cohen and Davidson 1990; Almog and Bendor 2004, 273, 280). Even if U.S. political leaders disagreed with some articles, the U.S. government can ratify the Convention while making a reservation to a specific article.

Despite the near universal ratification of the Convention, the signal the U.S. government sends by not ratifying the Convention is the wrong one (Almog and Bendor 2004, 273, 284). Failure to ratify the Convention indicates that the United States does not see fit to enforce the rights of its youngest and, in many ways, most vulnerable citizens and residents. Failure to ratify suggests U.S. leaders and others are afraid that a balance cannot be struck between the rights and interests of children and others, including their parents. Would not most parents want their children to possess the rights identified in the Convention?

By ratifying and implementing the Convention, the United States can benefit children not only within its own borders, but children across the world. The extensive resources of the United States could be deployed to tackle problems crossing borders that strike children. The United States should continue to move forward on the optional protocols on trafficked children and children forced to fight others' wars by seeking to help children who are hidden in the darkest corners of global economies.

REFERENCES

Almog, Shulamit, and Ariel L. Bendor. 2004. "The UN Convention on the Rights of the Child Meets the American Constitution." *The International Journal of Children's Rights* 11: 273–289.

Bitensky, Susan H. 1990. "Educating the Child for a Productive Life." Pages 167–196 in *Children's Rights in America*, ed. Cynthia Price Cohen and Howard A. Davidson. Washington, D.C.: American Bar Association.

Blau, Judith, and Alberto Moncada. 2007. *Freedoms and Solidarities: In Pursuit of Human Rights.* New York: Rowman and Littlefield.

———. 2006. *Justice in the U.S.: Human Rights and the U.S. Constitution.* New York: Rowman and Littlefield.

Boskey, James B. 1990. "Preventing Exploitation of the Child." Pages 303–314 in *Children's Rights in America*, ed. Cohen and Davidson.

Davidson, Howard A. 1990. "The Child's Right to be Heard and Represented." Pages 151–165 in *Children's Rights in America*, ed. Cohen and Davidson.

Detrick, Sharon. 1999. *A Commentary on the United Nations Convention on the Rights of the Child.* Boston: Martinus Nijhoff.

Ellis, Jane. 1990. "The Best Interests of the Child." Pp. 3–18 in *Children's Rights in America*, ed. Cohen and Davidson.

Grover, Sonja. 2004. "On Recognizing Children's Universal Rights: What Needs to Change in the Convention on the Rights of the Child." *The International Journal of Children's Rights* 12: 259–271.

Guggenheim, Martin. 1990. "The Child's Access to Diverse Intellectual, Artistic, and Recreational Resources." Pages 289–301 in *Children's Rights in America*, ed. Cohen and Davidson.

Janoski, Thomas. 1998. *Citizenship and Civil Society.* New York: Cambridge University Press.

Johnson, Kay A., and Molly McNulty. 1990. "Assuring Adequate Health and Rehabilitative Care for the Child." In *Children's Rights in America*, ed. Cohen and Davidson.

Johnson, Thomas A. 1990. "Involvement of the Child in Armed Conflict." Pages 325–334 in *Children's Rights in America*, ed. Cohen and Davidson.

Lansdown, Gerison. 1998. "The Rights of Disabled Children." *The International Journal of Children's Rights* 6: 221–227.

Lantier, Greg. 2006. "Freedom of Thought, Conscience, and Religion." Pages 151–162 in *The UN Convention on the Rights of the Child*, ed. Jonathan Todres, Mark E. Wojcik, and Cris R. Revaz. Ardsley, NY: Transaction.

Lee, Siyeon. 2006. "Children's Right of Access to Information." Pages 177–188 in *The UN Convention on the Rights of the Child*, ed. Jonathan Todres, Mark E. Wojcik, and Cris R. Revaz. Ardsley, NY: Transaction.

Marshall, T. H. 1950. *Citizenship and Social Class.* New York: Cambridge University Press.

Mason, Elisabeth. 2006. "The Best Interests of the Child." Pp. 121–126 in *The UN Convention on the Rights of the Child*, edited by Jonathan Todres, Mark E. Wojcik, and Cris R. Revaz. Ardsley, NY: Transaction.

Matthews, Martha. 2006. "Freedom of Expression." Pp. 143–150 in *The UN Convention on the Rights of the Child*, edited by Jonathan Todres, Mark E. Wojcik, and Cris R. Revaz. Ardsley, NY: Transaction.

Myers, John E. B. 1990. "The Child, Parents, and the State." Pages 87–107 in *Children's Rights in America*, ed. Cohen and Davidson.

Pates, Michael. 2006. "The UN Convention on the Rights of the Child and Corporal Punishment." Pages 201–206 in *The UN Convention on the Rights of the Child*, ed. Jonathan Todres, Mark E. Wojcik, and Cris R. Revaz. Ardsley, NY: Transaction.

Price Cohen, Cynthia, and Howard A. Davidson. 1990. *Children's Rights in America*. Washington, DC: American Bar Association.

Remple, Evelynn Brown, and Mark E. Wojcik. 2006. "Capital Punishment and Life Sentences for Juvenile Offenders." Pages 277–292 in *The UN Convention on the Rights of the Child*, ed. Jonathan Todres, Mark E. Wojcik, and Cris R. Revaz. Ardsley, NY: Transaction.

Revaz, Cris R., and Jonathan Todres. 2006. "The Optional Protocols to the UN Convention on the Rights of the Child and the Impact of U.S. Ratification." Pp. 293–309 in *The UN Convention on the Rights of the Child,* edited by Jonathan Todres, Mark E. Wojcik, and Cris R. Revaz. Ardsley, NY: Transaction.

Roper v. Simmons, 543 U.S. 551 (2005).

Sheperd, Robert E., Jr. 1990. "Civil Rights of the Child." Pages 135–149 in *Children's Rights in America*, ed. Cohen and Davidson.

Shi, L., J. Macinko, B. Starfield, J. Xu, J. Regan, R. Politzer, and J. Wulu. 2004. "Primary Care, Infant Mortality, and Low Birth Weight in the States of the USA." *Journal of Epidemiology and Community Health* 58: 374-380.

Skoler, Daniel L. 2006. "Anti-Discrimination Guarantees under the UN Convention on the Rights of the Child—Issues and Impact for U.S. Ratification." Pp. 99–126 in *The UN Convention on the Rights of the Child,* ed. Jonathan Todres, Mark E. Wojcik, and Cris R. Revaz. Ardsley, NY: Transaction.

Sobie, Merrill. 1990. "Rights of the Child Charged with Violating the Law." Pages 315–323 in *Children's Rights in America*, ed. Cohen and Davidson.

Szaj, Christine M. 2006. "The Right of the Child to Be Heard." Pages 127–142 in *The UN Convention on the Rights of the Child*, ed. Jonathan Todres, Mark E. Wojcik, and Cris R. Revaz. Ardsley, NY: Transaction.

Taylor, Catherine S. 2006. "Children's Right to an Adequate Standard of Living." Pages 237–250 in *The UN Convention on the Rights of the Child*, ed. Jonathan Todres, Mark E. Wojcik, and Cris R. Revaz. Ardsley, NY: Transaction.

Todres, Jonathan. 2006. "The Right to Health under the UN Convention on the Rights of the Child." Pages 221–236 in *The UN Convention on the Rights of the Child*, ed. Jonathan Todres, Mark E. Wojcik, and Cris R. Revaz. Ardsley, NY: Transaction.

Tosado, Rebekah. 2006. "Children's Rights to Freedom of Association, Assembly, and Privacy." Pp. 189–200 in *The UN Convention on the Rights of the Child,* edited by Jonathan Todres, Mark E. Wojcik, and Cris R. Revaz. Ardsley, NY: Transaction.

Turner, Bryan S. 1993. "Outline of a Theory of Human Rights." *Sociology* 27, no. 3: 489–512.

Weill, James. 1990. "Assuring an Adequate Standard of Living for the Child." Pages 197–217 in *Children's Rights in America*, ed. Cohen and Davidson.

Whiteford, Peter. 2007. "Child Poverty, Joblessness and Welfare Reform in the UK—an OECD Perspective." Available at: http://www.oecd.org/dataoecd/13/15/38343085.pdf. (Accessed March 29, 2008.)

∼

CHAPTER SIX

Rights of Migrants and Minorities

CECILIA MENJÍVAR
AND RUBÉN G. RUMBAUT

The law, in its majestic equality, forbids the rich as well as the poor to sleep under bridges, to beg in the streets, and to steal bread.
—Anatole France

In this chapter we contrast the goals and principles enshrined in two UN treaties—the International Convention on the Elimination of All Forms of Racial Discrimination and the International Convention on the Protection of the Rights of All Migrant Workers and Members of Their Families—with their implementation in the United States. We expose the gaps between de jure declarations based on universal principles of human rights and de facto practices, between rhetoric and reality, while noting increasing trends toward the erosion of personhood rights. We underscore the consequences of universal human rights violations for various communities in the United States, noting the social suffering and harm that it engenders. In doing so, we note the discrepancies and the dissonance between contemporary laws contained in national edicts that are in principle unbiased and "neutral" and the gross violations of the rights of the individuals that they putatively protect.

Such contradictions, to be sure, have existed since before the founding of the nation. More than six decades ago, *An American Dilemma: The Negro Problem and Modern Democracy* (Myrdal 1944) painstakingly documented the gulf that existed between the lofty ideals of the "American Creed" and the racial oppression of the country's black minority, whose civil and political rights had been categorically denied in the generations following the end of slavery. That landmark work influenced the Supreme

Court's 1954 decision in *Brown v. Board of Education* to outlaw de jure segregation in U.S. public schools. And yet by 2007, with the promise of *Brown* unfulfilled in a national context of increased racial and ethnic diversity and renewed residential and school segregation (Merritt and Lee 2003), a conservative Supreme Court majority effectively reversed its reasoning in *Brown* and, in what a dissenting justice called a "cruel irony," actually cited *Brown* to justify its prohibition of school districts in Seattle and Louisville from implementing their efforts to promote racial integration. Instead of a straight march toward equality and human rights, we recognize that "uncivil times for civil rights have been a recurrent theme in U.S. history. Ebbs and flows of racism and nativism have deeply affected racial and other minorities in the country.... In the struggle for social justice, backlashes against [minority] groups often are related in a complex matrix" (Johnson 2003).

Despite the U.S. ratification of the UN Convention on the Elimination of All Forms of Racial Discrimination, and notwithstanding the legal rights that racial minorities won in the modern civil rights era in the United States, the legacies of centuries of racial oppression persist in what Joe Feagin has called "systemic racism" (2006) and in what Michael Burawoy (2006) describes as a "color-blind racism" that give rise, for example, to the staggering rates of incarceration among African Americans, as well as the governmental abandonment of African American victims of Hurricane Katrina (Hanson and Hanson 2006). We also refer to the intensifying immiseration and stigmatization of vulnerable migrant laborers and their families, and to the legal violence that results in the gross violations of human and personhood rights of immigrant parents who are forced to live apart from their children and permanently deported without recourse to appeal (Human Rights Watch 2007). As such, our discussion is linked to the distinction that Blau and Moncada (2006) have made between *human rights* as comprehensively global as well as national, and *liberal rights,* which relate to individual citizenship rights within the nation-state. Human rights encompass civil and political rights, but also social and economic rights such as food security and the rights to education, a job, housing, and health care—that is, rights inherent to a shared humanity that the state must protect and foster, and to the means by which people can live fulfilling lives.

The conventions that we examine are related, but differ from each other in distinct ways. While the United States has signed and ratified the Convention on the Elimination of All Forms of Racial Discrimination, it has *not* done so with the Convention on the Protection of the Rights of All Migrant Workers and Members of Their Families. Indeed, the former has counterparts in legal rights that the United States accords formally to individuals from all ethnic and racial groups. In contrast, far from having legal counterparts, the latter has met opposition in U.S. legal frameworks, enacting laws and ordinances that go *against* the basic principles enshrined in the convention. Importantly, however, whether the conventions are signed and/or ratified, or even whether there exist compatible legal rights at the national level, the end result is not notably different. The groups that those conventions supposedly protect are, in reality, excluded and marginalized and given unequal access to the goods and benefits of society. In the end, the structural obstacles present in the United States that prevent the full implementation of these conventions also keep these groups out. In the case of migrants, such obstacles are manifested in the form of exclusionary immigration policies that seek not merely to expel or keep them out of the country, but to exploit them in multiple ways while they are in the country, curtailing the full enjoyment of their social, economic, and political rights.

THE TWO INTERNATIONAL CONVENTIONS

The International Convention on the Elimination of All Forms of Racial Discrimination[1] was adopted by the General Assembly of the United Nations in resolution 2106 on December 21, 1965, and in accordance with Article 19, it entered into force on January 4, 1969. One hundred and seventy countries have signed it or ratified it. The United States signed it on September 28, 1966, but did not ratify it until almost three decades later, on October 21, 1994.

This convention seeks to condemn and eliminate by all appropriate means and without delay racial discrimination in all its forms, particularly segregation and apartheid. In addition, according to Article 5 of this convention, states parties also agree to guarantee the right to equality before the law without distinction of race, color, or national or ethnic origin, particularly with relation to the following rights: "to equal treatment before the tribunals and all organs administering justice; to security of person and protection by the state against violence or bodily harm, whether inflicted by government officials or by any individual group or institution; to political rights, particularly the right to participate in elections—to vote and to stand for election—and to have equal access to public service; the right to nationality; the right to marriage and choice of spouse; the right to own property alone as well as in association with others; the right to inherit; the right to freedom of thought, religion, opinion, expression and peaceful assembly; the right to housing; the right to public health, medical care, social security and social services; the right of access to any place or service intended for use by the general public, such as hotels, restaurants, cafes, theatres and parks; the right to equal participation in cultural activities; and the right to education and training." Article 6 of this convention further specifies that states parties shall assure everyone effective protection against any acts of racial discrimination that violate human rights and fundamental freedoms, as well as the right to seek from tribunals just and adequate reparation or satisfaction for any damage suffered as a result of such discrimination.

The Committee on the Elimination of Racial Discrimination (CERD) monitors the implementation of the convention by the states parties. All states parties are obligated to submit regular reports to the CERD on how rights are being implemented, and the committee in turn assesses the reports and produces its recommendations in the form of "concluding observations." The convention has in place three mechanisms through which it monitors the implementation of rights. It has an early warning procedure, it examines interstate complaints, and it also takes individual complaints. For instance, the United States, along with Brazil, Belize, and Peru, was sent an early warning letter in March 2007 because the regular reports due in 2003 and 2005 had not been submitted.[2] Furthermore, in resolution 1993/20 the Commission on Human Rights decided to appoint, for a three-year period, a special rapporteur on contemporary forms of racism, racial discrimination, and xenophobia. The rapporteur is charged in particular to examine incidents of racial discrimination, xenophobia, anti-Semitism, Negrophobia, or any form of discrimination against blacks, Arabs, and Muslims, and related intolerance, and to report to the commission annually.

The International Convention on the Protection of the Rights of All Migrant Workers and Members of Their Families was adopted by Resolution 45/158 on December 18, 1990, at the forty-fifth session of the General Assembly of the United Nations in New York. In accordance with Article 87 (1), it entered into force on July 1, 2003. The convention is open for signature by all states in accordance with its Article 86. Notably—in an age of widening global inequality when international migration flows largely from less to more developed countries have increased—*none of the wealthiest receiving countries of international migrants, including the United States, have signed it or ratified it.* Indeed, the UN special rapporteur on migrants' human rights has noted this situation and attributes it to issues related to national interests as well as reluctance, on the part of the major receiving countries, to explicitly recognize the demand for immigrants' labor. He also notes that this unwillingness is related to anti-immigrant ideologies, often tinged with xenophobia and racism, in the countries that receive the most immigrants today (Bustamante 2005). Fifty-one countries either have signed or ratified it, with several expressing reservations. The Committee on the Protection of the Rights of All Migrant Workers and Members of Their Families (CMW) monitors implementation of this convention by its states parties. It is the newest treaty body and it held its first session in March 2004. According to its website, all states parties must submit regular reports to the committee on how the rights are being implemented. States parties report one year after acceding to the convention and then every five years. The CMW then examines the report and addresses its recommendations to the state party in the form of "concluding observations."[3]

The Convention on the Protection of the Rights of All Migrant Workers and Members of Their Families reaffirms the basic rights included in other conventions into a comprehensive one that has universal applicability for migrants.[4] Since we cannot cover in detail its ninety-three articles here, we have selected a few that capture the major discrepancies between what the UN convention aims to do and what the United States does through its immigration laws and treatment of migrants on its soil (encompassing a range of U.S. statuses from legal permanent residents to refugees, asylees, and undocumented migrants).

The convention is applicable to all migrant workers, regardless of sex, race, language, age, nationality, religion, ethnic or social origin, marital status, political opinion, or birth status, and it applies to the entire migration process and entire period of stay. This convention states that migrant workers and members of their families should have the right at any time to enter and remain in their country of origin; that migrant workers or members of their families should not be subjected to arbitrary or unlawful interference with their privacy, family, home, correspondence or other communications, or to unlawful attacks on their honor and reputation. It affirms that migrant workers and members of their families shall have the right to the protection of the law against such interference or attacks, and that they are not to be subjected individually or collectively to arbitrary arrest or detention. If migrant workers and members of their families are arrested or detained on a criminal charge, they should be brought swiftly before a judge or other authorized officer and be entitled to trial within a reasonable time. As a general rule, they should not be detained while awaiting trial. And if they are detained for violations of immigration provisions, they should be held, if at all possible, separately from convicted persons or persons detained pending trial. The convention also states that migrant workers and their families shall not be liable to be tried or punished for an offense for which they have already been convicted or acquitted in accordance with the law and penal procedure.

The convention stipulates that migrants and their children should have access to a variety of social services, including educational institutions, vocational guidance, placement services, and training on the basis of equality of treatment for their children; access to housing, including subsidies for housing, and protection from exploitation with respect to rents; and access to health services, provided that requirements to participate in the programs are met. Noteworthy, the convention and signatory parties recognize the family as the natural and fundamental unit of society, and, as such, they require that this unit be protected by society and that the state should take appropriate measures to protect the unity of migrant workers' families. And when workers are separated from their spouses or other family members, particularly minor dependent children, the states parties are to take appropriate measures to facilitate their reunification. In those respects, actual realities in the United States today appear to be grossly discrepant.

THE UNITED STATES AND THE CONVENTION ON THE ELIMINATION OF ALL FORMS OF RACIAL DISCRIMINATION

In 1954 the U.S. Supreme Court ruled in *Brown v. Board of Education* that segregated education is inherently unequal—overturning its infamous 1896 decision in *Plessy v. Ferguson*—and subsequently ordered the nation's schools to integrate "with all deliberate speed." Schools, school buses, and public buildings, parks, and playgrounds were to be opened up to everyone, regardless of race. The civil rights movement of the 1960s further pushed for racial equality in other spheres of life, seeking to dismantle the institutional edifice of Jim Crow caste segregation and secure guarantees to equal access to social goods and basic human rights to all regardless of race. Once the Johnson administration's Justice Department became committed to enforcing the Civil Rights Act of 1964 and the Voting Rights Act of 1965, local governments felt formally compelled to promote racial integration in schools and workplaces and public spaces. Thus, de jure recognition of the equality of racial minorities was inscribed in the law. However, this rhetoric hardly squared with reality, because racial discrimination and the violation of basic rights of minorities persisted. The expression of biased treatment changed, shifting from overt discrimination prior to the civil rights movement to covert, latent forms, so that it would not prompt legal disputes or charges. The result was "statistical discrimination" (Massey and Denton 1993, 96), which happens when race and socioeconomic characteristics become intertwined and discrimination is not directed at race per se but at the characteristic that is strongly associated with race. This form of discrimination is pernicious and becomes a moving target, difficult to pinpoint, resulting in insidious forms of rights violations. Importantly, it is encoded in formal institutions, in the frameworks of those in positions of power to allocate resources. African Americans remain deeply excluded and far from achieving parity with whites on practically all social indicators nationally, such as education, health, income, home ownership, and representation in the justice system.

A recent example of how this new form of indirect or "statistical discrimination" seeps through formal structures is the Supreme Court's five-to-four ruling in the Seattle and Louisville school district cases mentioned earlier. Ironically, as immigration has increased and the nation has become more diverse ethnically and racially, its public schools, with the Supreme Court's authoritative approval, have become more segregated. The landmark ruling responsible for the integration of schools is no longer upheld, and the Court has essentially stripped the ruling in *Brown* of much of its power and significance. These developments have paralleled regional and state-level ones, such as the banning of affirmative action in the states of Texas and California.

The Mexican-origin population has a parallel history of rights abuses, and like African Americans, there also have been treaties and court decisions to redress them. When nearly half of Mexico's territory became part of the United States through the Treaty of Guadalupe Hidalgo in 1848, the rights of Mexicans in the annexed territories were supposed to be protected, but Mexicans really never enjoyed full citizenship rights (Johnson 1998). More than a century later, in *Hernández v. Texas* (a case decided two weeks before *Brown* in 1954, the same year of the mass raids and deportations of Mexicans by U.S. government agents during "Operation Wetback," and the first case to be tried by Mexican American lawyers before the U.S. Supreme Court), the Court ruled that the systematic exclusion of persons of Mexican ancestry from juries in Jackson County, Texas, violated the Constitution, thereby expanding the Equal Protection Clause of the Fourteenth Amendment (Olivas 2006). And in another landmark case in 1982, the Supreme Court ruled in *Plyler v. Doe* that public schools were prohibited by the Fourteenth Amendment from denying the children of undocumented Mexican immigrants access to a public education. Those children, according to the ruling, were to have the same right to a public education as U.S. citizens and permanent legal residents. Importantly, it specifically forbade public schools from adopting policies that would deny students the right to a public educa-tion based on their immigration status or that of their parents. But in recent years, in the context of an increasingly more hostile climate toward immigrants, states and local governments have attempted on numerous occasions to take away this right. Perhaps best known is Proposition 187 in California, a 1994 ballot measure that aimed to "Save Our State" (SOS) by denying social and health services and access to public schools to undocumented immigrants and their children, and required school districts to verify the legal status of students' parents and report any persons suspected of being in the United States unlawfully so that they may be detained and deported. The measure was approved by the voters in a landslide but struck down as unconstitutional by the federal courts three years later (in part because it violated the Supreme Court's ruling in *Plyler*). We take note of more recent such efforts in the next section.

THE UNITED STATES AND THE CONVENTION ON THE PROTECTION OF THE RIGHTS OF ALL MIGRANT WORKERS AND MEMBERS OF THEIR FAMILIES

With regard to the basic principles contained in this convention, we limit ourselves to highlighting some of the more serious and salient discrepancies in the recent record of the United States. The history of U.S. immigration law is replete with such cases— the Alien and Sedition Acts of 1798, the Chinese Exclusion Act, the post–World War I Palmer Raids, the World War II internment of Japanese Americans, and the forced repatriations of persons of Mexican ancestry, among others (Kanstroom 2007; Motomura 2006; Ngai 2004; Pfaelzer 2007; Zolberg 2006)—but we focus only on those that have been enacted since the mid-1990s, when the convention was adopted. Far from paralleling the UN convention, these and related laws counteract and conflict with the convention on basic points. United States immigration law, far from adhering to international treaties and conventions, seems geared to undermine certain categories of migrants by legalizing the denial of basic human rights. Immigration law leaves a large number of individuals without protection and, as such, not existing legally. Even though legal nonexistence has not precluded these immigrants' social presence in the United States, legal nonexistence is a state of subjugation that results in vulnerability to deportation, confinement to low-wage jobs, and the denial of basic human needs, such as access to decent housing, education, food, and health care (Coutin 2000; Menjívar 2006). Legal nonexistence can mean erasure of rights and personhood, making violence against people in this condition legitimate or perceived as such (Coutin 2000). We focus here on specific cases that directly contradict universal understandings of basic human rights.

In efforts both to demagogue and to appease a public that blamed immigrants for a range of social and economic woes, the U.S. Congress attached a series of provisions to the 1996 federal welfare reform bill (the Personal Responsibility and Work Opportunity Reconciliation Act, or PRWORA) to bar immigrants from access to a number of public assistance programs, and it passed the Illegal Immigration Reform and Immigrant Responsibility Act (IIRIRA) of 1996. The latter sought to enact policies to discourage unauthorized migrants from coming to the United States, but in reality punished severely those who were already in the country. This perverse legal maneuver has had many negative consequences not only for migrants but for larger segments of society, as it has profoundly affected the lives of family members, children, and spouses of the migrants. Among the articles contained in IIRIRA, two under Title III are particularly pernicious for the migrants and their families. An objective of the act was to open up new grounds for mandatory deportation and to foreclose avenues of appeal of deportation decisions. It mandates that individuals who have been lawfully admitted as nonpermanent migrants but who overstay their visas for a period of between 180 to 365 days be penalized by a three-year period of exclusion from the country, during which they would be ineligible to return legally to the United States. If these individuals overstay their visas for more than 365 days, they are subject to a 10-year period of exclusion. Another article in this act makes permanent legal residents deportable under an array of new offenses, retroactive to offenses that may have been committed years or even decades earlier that did not trigger deportation at the time. A permanent legal resident is now deportable if he or she is convicted, at any time after entry, of a crime of domestic violence, stalking, child abuse, neglect, or abandonment, among other offenses; indeed, noncitizens have been forced into permanent exile for petty shoplifting or for possessing small amounts of narcotics. And because this punishment is retroactive, an individual who entered the country legally as a child, committed a crime in adolescence, served his or her sentence, formed a family and remained law-abiding ever since (in some cases for more than thirty years) is now deportable to a country she or he hardly knows. Since IIRIRA was implemented, an estimated 74,000 immigrants were deported from the United States every year between 1997 and 2005; many of those deported were lawful permanent residents and refugees (not solely undocumented migrants), and left behind at least 1.6 million spouses and children, many of whom are U.S. citizens. Of all those deported in fiscal 2005, 65 percent were deported for nonviolent offenses (including illegal entry, drug offenses, theft), 20 percent for unspecified "other" reasons, and less than 15 percent for the commission of a crime involving any form of violence. Hearings before a judge to consider immigrants' ties to the United States, especially family ties, were stopped in 1996 for a long list of offenses (Human Rights Watch 2007).

The IIRIRA at once undermines several principles of the UN convention and those of other treaties that the United States has signed or ratified. The manner in which it is being applied has led to multiple consequences that threaten the lives and well-being of the immigrants themselves and of their U.S.-born children. A particularly insidious practice that has resulted from this law is the routine deportation of immigrants, often one member of a family, which leads to all forms of violations of rights, not least the separation of parents and their minor children (some of whom have even been put up for adoption in the United States after the forced removal of their parents), of married couples, and of siblings. The Department of Homeland Security's Immigration and Customs Enforcement (ICE) has named the latest offshoot "Operation Return to Sender," which started in May 2006 and has involved ICE raids in private homes, parking lots of malls, farms, meatpacking plants, and other workplaces across the country. This "operation" is aimed at removing immigrants classified as "fugitive aliens," even though they might be legal permanent residents or the "collateral catch" of these raids for whom there were no warrants. The result is not only huge financial vulnerability for the families but also indefinite periods of separation that carry deeply detrimental consequences for all involved. Thousands of U.S.-born children (American citizens) have lost their parents in this manner; it is estimated that more than 18,000 fathers had been deported as a result of this operation by mid-2007 (Dandicat 2007). And often, in direct violation of the International Convention on the Protection of the Rights of All Migrant Workers and Members of Their Families, those who are detained are treated as criminals, with few if any rights, even those that conventionally are accorded to detained persons. Detainees are easily cut off from communication with family members or from legal representation through a strategy of moving them seemingly randomly from one detention facility to another, often in the middle of the night (Dow 2004). Many remain in detention for months, if not years, without knowing the nature of the charges against them because they have not committed crimes recently or they already have served sentences for the crimes they committed in the past. Ironically but tellingly, such deportations were accelerated on the heels of the mass protests of spring 2006, when millions marched on the streets of cities across the country to demand more ethical and just immigration laws that would not break up families or pillory vulnerable workers.[5]

Those protest marches—among the most extraordinary reactive mobilizations in U.S. history—were triggered by H.R. 4437, a bill passed by the U.S. House of Representatives in December 2005 that would have made felons of undocumented immigrants and criminalized those who would assist them. The bill was so brazen in its hard line that Cardinal Roger Mahony, head of the Los Angeles archdiocese, the largest Catholic archdiocese in the United States, published an op-ed in the *New York Times* in March 2006 justifying a call for civil disobedience should H.R. 4437 become law. The U.S. Senate, in turn, was stymied in its attempt to pass alternative legislation to regularize the status of undocumented immigrants under a set of strict conditions. The vacuum left by the failure of the federal government to pass "comprehensive immigration reform"—the result of irreconcilable political conflict between those who sought "enforcement" solutions to the presence of millions of migrant workers (from their criminalization and deportation to fencing the entire southern border) to those who sought to forge paths to their eventual legalization and integration (denigrated as "amnesty" by opponents)—has been filled by hundreds of attempts by state and local governments to assume immigration control functions in a growing climate of fear and enforced opprobrium.

In the first half of 2007 alone, more than 1,700 immigration-related bills were introduced in state legislatures, and 170 were enacted; a year before, in the first half of 2006, more than 500 immigration-related bills were introduced in 33 state legislatures, and 79 enacted. Many of these state statutes have been blatantly restrictionist; Georgia's exceeded the scope of California's Proposition 187 (Olivas 2007). They affect a gamut of issues including education, employment, identification, driver's licenses, law enforcement, legal services, public benefits, housing and rents, alcohol and tobacco purchases, gun and firearm permits, flag displays, and juvenile reporting requirements. These in turn have been matched by an even larger set of new municipal and county ordinances across the country, from San Bernardino and Escondido, California; to Maricopa County, Arizona; Farmers Branch, Texas; Carpentersville, Illinois; Hazleton, Pennsylvania; Bogota, New Jersey; and Prince William County, Virginia, with harsh provisions aimed at immigrant renters, English-only documents, even the use of the public library. Older codes, such as long-standing trespass and loitering ordinances, have been selectively reapplied to conduct alien sweeps, to prevent day laborers from congregating, and even (in a New Orleans parish) to prohibit trucks from selling Mexican food. Many of them have been withdrawn, repealed, or struck down in courts on the grounds that they exceeded their constitutional authority or failed basic requirements of due process (as in the *Hazleton* case in 2007),[6] but more are pending. Their effects, in any event, coupled with nationwide ICE raids and uninhibited nativist hostility, are measurable in a palpable sense of dread and even terror in populations of workers and students, including permanent legal residents among them, who become subject to racial profiling (Freedman 2007). As Olivas (2007) argues in a forceful critique of these "pigtail ordinances in modern guise," "the blowback in affected communities, and the resultant prejudice sure to follow from [them] ... are sure signs of an ethnic and national origin 'tax' that will only be levied upon certain groups, certain to be Mexicans in particular, or equally likely, Mexican Americans."

DISCUSSION

Article 22 of the convention against all forms of racial discrimination states that "disputes between two or more states parties with respect to the interpretation or application of this Convention, which are not settled by negotiation or by the procedures expressly provided for in this Convention, shall, at the request of any of the parties to the dispute, be referred to the International Court of Justice for decision, unless the disputants agree to another mode of settlement." Upon ratification, however, the United States stipulated that "with reference to Article 22 of the Convention, before any dispute to which the United States is a party may be submitted to the jurisdiction of the International Court of Justice under this article, the specific consent of the United States is required in each case." That last reservation specifies that "the United States declares that the provisions of the Convention are not self-executing."[7] In practice this means that since ratification does not have any impact on U.S. domestic law, ratifying the convention is mainly an empty, symbolic gesture. Until recently, at least on paper, the United States had sought not to clash so starkly with international agencies regarding the protection of minorities' and migrants' rights, even when international treaties had no bearing on U.S. soil. This changed dramatically, and not only in the United States, after September 11, 2001.

The end result is the erosion of rights under a new regime of national security and border enforcement. Although domestic minorities might enjoy de jure protections, they continue to be excluded through new forms of discrimination and structural disadvantage. Many immigrants lose the small gains they achieved and have become newly vulnerable, legally and socially. Both are tied in forms of discrimination that have become at once more ingrained and more insidious, regressing any gains in the area of rights that were made earlier. As Johnson (2004) points out, although domestic minorities and lawful immigrants might enjoy certain protections de jure, the fact remains that they are regarded as subordinate groups and continue to suffer discrimination. And the events of September 11 galvanized such sentiments.

There is clearly a trend toward the increasing abrogation of rights of racial minorities and immigrants in the United States, with legal structures either enacted or changed to support this trend. Legal statutes written to protect the rights of racial minorities in the latter half of the twentieth century rarely reached their goals, but the fact that they existed and paralleled those enshrined in the UN resolutions was important, offering legal recourse to redress serious violations of rights. The civil rights movement pushed for changes that lent U.S. legal structures a semblance of compliance with international treaties on the protection of rights. However, in recent years, many of these gains have been reversed, and the climate for the protection of rights has decidedly changed. We now see reversals in key Supreme Court decisions, the outright violation of civil rights, and a climate that demonizes entire categories of immigrants (the racial and ethnic minorities of the future) for the very conditions that make them desirable: as sources of cheap labor for an increasingly brutal economic system.

In no small part, September 11 and its immediate legislative outcome, the USA PATRIOT Act (an acronym for Uniting and Strengthening America by Providing Appropriate Tools Required to Intercept and Obstruct Terrorism Act of 2001), served as catalysts for this accelerated reversal in the protection of rights. To be sure, these developments did not *cause* the trend, but they occurred in and were exacerbated by a climate that was already moving in the direction of increased discrimination, racism, and enmity against immigrants. After September 11, Akram and Johnson (2002) saw that "the centralization of immigration power in the hands of the federal government may exacerbate the civil rights impacts of the enforcement of the immigration laws. The federal government has acted more swiftly and uniformly than the states ever could, with severe consequences for the Arab and Muslim community in the United States" (4–5). In this exclusionary climate, Arabs who might have been granted admittance by the United States as bona fide refugees have instead been denied. Thus, one of the consequences of the U.S. invasion of Iraq in 2003 was that by 2007 there were more than 4 million refugees and displaced Iraqis, over 2 million having fled to neighboring countries like Syria and Jordan, and another 2 million internally displaced—including many who aided the United States and now find themselves persecuted for it. But from April 2003 to April 2007 fewer than 500 Iraqis were allowed into the United States as refugees (Husarska 2007). This denial stands in contrast to the period after the Vietnam War, when the United States accepted a historic responsibility for the resettlement of hundreds of thousands of Indochinese refugees.

Other groups have suffered the consequences as well, as measures in the name of national security and the "war on terror" have allowed the federal government and law enforcement agencies to trample the rights of many, including U.S. citizens "suspected" of activities against the state. Massey (2007, 146) refers to this as "postmodern racism," a context facilitated by the government as well as by pundits and politicians in which immigrants become dehumanized or not fully human in the eyes of the public and thus are perceived as having no rights, and which "opens the door to the harshest, most exploitative, and cruelest treatment that human beings are capable of inflicting on one another" (150). Similarly, in an analysis of court case records, Varsanyi (2007) notes a similar process of dehumanization, of stripping immigrants of personhood and humanity, as in the case of a Texas statute seeking to deny public education to undocumented children. These children were physically present in Texas but legally absent due to their undocumented status (Coutin 2000); the judges considered them immigrants, *not* people, and thus not eligible for protection under the Fourteenth Amendment. Varsanyi calls this the production of neoliberal subjects, and it occurs within a two-tiered system of membership, with citizens on the one hand and noncitizens, who are marginalized, exploited, and scapegoated, on the other. This decoupling of personhood from the immigrant is reaffirmed in the actions and words of public officials, as when Maricopa County Sheriff Joe Arpaio seeks to arrest and prosecute undocumented immigrants for conspiracy to smuggle themselves into the country, or when Representative Russell Pearce (R-AZ) hopes that the barrage of anti-immigrant laws in his state will lead immigrants to "self-deport" and go home (González 2007). The parallels to the forced "repatriations" of the 1930s are evident (Johnson 2005; Kanstroom 2007).

The larger context extends beyond national borders. The United States exerts considerable pressure on the governments of countries with either "weaker" states or with whom it maintains close ties. As it has done historically, it demands loyalty and service in exchange for aid or other economic incentives. In efforts to restrict immigration, it has enlisted the help of governments south of the border, such as Mexico and Guatemala and even Costa Rica, so that migrants are stopped even before they reach the southern U.S. border. In the name of national security and the "war on terror," the United States has mustered the assistance of these governments to expand its borders beyond their physical location while seeking to implement similar "counterterrorism" measures that infringe individuals' rights in other countries. In the process, those countries, willingly or unwillingly, join the "rogue" state in dehumanizing people and stripping them of their civil and human rights.

Like other self-fulfilling prophecies, *inclusionary* as well as *exclusionary* models of membership are influenced by the very phenomena they purport to be classifying. In the end, as Aleinikoff and Rumbaut (1998) observed a decade ago, "the way people are welcomed to become members of a society influences their joining behavior which, in turn, influences how the society invites others to join it." Thus, a state concerned about the successful integration of a large and growing resident immigrant population adopts policies that help orient and acculturate immigrants, provide skills and access, and foster tolerance and nondiscrimination. But the inclusionary political model of membership that generally prevailed in the United States in the latter half of the twentieth century has been buffeted by recent events and changing circumstances. Anti-immigrant policies are not integrative policies. In a vicious cycle, an unwelcoming polity that pillories and dehumanizes entire categories of migrant workers, makes entry and attainment of citizenship difficult or impossible, and requires would-be members to change drastically to conform to their new home is likely to produce an immigrant population less willing to choose to conform, and such behavior may then reaffirm for the polity its view of immigrants as persons in need of reform—or deportation. In the dialectics of inclusion and exclusion, what goes around comes around. States, too, reap what they sow.

NOTES

1. See http://www.ohchr.org/english/law/cerd.htm.
2. See http://www.ohchr.org/english/bodies/cerd.
3. See http://www.ohchr.org/english/bodies/cmw.
4. See http://www.ohchr.org/english/law/cmw.htm.
5. Of course, massive deportations are not new in the history of U.S. immigration policies, as seen in "Operation Wetback" in 1954 and in the forgotten forced removals of the 1930s, when more than a million people of Mexican ancestry (including U.S. citizens) were "repatriated" with dire consequences (Johnson 2005; Kanstroom, 2007; Ngai 2004).

6.   For the federal judge's ruling in *Lozano v. Hazleton,* see http://coop.pamd.uscourts. gov/06v1586.pdf.

7.   See http://www.ohchr.org/english/countries/ratification/2.htm#reservations.

REFERENCES

Akram, Susan Musarrat, and Kevin R. Johnson. 2002. "Race, Civil Rights, and Immigration Law after September 11, 2001: The Targeting of Arabs and Muslims." *New York University Annual Survey of American Law* 58: 4–5.

Aleinikoff, T. Alexander, and Rubén G. Rumbaut. 1998. "Terms of Belonging: Are Models of Membership Self-Fulfilling Prophecies?" *Georgetown Immigration Law Journal,* 13 no. 1: 1–24.

Blau, Judith, and Alberto Moncada. 2006. *Justice in the U.S.: Human Rights and the U.S. Constitution.* Lanham, MD: Rowman and Littlefield.

Brown v. Board of Education of Topeka, 347 U.S. 483 (1954).

Burawoy, Michael. 2006. "A Public Sociology for Human Rights." Pp. 1–20 in *The Public Sociologies Reader,* edited by Judith Blau and Keri Iyall Smith. Lanham, MD: Rowman and Littlefield.

Bustamante, Jorge. 2005. Interim Report of the Special Rapporteur of the Commission on Human Rights on the Human Rights of Migrants. Available at http://ap.ohchr.org/ documents/dpage_e.aspx?m=97. (Accessed February 11, 2008.)

Coutin, Susan B. 2000. *Legalizing Moves: Salvadoran Immigrants' Struggle for U.S. Residency.* Ann Arbor: University of Michigan Press.

Dandicat, Edwidge. 2007. "Impounded Fathers." *New York Times,* June 17, available at http://www.nytimes.com/2007/06/17/opinion/17danticat.html. (Accessed March 30, 2008.)

Dow, Mark. 2004. *American Gulag: Inside U.S. Immigration Prisons.* Berkeley: University of California Press.

Feagin, Joe. 2006. *Systemic Racism: A Theory of Oppression.* New York: Routledge.

Freedman, Samuel G. 2007. "Immigration Raid Leaves Sense of Dread in Hispanic Students." *New York Times,* May 23, available at http://www.nytimes.com/2007/05/23/ education/23education.html?ex=1337572800&en=1d55e9a1a24d9cfb&ei=5088& partner=rssnyt&emc=rss. (Accessed March 30, 2008.)

González, Daniel. 2007. "Migrants Fleeing as Hiring Law Nears." *Arizona Republic,* Sunday, August 27, A-1.

Hanson, Jon, and Kathleen Hanson. 2006. "The Blame Frame: Justifying (Racial) Injustice in America." *Harvard Civil Rights–Civil Liberties Law Review* 41: 413–480.

Hernandez v. Texas, 347 U.S. 475 (1954).

Human Rights Watch. 2007. *Forced Apart: Families Separated and Immigrants Harmed by U.S. Deportation Policy.* HRW 18, no. 3, available at http://hrw.org/reports/2007/us0707. (Accessed February 11, 2008.)

Husarska, Anna. 2007. "There's No 'U.S.' in Refugees." *Los Angeles Times,* September 29.

Johnson, Kevin. 2005. "The Forgotten 'Repatriation' of Persons of Mexican Ancestry and Lessons for the 'War on Terror.'" *Pace Law Review* 26, no. 1: 1–26.

———. 2004. *The "Huddled Masses" Myth: Immigration and Civil Rights.* Philadelphia: Temple University Press.

————. 2003. "Immigration, Civil Rights, and Coalitions for Social Justice." *Hastings Race and Poverty Law Journal* 1: 181.

————. 1998. "An Essay on Immigration, Citizenship, and U.S./Mexico Relations: The Tale of Two Treaties." *Southwestern Journal of Law and Trade in the Americas* 5: 121.

Kanstroom, Daniel. 2007. *Deportation Nation: Outsiders in American History.* Cambridge, MA: Harvard University Press.

Mahony, Roger. 2006. "Called by God to Help." *New York Times,* March 22, available at http://www.nytimes.com/2006/03/22/opinion/22mahony.html. (Accessed March 30, 2008.)

Massey, Douglas S. 2007. *Categorically Unequal: The American Stratification System.* New York: Russell Sage Foundation

Massey, Douglas S., and Nancy A. Denton. 1993. *American Apartheid: Segregation and the Making of the Underclass.* Cambridge, MA: Harvard University Press

Menjívar, Cecilia. 2006. "Liminal Legality: Salvadoran and Guatemalan Immigrants' Lives in the United States." *American Journal of Sociology* 111, no. 4: 999–1037.

Merritt, Deborah J., and Bill Lann Lee. 2003. Amicus Curiae Brief of the American Sociological Association in *Grutter v. Bollinger,* 539 U.S. 306, available at http://asanet.org/galleries/default-file/AmicusBrief_ASA.pdf. (Accessed March 30, 2008.)

Motomura, Hiroshi. 2006. *Americans in Waiting: The Lost Story of Immigration and Citizenship in the United States.* New York: Oxford University Press.

Myrdal, Gunnar. 1944. *An American Dilemma: The Negro Problem and Modern Democracy.* 2 vols. New York: Harper.

Ngai, Mae N. 2004. *Impossible Subjects: Illegal Aliens and the Making of Modern America.* Princeton, NJ: Princeton University Press.

Olivas, Michael A. 2007. "Lawmakers Gone Wild? A Response to Professor Kobach." *SMU Law Review* (in press).

Olivas, Michael A., ed. 2006. *"Colored Men" and "Hombres Aquí":* Hernández v. Texas *and the Emergence of Mexican-American Lawyering.* Houston, TX: Arte Público Press.

Pfaelzer, Jean. 2007. *Driven Out: The Forgotten War Against Chinese Americans.* New York: Random House.

Plessy v. Ferguson, 163 U.S. 537 (1896).

Plyler v. Doe, 457 U.S. 202 (1982).

Varsanyi, Monica. 2007. "Neoliberalism and the Rescaling of National Membership." Unpublished manuscript, Arizona State University.

Zolberg, Aristide R. 2006. *A Nation by Design: Immigration Policy in the Fashioning of America.* New York and Cambridge, MA: Russell Sage Foundation and Harvard University Press.

ADDITIONAL RESOURCES

International Center for Migration, Ethnicity and Citizenship:
http://www.newschool.edu/icmec.

International Convention on the Protection of the Rights of All Migrant Workers and Members of Their Families:
http://www.ohchr.org/english/law/cmw.htm.

Migrants Rights International:
http://www.migrantwatch.org.

UN International Migration and Development:
   http://www.un.org/esa/population/migration/index.html.
UNESCO. International Migration and Multicultural Policies:
   http://portal.unesco.org/shs/en/ev.php-URL_ID=1211&URL_DO=DO_
   TOPIC&URL_SECTION=201.html.

CHAPTER SEVEN

~

Women's Rights

TOLA OLU PEARCE

This chapter examines women's attempts to redress the injustices and inequalities experienced by virtue of the fact that they are women. It takes as axiomatic the fact that women belong to diverse groups and that the discourse has moved beyond the woman/women debate. Although systemic and systematic practices by states and private individuals (Burrows 1986; MacKinnon 2006) have been resisted over the centuries (well-known voices include: Wollstonecraft, Tubman, Truth, Bhaduri, Ransome-Kuti, El Saadawi, etc.), much of the language for understanding these issues is new. Further, gender concerns did not receive the degree of validation women sought until they were catapulted onto the human rights platform by the United Nations in 1995. Neither the Universal Declaration of Human Rights (UDHR) (1948) nor the Committee on the Elimination of Discrimination Against Women (CEDAW) (1979) achieved this kind of legitimacy for the women's movement. Beijing (1995) and its aftermath signaled shifts: a central position for gender issues in the human rights movement and more compelling protection for local activists and theorists working in a wide variety of environments. Thus, gendering human rights puts us firmly in the murky terrain of politics.

This chapter draws attention to four issues. First I examine conceptual tensions over what human rights entail, and whether accepting the Euro-American liberal approach is sufficient. Next, I discuss the analytic frame developed by African American women and its uses in gendering human rights. Third, I review attempts to confront human rights violations and the knotty issue of cultural relativism. Finally, I comment on the significance of neoliberal globalization for women's human rights.

CONCEPTUALIZING HUMAN RIGHTS

After World War II, the United States took charge of the global human rights project. Both government and mainstream academic perspectives on "rights" and on human rights as a special category are grounded in the liberal tradition based on the arguments of scholars like John Locke (1632–1704). Briefly stated, liberalism focuses on the rational individual, his freedoms, autonomy, and independence. To have a right is to have a just claim, an entitlement that neither persons nor institutions can trample on. This focus on negative rights was particularly directed at the state (hypothetically established by social contract among individuals), which is legally constrained from interfering with an individual's legal rights. The state must also ensure that others do not infringe on an individual's entitlements. Within this liberal perspective, human rights therefore concentrate on the individual as the bearer of rights and the centrality of the state-individual relationship. Donnelly has summarized the perspective thus: "Human rights—equal and inalienable entitlements of all individuals that may be exercised against the state and society—are a distinctive way to seek to realize social value as justice and human flourishing" (Donnelly 2007, 284). As opposed to other types of rights, this category requires only that one be human.

Donnelly however goes on to argue that only "modern" Western societies developed the concept of human rights because they evolved in response to the specific "social, economic, and political transformations of modernity" (Donnelly 2007, 287). He believes that other societies may well find such ideals relevant once they begin to experience turmoil and threats to dignity on the road to modernity. One problem, however, is the difficulty in separating the indignities of modernity from the specific experience of being pressed into modernity under colonization, neocolonialism, and neoliberal globalization domination. I have also critiqued elsewhere the tendency of some Western scholars to define human achievements so narrowly (e.g., towns, cities, theater, etc.) that only Western expressions fit the bill (Pearce 2001). I extend my concern here to the impact of definitions on women.

The liberal framework summarized above, which privileges the individual, the state, and the public sphere, is problematic for women both in North America and across the globe. Following Pateman's (1988) seminal work on the sexual contract, American feminists have outlined the ways in which the liberal public-private divide impedes their efforts to claim human rights (Cook 1994). Not only does the state have a history of sanctioning this divide and relegating women to the private sphere, but it has also been aggressively active in the construction of gender differences (Brush 2003) such that females within any group or strata are understood to be unequal to males in that category, with fewer rights in the public sphere. It soon became clear after 1948 that UDHR did not solve women's problems, any more than today's increased political representation does. Elected officials are regarded as "honorary men" and pressured to shed "feminine" traits in the quest for political leadership.

Thus, as recently as 2006, MacKinnon was still able to ask: "Are women human?" in a collection of essays, which included experience from North America. Unless women are constructed anew within the private sphere, stepping out into the public sphere does not alter who they are in society, nor does it automatically confer the substantive human rights bestowed on men. It does so only in theory. Under these conditions, being woman "is not yet a name for a way of being human" (MacKinnon 2006, 43). One may also note that the liberal framework makes it easier for the United States to opt out of ratifying CEDAW, by insisting that it expects women to use the existing platform of first-generation human rights (i.e., political and civil rights) to seek redress. All this is not to deny that several groups (class, race, sexual minorities, the elderly) are also perceived by the state as "other" and thus less entitled.

Across the United States women of color have also critiqued the liberal perspective on rights. Dorothy Roberts (1997) shows that negative obligations and freedom from state interference are too limiting and serve to relegate other freedoms (e.g., from want, or hunger) to the back burner. She states emphatically: "The abstract freedom to choose is of meager value without meaningful option from which to choose and the ability to effectuate one's choice. Defining the guarantee of personhood as no more than shielding a sphere of personal decisions from the reach of government—merely ensuring the individual's 'right to be let alone'—is inadequate to protect the dignity and autonomy of the poor and oppressed" (309). Roberts not only argues that women's reproductive rights are human rights, but adds that society has a responsibility to address the material conditions of vulnerable women whose rights to public resources are not granted legitimacy.

In other societies women are equally affected by the liberal project, since the rational economic citizen has become the target of the new neoliberal economic policies, which reduce the availability of local resources and augment national debts. Further, since the United States does not endorse second (i.e., social, economic, and cultural rights) and third (i.e., right of self-determination and development) generation human rights, there is always the question of the legitimacy of claims at multilateral meetings. In 2001, for instance, the United States rejected a UN report on the Right to Development, arguing that such claims are "at best" goals, not entitlements or universal human rights (Raghavan 2001). Over the years, non-Western scholars have consistently argued for decentering the Euro-American framework. But their arguments have generally been dismissed as not relevant because indigenous values are not rights that citizens are able to claim against a state. Using African constructions, I will argue that other models draw attention to aspects of the human condition that precede state formation. This is significant for gendering human rights.

Although the African continent has hundreds of ethnic groups, several scholars suggest there are some indigenous ideas that ground local perspectives on human rights. If one accepts that cultural constructs are "fictions" (Kahn 1995), the African fiction of the interdependent being is as valid as the Euro-American fiction of the autonomous person (Comaroff and Comaroff 2001). African societies believe that groups are the backbone of individuals and that humans are "beings-in-relation" (Awolalu 1972). While agency is important (Nyamu-Musembi 2002), the self is generally construed in terms of mediatory agency (Shaw 2000) and is viewed as diffuse, fluid, and permeable (Babatunde 1992). Piot concludes that in Africa, persons are generally perceived as *constituted by relationships rather than situated in them* (Piot 1999, 18). This perspective is marked by a belief in radical reliance on others. By and large, the human condition is one of dependency, not austere self-sufficiency. From this insight, the most basic of all human rights is *the right to call for assistance.* It is universal, predates state formation, is no cause for shame, and is above all *reciprocal.* Which human being is actually self-made? The social support needed for a newborn will necessarily differ from that required by an adult (Wiredu 1992), a widowed father, or a pregnant female.

Unfortunately, African communities have not always lived up to the ideals of benign human interdependence. But the world has never judged the ideals of democracy by the practice of Jim Crow democracy. The point is that the African axiom on human rights is necessary for forging a humane vision of our future, where, as Donnelly himself argues, the human rights discourse is just one strategy for building future possibilities: It's "less about the way people 'are' than about what they might become" (Donnelly 2003, 15).

INTERSECTIONALITY

Feminist theorizing within the United States was significantly enhanced with the development of "intersectionality," an analytical tool developed by African American women. Beginning in the late 1960s with Beale's "double jeopardy," intersectionality emerged as a way of theorizing black female experience such that race, class, and gender systems could be understood as "mutually constructing systems" (Collins 1998, 116). By the 1980s black women had expanded this frame to other social categories (age, prisoners, sexualities) and several disciplines. The concept underscores the experiences of marginalized groups and sees them as agents of knowledge about their own lives and their relationship to hegemonic systems. Intersectionality later became a national imperative for anyone working on gender—including whites and males. In exposing discriminatory practices, differential identity constructions, etc., the paradigm has gone global (Basu 1995; Kabeer 1994). Sonia Alvarez, for instance, reports that the road to Beijing brought out new sets of actors in South America "whose discourses emphasized the ways in which race/ethnicity, class, sexuality, age and so on are constructive of gender identities" (Alvarez 1998, 301).

As an analytical tool, intersectionality, along with standpoint, is indispensable in exposing human rights violations and justifying the claims of subordinated groups. By legitimizing the experience, voice, and knowledge from various locations, intersectionality brings to the fore what Dagnino calls the "right to have rights" (2005, 153), in that no marginalized experience can be ignored. For women in the United States, much of the struggle is still at the level of the right to have rights, insofar as CEDAW, the International Covenant on Economic, Social and Cultural Rights, and other instruments have not been ratified. For example, dealing with pornography merely in terms of obscenity laws and not human rights does nothing to hold perpetrators operating away from public view accountable, nor does it empower women in general (MacKinnon 2006).

In exposing experiences in order to make claims, a major task has been to develop the language, concepts, and frameworks that depict experiences. The ability to name what is going on in daily life has been the concern of scholars like Dorothy

Smith (1987). Concepts like "ruling relations," the "glass ceiling," marital rape, and gender power are part of the effort to bring to light women's realities. In addition, to understand *how* systems work, we need to go beyond an essentialist focus on "intersectional bodies" that are merely added to the mix. Women are studying just how states, communities, or household members generate reality (Naples 2007). Solinger (1994), for example, discusses how social, cultural, and economic practices merged in post–World War II United States to define unwed pregnancy differently for blacks and whites. While the former were consistently defined in pathological terms, whites were rehabilitated through a mandate that allocated resources for adoption. White girls were then reconstructed as mature, marriageable ladies.

In recognition of differences in global experience, mutual understanding is developing between human rights workers in different regions. Moghadam (2007) believes that a positive shift, between first- and third-world feminists, occurred during the 1980s partly because of changes in the global economy. Tensions decreased as a result of the slow and steady attempts by transnational feminist networks (TFNs) like Development Alternatives with Women for a New Era (DAWN), Women Living Under Muslim Laws (WLUML), MADRE, and Women's Caucus for Gender Justice to address ideological divides. Local or regional organizations determine their own priorities prior to transnational collaboration, and pre- or postconference forums have emerged as an important strategy for retaining independence (e.g., prior to UN or global NGO meetings). Transnational feminist networks now have a track record in working with community, national, and global policymakers. On human rights, successes include contributions to final documents such as the Vienna Declaration and Programme of Action adopted by 171 countries in 1993.

Finally, intersectionality also highlights the problem of representation: Who speaks for whom? This is relevant at every level where women congregate to develop a public voice. Thus Collins (1998) observes that all group standpoints require open discussion between members to prevent domination from within the group. Representation draws attention to another problem, one suggested by the famous essay "Can the Subaltern Speak?" (Spivak 1988). Although numerous interpretations to Spivak's essay exist, one of note is that even when women act, speak, and assess their own situation, this is not sufficient to ensure they are "heard." A woman's message is easily ignored in the crossfire of public discourses on cultural, religious, and economic principles (Morton 2007).

HUMAN RIGHTS VIOLATIONS AND CULTURAL RELATIVISM

When a UN human rights instrument is crafted, a nation can sign, ratify (with or without reservations), implement, or ignore it. Cultural outlook generally affects what happens, for example, whether there is an emphasis on cultural diversity or not (Blau and Moncada 2005), and the UN Educational, Scientific, and Cultural Organization (UNESCO) has garnered a declaration of its own affirming the importance of cultural diversity (UNESCO 2001). However, instruments like CEDAW developed to empower women are the least likely to be implemented, even when signed and ratified.

Nonetheless, progress is being made. In 2000, the Optional Protocol to CEDAW was passed with no reservations allowed.

The above developments aside, disagreements on cultural relativism are far from settled even among feminists. From well-known attacks on the evolutionary paradigm that places Euro-American cultures at the pinnacle of human development, to the argument that insiders' judgments are absolute, cultural relativism is used in different ways for different political purposes. In the United States it was employed by the state to wiggle out of addressing women's human rights. Shachar (1998) discusses the Supreme Court's refusal to rule on a case involving the petition of a Pueblo woman, married outside the group, who wanted the right to bestow Pueblo citizenship on her child, a right reserved for males. The court's ruling was based on the concept of multicultural accommodation. As a solution Shachar develops two intersectionist models premised on the fact that individuals are simultaneously members of different groups (Pueblo, female, and U.S. citizen). In one model, (the horizontal) legal jurisdiction is structured in layers with the identity group responsible for certain legal areas. The second model (the vertical) calls for "joint governance," where any issue could have coordinated input from both legal systems. Though both models have their critics, each at least begins to address the practical problems women face, in that each goes beyond the untenable dichotomous (either/or) perspective.

Although the United States often points to human rights violations in other countries, its own relativist perspective nonetheless affects the lives of American women. In his study of single mothers, Neubeck (2006) reviews the obstacles facing poor women that stem from the government's refusal to adopt the International Covenant on Economic, Social and Cultural Rights (1966). The limited assistance awarded them tends to leave single mothers worse off than their European counterparts. Further, the United States believes that "the attainment of the rights to an adequate standard of living is a goal or aspiration to be realized progressively that does not give rise to any international obligation or any legal entitlements.... *Additionally, the United States understands the right of access to food to mean the opportunity to secure food and not a guaranteed entitlement*" (quoted in Neubeck 2006, 11, emphasis added). According to Neubeck, this official perspective was borne out by the 1996 welfare reform, which upheld labor participation as the solution to poverty. However, structural changes in the economy have sifted these women into dead-end jobs with lows wages and few benefits. The well-being of mothers and children was secondary to their "use" in the system as cheap labor.

Cultural relativism remains a source of tension between Euro-American and other cultures. The civilizing mission was a convenient weapon used during colonial occupation to justify political and economic domination. Mutua argues that as part of the human rights movement, Western societies proceeded to "descend on 'backward' nations in the Third World with the human rights mission to free them from the claws of despotic governments and benighted cultures" (Mutua 2003, 2). Similarly, while deploring attempts by other regions to interpret the UDHR culturally, the United States employs its own interpretations. Article 5 of UDHR rejects cruel, inhuman, or degrading treatment or punishment. Most European nations interpret the death penalty as inhuman, but the United States does not.

Cultural relativism becomes even more contentious with women's human rights, where reservations to the UN instruments are standard fare. In fact, CEDAW "is the treaty with the greatest number of substantive reservations" (Mertus 2005, 104) focused on tradition, nationality, legal capacity, marriage, and family relations. Even before CEDAW, Western nations often politicized women's lives in other cultures in order to demand widespread societal changes. Given Western discourses on practices such as female genital cutting, the veil, sati, widowhood norms, "honor killings," etc., third-world scholars have attacked the politics behind Western official and academic maneuvering (Abu-Lughod 2002). Many third-world feminists have also critiqued these practices. The problem, however, lies with the uses to which Western searchlights have been put, including the "white men saving brown women from brown men" syndrome (Spivak 1988, 297).

In addition to the complicated relationships between female and male persons of color and Euro-American cultures, there is still the complicated job of analyzing gender relations within local communities. Precolonial issues, the impact of colonization, and interactions between indigenous and imported phenomena require analysis. I am in agreement with Coomaraswamy who critiques the tendency to romanticize precolonial India and notes that "the rigors of the caste system or sex-based oppression cannot all be laid at the doorstep of colonial India" (Coomaraswamy 1994, 44). Ditto for Africa, Asia, and the Middle East. All the same, women did not experience unmitigated benefits during colonization (Pearce 1965). Results were mixed, not only between different categories of women, but across different spheres of a woman's life. Everywhere, including the United States (Cole and Guy-Sheftall 2003), community members bristle at unfavorable depictions of local gendered structures and attitudes. Any revelation generates accusations of race, ethnic, and national disloyalty or blind support for all things Western. Nonetheless, TFNs have become adept at unraveling the specifics of gendered experiences through dialogue, sharing information, or resources, and organizing collective interventions that expose "collusions of patriarchies" (WLUML cited in Moghadam 2007, 154).

WOMEN'S RIGHTS IN THE AGE OF GLOBALIZATION

Any story can be told from more than one perspective. Thus, in opposition to the grand narrative on modernity, Bauman examines the steady trail of environmental and human wastage. Industrial capitalist modernity by its very *design* requires much of humanity to be left behind as waste: "*Homo sacer* (a creature stripped of human and divine significance in Roman law, the worthless other) is the principal category of human waste laid out in the course of the modern production of orderly ... sovereign realms" (Bauman 2004, 33).

In the age of globalization, women's human rights are at the center of attempts to counter "order building" that increases human wastage. In theorizing the meaning and impact of the neoliberal policies and treaties set in motion for global capitalist restructuring, an intersectionist gender analysis helps to contextualize different experiences and asks: How is globalization affecting and reconstituting lives, or repositioning geographic regions? Who benefits, who gets excluded, what practices are involved, and what are the substantive rights of the included?

There is overwhelming evidence that women have suffered disproportionately from the restructuring of national economies worldwide. Neoliberal policies have shrunk the formal sector, creating an expanding ring of informal employment (subcontracting, home-based work, sweatshops, day care) that avoid government regulation and employee benefits. Women are often the preferred workers because of their desperation and norms of femininity. The casualization of work has also increased part-time and temporary labor. Overall, labor costs are constantly sacrificed to maximize profit. Women often become the main providers in poor households when partners are laid off formal-sector jobs. Many seek additional work, but tensions build and domestic violence increases (Mexico, Sierra Leone, India). In sum, women are increasingly at risk both inside and outside the home. Nonetheless, some women have gained economically. These tend to be educated, professional, or upper-class women in all regions, although women living in First World nations are further cushioned by the economic policies developed by the global North (Ilumoka 1994).

Many of the problems sparked by global restructuring involve migration and the situation of job seekers affected by jobless economic growth. One major concern is the chain of emigration as women from poorer nations seek domestic and care work in richer countries, leaving young children and family members behind over extended periods. Research is mounting on the consequences for all parties, both in exporting and importing nations. For migrants, problems include horrendous working conditions, passport seizure by employers, emotional distress, sexual harassment, care crises back home, and pressure from governments eager for wage remittance in foreign currency (Ehrenreich and Hochschild 2002). Female migrant workers are at the forefront in seeking to have a human rights perspective applied by host countries, particularly that individuals be treated as "persons/humans" regardless of nationality (Zimmerman, Litt, and Bose 2006). Not surprisingly, there is growing interest in the concept of transnational citizenship among these workers.

Of great concern is the impact of globalization on the trafficking of women and children. United Nations instruments prohibiting human trafficking are among the earliest conventions, even predating UDHR (e.g., the 1921 Convention). Besides instruments specifically targeted at trafficking (1949, 1950), others make reference to the prevention, condemnation, and prosecution of traffickers (e.g., CEDAW in 1979; African Charter in 1981). Yet, the United Nations estimated in 2004 that the annual flow of persons was close to 4 million (UNESCO 2004). This traffic has prompted widespread counteractivities, such as those undertaken by the Asia Foundation (2002), which has seventeen offices across Asia working with local groups to educate, provide material support to victims, train local staff, and pursue offenders. Several nations including the United States, Nigeria, South Africa, Cambodia, and Thailand have passed protective laws. But progress is slow and dangerous given the links to organized crime and profit making.

Finally, one must note that the liberal perspective that emphasizes state-individual relations is seriously compromised by neoliberal economic globalization, since governments are now pressured to accept free market reforms in order to gain a competitive edge on the global market. Civil society is pressed away from the politics of resource redistribution, systemic injustice, and social rights to developing programs aimed at merely increasing the economic efficiency of citizens within a *preformulated economic framework* (Jayasuriya 2006). But the task of gendering human rights requires something else entirely: that *political* deliberations on social rights, the shape of structures, the meaning of democracy, and so forth, be at the very center of the way forward.

CONCLUSION

A focus on women helps to reconstitute both the discourse and practice of human rights. The knowledge and experience of various groups makes it imperative that we move beyond the liberal mainstream model in North America. This chapter has shown that social life beyond the political sphere of individual-state interaction is important. There is a natural integration among all three generations of human rights, and all are required for each to work. We thus need a holistic perspective to human rights. We also need to incorporate the experiences and perspectives of many groups, and a global intersectionist gender analysis legitimizes other voices. In actively choosing our future, the world needs more than the Euro-American perspective in the human rights project.

REFERENCES

Abu-Lughod, Lila. 2002. Asia Source Interview, available at: http://www.asiasource.org/news/special_reports/lila/cfm. (Accessed August 15, 2007.)

Alvarez, Sonia. 1998. "Latin American Feminists 'Go Global': Trends of the 1990s and Challenges for the New Millennium." Pp. 293–324 in *Cultures of Politics, Politics of Cultures,* edited by Sonia Alvarez, Evelina Dagnino, and Arturo Escobar. Boulder, CO: Westview Press.

Awolalu, Omisade. 1972. "The African Traditional View of Man." *Orita* 6, no. 2: 101–118.

Babatunde, Emmanuel. 1992. *A Critical Study of Bini and Yoruba Value Systems of Nigeria in Social Change.* Lewiston, ID: Edwin Mellen Press.

Basu, Amrita, ed. 1995. *The Challenges of Local Feminisms.* Boulder, CO: Westview Press.

Bauman, Zygmunt. 2004. *Wasted Lives: Modernity and Its Outcasts.* Cambridge, UK: Polity.

Beale, Frances. 1969. "Black Women's Manifesto; Double Jeopardy: To Be Black and Female." Pamphlet submitted to the Third World Women's Alliance, New York, available at http://www.hartford-hwp.com/archives/45a/196.html. (Accessed September 17, 2007.)

Blau, Judith, and Alberto Moncado. 2005. *Human Rights.* Lanham, MD: Rowman and Littlefield.

Brush, Lisa. 2003. *Gender and Governance.* Walnut Creek, CA: Altamira.

Burrows, Noreen. 1986. "International Law and Human Rights: The Case of Women's Rights." Pp. 80–98 in *Human Rights: From Rhetoric to Reality,* edited by Tom Campbell, Dave Goldberg, Sheila McLean, and Tom Mullen. New York: Blackwell.

Cole, Johnetta, and Beverly Guy-Sheftall. 2003. *Gender Talk.* New York: Ballantine.

Collins, Patricia Hill. 1998. *Fighting Words.* Minneapolis: University of Minnesota Press.

Comaroff, John L., and Jean Comaroff. 2001. "On Personhood: An Anthropological Perspective from Africa." *Social Identities* 7, no. 2: 267–283.

Cook, Rebecca, ed. 1994. *Human Rights of Women.* Philadelphia: University of Pennsylvania Press.

Coomaraswamy, Radhika. 1994. "To Bellow Like a Cow: Women, Ethnicity and the Discourse of Rights." Pp. 39–57 in *Human Rights of Women,* edited by Rebecca Cook. Philadelphia: University of Pennsylvania.

Dagnino, Evelina. 2005. "'We All Have Rights, But … ': Contesting Concepts of Citizenship in Brazil." Pp. 149–163 in *Inclusive Citizenship,* edited by Naila Kabeer. London: Zed.

Donnelly, Jack. 2007. "The Relative Universality of Human Rights." *Human Rights Quarterly* 29: 281–306.

———. 2003. *Universal Human Rights in Theory and Practice.* 2d ed. Ithaca, NY: Cornell University Press.

Ehrenreich, Barbara, and Arlie Russell Hochschild. 2002. *Global Woman.* New York: Metropolitan/Owl Books.

Ilumoka, Adetoun. 1994. "African Women's Economic, Social and Cultural Rights—Toward a Relevant Theory and Practice." Pp. 307–325 in *Human Rights of Women,* edited by Rebecca Cook. Philadelphia: University of Pennsylvania Press.

Jayasuriya, Kanishka. 2006. *Statecraft, Welfare and the Politics of Inclusion.* New York: Palgrave Macmillan.

Kahn, Robbie. 1995. *Bearing Meaning: The Language of Birth.* Urbana: University of Illinois Press.

MacKinnon, Catharine. 2006. *Are Women Human?* Cambridge, MA: Belknap Press of Harvard University Press.

Mertus, Julie. 2005. *The United Nations and Human Rights.* New York: Routledge.

Moghadam, Valentine. 2007. *Globalizing Women.* Baltimore, MD: Johns Hopkins University Press.

Morton, Stephen. 2007. *Gayatri Spivak.* Cambridge, UK: Polity.

Mutua, Makau. 2003. "A Third World Critique of Human Rights." Paper presented at the Central European University, Budapest, January 29, 2007, available at http://www.ceu.hu/legal/universalism%20and%20local%20knowledge%20in%20HR%202003/Makua_text.htm. (Accessed April 2, 2008.)

Naples, Nancy. 2007. Intersectional Approaches to Citizenship, States, and Politics. Panelist in Special Session at the American Sociological Association Meeting. New York, August 13.

Neubeck, Kenneth. 2006. *When Welfare Disappears: The Case for Economic Human Rights.* New York: Routledge.

Nyamu-Musembi, Celestine. 2002. "Are Local Norms and Practices Fences or Pathways? The Example of Women's Property Rights." Pp. 126–150 in *Cultural Transformation and Human Rights in Africa,* edited by Abdullahi A. An Na'im. London: Zed.

Pateman, Carole. 1988. *The Sexual Contract.* Palo Alto, CA: Stanford University Press.

Pearce, Tola. 2001. "Human Rights and Sociology: Some Observations from Africa." *Social Problems* 48, no. 1: 48–56.

———. 1965. "The Changing Status of African Women South of the Sahara." Paper presented at the Southwestern Anthropological Association. San Francisco.

Piot, Charles. 1999. *Remotely Global.* Chicago: University of Chicago Press.

Raghavan, Chakravarthi. 2001. "Economic, Cultural and Social Rights Only 'Goals,' Says U.S." *South-North Development Monitor,* available at: http://www.twnside.org.sg/title/cultural.htm. (Accessed March 30, 2008.)

Roberts, Dorothy. 1997. *Killing the Black Body.* New York: Pantheon Books.

Shachar, Ayelet. 1998. "Group Identity and Women's Rights in Family Law: The Perils of Multicultural Accommodation." *Journal of Political Philosophy* 6, no. 3: 263–285.

Shaw, Rosalind. 2000. "Tok Af, Lef, Af: Political Economy of Temne Techniques of Secrecy and Self." Pp. 25–49 in *African Philosophy as Cultural Inquiry,* edited by Ivan Karp and D. A. Masolo. Bloomington: Indiana University Press.

Smith, Dorothy. 1987. *The Everyday World as Problematic: A Feminist Sociology.* Toronto: University of Toronto Press.

Solinger, Rickie. 1994. "Race and 'Value': Black and White Illegitimate Babies, 1945–1965." Pp. 287–310 in *Mothering: Ideology, Experience, and Agency,* edited by Evelyn Nakano Glenn, Grace Change, and Linda Kennie Forcey. New York: Routledge.

Spivak, Gayatri. 1988. "Can the Subaltern Speak?" Pp. 271–313 in *Marxism and the Interpretations of Culture,* edited by Cary Nelson and Larry Grossberg. Urbana: University of Illinois Press.

UNESCO. 2004. Data Comparison Sheet #1. Worldwide Trafficking Estimates by Organizations, available at http://www.unescobkk.org/culture/trafficking. (Accessed August 24, 2007.)

Wiredu, Kwasi. 1992. "The African Concept of Personhood." Pp. 104–117 in *African-American Perspectives on Biomedical Ethics,* edited by Harley Flack and Edmund Pellegrino. Washington, DC: Georgetown University Press.

Zimmerman, Mary, Jacquelyn Litt, and Christine Bose. 2006. *Global Dimensions of Gender and Carework.* Palo Alto, CA: Stanford University Press.

ADDITIONAL RESOURCES

Collins, Patricia Hill. 1998. *Fighting Words: Black Women and the Search for Justice.* Minneapolis: University of Minnesota Press.

Epstein, Cynthia Fuchs. 1988. *Deceptive Distinctions: Sex, Gender, and the Social Order.* New Haven, CT: Yale University Press.

Ferree, Myra Marx, Valerie Sperling, and Barbara Risman. 2005. "Feminist Research and Activism: Challenges of Hierarchy in a Cross-National Context." Pp. 137–156 in *Rhyming Hope and History: Activists, Academics, and Social Movements Scholarship,* edited by D. Croteau, W. Hoynes, and C. Ryan. Minneapolis: University of Minnesota Press.

Gerson, Kathleen. 1985. *Hard Choices.* Berkeley: University of California Press.

Gouldner, Alvin. 1970. *The Coming Crisis of Western Sociology.* New York: Basic.

hooks, bell. 2000. *Feminist Theory: From Margin to Center.* Cambridge, MA: South End.

Kabeer, Naila. 1994. *Reversed Realities: Gender Hierarchies in Development Thought.* London: Verso.

Kanter, Rosabeth. 1977. *Men and Women of the Corporation.* New York: Harper and Row.

Lorber, Judith. 2005. *Breaking the Bowls: Degendering and Feminist Change.* New York: Norton.

Risman, Barbara J. 2004. "Gender as a Social Structure: Theory Wrestling with Social Change." *Gender & Society* 18: 429–450.

Sprague, Joey. 2005. *Bridging Differences: Feminist Methodologies for Critical Researchers.* Lanham, MD: Rowman and Littlefield.

Chapter Eight

~

Rights of People with Disabilities

Jean Lynch

The most recent human rights instrument, open for state signature and ratification in March 2007, is the Convention on the Rights of Persons with Disability. The convention consists of a preamble, followed by fifty articles. The preamble states that "disability is an evolving concept and that disability results from the interaction between persons with impairments and attitudinal and environmental barriers that hinder their full participation in society on an equal basis with others." The preamble provides a series of statements outlining specific concerns involved in achieving rights for people with disabilities, such as diversity of the community, the negative impact of poverty, and the special needs of women and children. Other statements speak to the inclusion of specific rights, such as autonomy and the inclusion of persons with disability in decisions about policies and programs that affect the community. The instrument specifies the importance of recognizing the disabled population's valuable contributions to society.

Articles 1 through 4 address the purposes of the convention, relevant definitions, general principles, and the expected obligations of ratifying states. The remainder of the instrument outlines the major obstacles confronting people with disabilities and delineates the institutions, social relationships, and attitudes that prevent the disabled population from realizing full inclusion and participation. The substantive areas addressed include the following: education; health; work and employment; an adequate standard of living and social protection; political and public life; justice and legal rights; and cultural life, recreation, leisure, and sports. The convention emphasizes specific rights of individuals with disability, including autonomy, freedom of decision making and choice, independent living and freedom of movement, freedom of expression and access to information, rights to privacy, and respect for family. Special attention is given to recognizing the greater risks faced by women and girls who have disabilities, emphasizing the need to incorporate a gender perspective in efforts to promote fully inclusive human rights for the disabled population. The convention speaks to the challenges that interfere with equality for people with disabilities, for example, poverty, discriminatory treatment, and the lack of public awareness regarding people with disabilities. Procedures for enhancing the images of disability include public awareness campaigns and the inclusion of disability education in school curriculums. Finally, the convention outlines international coordination of disability rights, including the periodic collection and analysis of data, cooperation between states through the sharing of experiences and best practices, a national implementation and monitoring system, and the establishment of a Committee on the Rights of Persons with Disability to oversee the progress of ratifying states.

Contrary to prevailing popular opinion, the treatment of people with disabilities in the United States is abysmal. Government policies and programs, public attitudes, and media images conspire to ensure that people with disabilities are marginalized or excluded from major social institutions, and, when all else fails, euthanized. Many people believe that life has improved for people with disabilities—after all, environmental alterations such as curb cuts, greater visibility in the workforce, the inclusion of disability issues and persons with disabilities in major media outlets, and the passage of the Americans with Disabilities Act (ADA) demonstrate victories for the disabled community. The reality differs. The effort to remedy physical accessibility is in its infancy, employment discrimination is rampant, and for the most part, media perceptions of people with disabilities fail to reflect the experiences of people with disabilities (Longmore 2003). The ADA has suffered the fate of most laws and policies that allegedly redress disadvantaged minority groups—challenges in court led to the erosion of its definitions and provisions (Erkulwater 2006). The resolution of these cases typically benefits employers and corporations, not people with disabilities, and what was touted as the "greatest piece of civil rights legislation" is being eroded section by section (Switzer 2003).

HISTORY OF TREATMENT OF PEOPLE WITH DISABILITIES

The exclusion and marginalization of people with disabilities is not a new phenomenon. People with disabilities were excluded from residing in the thirteen American colonies unless they could demonstrate financial viability. Those that could gain residency led a marginalized existence; isolated and hidden away in their homes, they were excluded from even minimal participation in community life. Early immigration policies prevented people with disabilities from entering the country due to fears of an increase in this population (Fleisher and Zames 2001).

Dominant thinking about work, success, and individual worth during the Industrial Revolution generated perceptions about the meaning and experience of disability. Industrial capitalism, with its emphasis on the glorification of work and the acquisition of wealth, sealed the fate of people with disabilities for the next few centuries. In the period of industrialization, capitalists defined the value of workers by their ability to function like machines. The harder a worker could be driven, the more valuable that laborer was to capitalist interests (Russell 1998). The American dream, with its Horatio Alger images of "pulling oneself up by the bootstraps," encouraged workers to exemplify those values that promised success and the potential acquisition of wealth—hard work, rugged individualism, unbridled competition, and independence. Based on these values, an individual employee's worth is attributable to individual input alone—those who succeed do so because of their hard work and ability; those who fail do so because of their weakness and inherent inferiority. They have no one to blame but themselves (Blau and Moncada 2006). Under the Spenserian philosophies of natural selection and social Darwinian survival of the fittest, people with disabilities could justifiably be excluded as unfit, left to join the ranks of the surplus population. Industrialization denied any possibilities for work accommodations for those who were different (e.g., flexible work schedules), and the physical environment erected barriers that prevented the participation of people with disabilities in the employment sector. Considering the significant value placed on a person's ability to work, people with disabilities were perceived as incompetent, unfit for employment, and incapable of economic independence (Russell 1998).

During most of U.S. history, people with disabilities have been viewed with suspicion, fear, and disdain, and those with any visible disability were assumed to be weak and dependent on others. In fact, until the 1950s, many people with disabilities were institutionalized despite their ability to live in the community. Suggested as the most benevolent solution for the child and family, parents were encouraged to place "defective" children in institutions. Institutionalization was the preferred solution for adults as well, promising invisibility and segregation from the "normal" population. Institutional care was primarily custodial with minimal attention given to training or education (Switzer 2003). The deinstitutionalization movement of the 1950s and 1960s changed little—except that people with disabilities were removed from institutions into an environment that was structurally and socially inaccessible with few programs and policies in place to address their needs. Public attitudes stigmatized people with disabilities, who then were marginalized and excluded from community participation (Fleischer and Zames 2001).

MODELS OF DISABILITY

Models of disability conceptualize disability by outlining the causes of and appropriate responses to disability. Models of disability shape public perceptions and suggest the roles and scripts able-bodied people and people with disabilities should assume in their interactions with each other. Following is a description of the moral, medical, and social models of disability. The transition from the medical model to the social model has not been entirely successful. Since the medical model (unfortunately) continues to provide the foundation for most programs and policies, it continues to be paramount in media representations and remains central in public perceptions of disability.

Why would using alternative means to perform an activity (such as using a wheelchair to enable mobility) justify stigmatizing, excluding, and denying privileges to a category of people (Silvers 1998)? One answer lies in the traditional models of disability. The earlier models—the moral and medical—both focus on limiting the negative impact people with disabilities have on society—usually with solutions that will relieve the discomfort of able-bodied people and prevent, as much as possible, the visibility of disability in society. Both focus on people with disabilities as socially and functionally deficient as well as physiologically or mentally impaired. The models use a deficit comparison conceptualization, emphasizing an ideal of normality against which disability is compared.

Moral Model of Disability

The earliest model of disability—the moral model—portrayed disability as resulting from the evil nature or moral lapse of an individual or of someone close to the person (such as an ancestor). Disability justified shunning and exclusion of that individual from participation in social life. Yet from early times able-bodied people realized their responsibility to provide for the maintenance of people with disabilities through economic compensation. Interestingly, disabilities were often believed to be accompanied by personal compensation as well; thus, for example, those suffering visual impairments might be compensated by highly acute hearing abilities (Silvers 1998). Vestiges of the moral model exist today; media depictions of people with disabilities frequently suggest a belief that they develop specialized or superior abilities that compensate them for their disabilities (Longmore 2003).

Medical Model of Disability

The medical model, welcomed as a much superior, more compassionate, rational, and scientific response to disability, replaced the moral model of disability. In reality, the medical model replaced terminology—sickness and pathology rather than evil and immorality, physiological or mental flaws rather than moral lapses, and medical treatment and rehabilitation rather than moral repentance and prayer—but improved neither the image of people with disabilities as inferior nor the treatment accorded them by the public (Longmore 2003).

The same philosophies and values that underscore the market economy provide justification and validation for the medical model of disability. In the medical model, able-bodiedness is a normative ideal against which disability is compared (Switzer 2003). The value of people with disabilities is measured according to the degree of their functionality (their capacity to work). The goal of treatment is to cure the individual or, when that is not possible, to rehabilitate people with disabilities so that they become as physically and mentally similar to able-bodied individuals as possible. Thus, the goals of cure and rehabilitation are paramount, with rehabilitation oriented toward increasing functional capacity (Silvers 1998).

The medical model rests on unquestioned ableist assumptions—disability is an individual flaw due entirely to natural causes and living with a disability is a "fate worse than death" (Fleischer and Zames 2001; Longmore 2003). The medical model fails to consider external sources that impact disability. No attention is paid to the social, economic, or physical barriers that limit the opportunities of people with disabilities or to the conflicts embedded in the social relations between people with disabilities and able-bodied people; the focus is on changing the individual, not on modifying the environment (Silvers 1998).

In the medical model, the disability becomes the person's sole identity. The person is infantilized and subject to other's perceptions and judgments (Longmore 2003). Medical practitioners and able-bodied people are the experts in conceptualizing disability and in determining the needs and desired outcomes for people with disabilities. Almost totally excluded from discourse are the true experts—people with disabilities themselves! Decisions about types of medical equipment, definitions of the quality of life, and euthanasia—when based on empirical data—more often emerge from data collected from able-bodied respondents' perceptions of the needs of people with disabilities and their lives (Silvers 1988; Timmermans 2001). In a society where public perceptions rest on stereotypic assumptions about people with disabilities, the findings from such questionable data collection procedures frequently yield policies and programs that further the exclusion and disadvantages already levied against this group (Silvers 1998).

The medical model, like the moral model, continues to place responsibility for disability squarely on the shoulders of people with disabilities themselves while at the same time limiting decisions about treatment options and goals. Not only is the cause frequently attributed to the individual (for example, poor health or genes), but the assumption is that the individual should comply with medical prescriptions regarding treatment plans and goals—whether or not the individual perceives such plans to be in his or her own best interest or aligned with his or her life goals. To the public, the presumptions of the medical model align exactly with their perceptions of disability. Normalization depicts people with disabilities as "other," as the victims of an arbitrary fate who, if they attend to and comply with medical directives, can overcome their inferiority (Fleischer and Zames 2001). To able-bodied people, the possibility of transforming people with disabilities into their own image resolves any contradictions whatsoever about the social problem of disability and the value of work. It unfortunately also prevents any recognition of the perspectives of many in the disabled community, who focus on goals other than cure.

SOCIAL MODEL OF DISABILITY

To a majority of those in the disabled community, the medical model completely fails to capture the experience of disability. The social model of disability attributes the disadvantages of disability to a hostile environment that can be transformed to lessen its handicapping effects (Silvers 1998). Rather than maintain an environment—physical, social and environmental—that reflects only the dominant group's preferences, the social model emphasizes inclusion and accessibility through modification of the environment (Switzer 2003). In the social model, the voices and the experiences of people with disabilities are central. In so doing, the paternalistic assumptions of functionality as realized only through the current modes of productivity, architectural designs, and environmental structures that benefit the dominant class are rejected. Rather, the social model recognizes the need for arrangements that promote maximum mainstream social and economic participation. In the social model, it is the structural environment and public attitudes that need alteration, not the individual with disabilities. The focus is no longer on cure as the ultimate or even most desirable goal of people with disabilities; rather, maximizing the potential and life satisfaction of individuals in accordance with their own preferences is paramount (Silvers 1998).

LEGISLATION

Two major pieces of legislation focused on improving accessibility and inclusion for people with disabilities, the Rehabilitation Act of 1973 and the Americans with Disabilities Act of 1990. The most important section of the former statute read "no otherwise qualified handicapped individual in the United States shall, solely by reason of his handicap, be excluded from participation in, be denied benefits of, or be subjected to discrimination under any program or activity receiving Federal financial assistance." Two decades later, the ADA extended the range of benefits to most aspects of civic life. Like most statutes aimed at civil rights, implementation was not forthcoming. It quickly became clear that the only way in which people with disabilities would benefit from the ADA was through litigation (Switzer 2003).

There are two major reasons why legislation implementing human rights fails in the United States. One reason is structural and the other is embedded in the social relations generated under capitalism. The former is primarily a problem of governmental division along federal and state lines and the separation of the federal government into branches (Blau and Moncada 2006). Legislation enacted at the federal level is subject to interpretation at the state level. Once passed, most laws pertaining to rights become enmeshed in endless litigation as people try to apply the law to specific situations. The only way to initiate implementation is to seek redress through the court system. The implementation of the ADA is no exception, but litigation has produced significant erosion of the original legislation. The ADA suffered from some limitations when it was written (most notably, the omission of an affirmative action requirement similar to what is found in civil rights statutes and other legislation addressing discrimination on the basis of minority group membership, for example, gender and race (Fleischer and Zames 2001).

One of the major difficulties in implementing the ADA is due to the fact that compliance is voluntary—without the establishment of a system to oversee compliance and with no sanctions in place for noncompliance, each individual case requires court litigation. In addition, vague phrases such as "undue hardship" and "reasonable accommodation" have been used by businesses to escape compliance with requested accommodations, claiming the requested changes would be a "significant difficulty or expense" (Colker 2005).

The historical conflict between the judicial system and the legislative branch also devastated the ADA. Although Congress expended effort to construct the bill, it was severely criticized by lower-court judges who claimed that the bill was not well conceived. In fact, in many cases, the lower courts ignored the original intentions of Congress and, rather than use the congressional record to resolve potential ambiguities, used the ambiguities that resulted to interpret the statute as narrowly as possible (Colker 2005).

Disability advocates believe the Supreme Court misinterpreted the ADA in some employment cases, treating them as if they revolved around benefits rather than discrimination—which led to decisions that disadvantaged people with disabilities. The Supreme Court also redefined the parameters of the definition of disability, excluding individuals if their medication allowed them to control their disability. Thus, certain populations clearly intended to be covered under the ADA were excluded and lost their protected status (Fleischer and Zames 2001).

In demonstrating the magnitude of the group that would benefit from the ADA, Congress cited the figure of 43 million as a minimum estimate. Yet the courts applied this figure as a ceiling, using it as a justification for limiting the scope of coverage for disability protections (Colker 2005). In effect, the legislation designed by Congress became subject to judicial interpretations that significantly weakened the statute's ability to lessen discrimination for people with disabilities.

The second reason why human rights cannot be integrated into the current system is that the inequalities naturally produced under capitalism and the competitive spirit capitalism generates pit all groups and individuals against each other in their individualistic pursuit of success and material acquisition. Success as defined under capitalism depends on competition between individuals, and state intervention is perceived as an unfair interference. The state is not supposed to act as an agent who can affect the outcome of the win-lose, every person for him-or herself foundation on which the market rests. Individuals succeed based on their own merits and abilities or lose based on their lack of ability and failings. If one group receives advantages (or seems to), success and failure no longer rest on individual merit alone. In addition, some groups are perceived as naturally inferior and occupy positions at the bottom of the stratification system. The protection of civil rights attempts to militate against this "natural inequality" by providing safety nets for those who have been disadvantaged by the system (Blau and Moncada 2005).

DISABILITY RIGHTS: CIVIL RIGHTS OR NOT?

While the former explains the negative attitudes the public holds toward civil rights and the programs and policies that aim at equalizing opportunities for groups defined as disadvantaged, it does not specifically explore the attitudes toward people with disabilities and the considerable resistance the disability movement confronts. What explains the resistance and the backlash that occurred following the development of legislation that sought to integrate people with disabilities into mainstream society? Over and above the negative repercussions that followed legislative attempts to redress grievances, there is clearly avoidance of and hostility toward the disability rights movement. There is an appalling lack of media coverage of actions taken by those on behalf of the disability rights community. With the exception of the Gallaudet uprising—which did receive national attention—few of the protests and other collective actions by the disabled community are covered by the media; when they do receive coverage, it is minimal at best (Fleischer and Zames 2001). Disability rights are often ignored, excluded from discussions of civil rights movements. Why is the disability movement perceived—even by those who should be allies—as somehow different from the struggles of other civil rights groups (Switzer 2003)? Why are scholars who pursue critical analysis of society unlikely to expand their analysis to the issues of disability (Longmore 2003)?

The disability movement is distinct from other civil rights movements because of the lack of a central identifiable figure (e.g., Gloria Steinem) or organized group that is publicly recognized as the "face" of the movement (Switzer 2003). More important than these differences, I contend that people are motivated to repel people with disabilities because of the images of disability that are perpetuated and the fear these representations engender in able-bodied people. Whereas other groups are stereotyped as having less ability to be productive members of society (such as being less intelligent or ambitious) or possessing personal characteristics that interfere with work excellence (such as being too emotional or submissive), people with disabilities are characterized as *incapable of working at all!* In fact, representations of people with disabilities expand beyond work incapacity; rather, people with disabilities are depicted as devoid of almost all of the most cherished American values of independence, autonomy, hard work, self-determination, and perseverance. People with disabilities are even perceived as demonstrating a lack of those qualities important to personal and intimate relationships—they are portrayed as unattractive and undesirable, sexless, and incapable of nurturing others. Silvers (1998, 3) claims that the presented images of people with disabilities are of people who live a "fringe existence." Because of limited physical access and other barriers to social inclusion encountered by people with disabilities, able-bodied people have few, if any, opportunities to understand people with disabilities and dispel such illusions. Nor do able-bodied people desire much contact with the disabled community; Silvers (1998, 36) claims "attempts at social participation are so extensively disallowed that, for most Americans, working side by side with a severely disabled person counts as extraordinary, while engaging in an intimate social relationship with such a person is unimaginable."

Yet, both people with disabilities and the able-bodied know (even if the latter both fear and deny this understanding) that the borders to the disability community are open—it is the only minority group that anyone can join at any moment. Given the images that are portrayed, is it any wonder that able-bodied individuals fear joining their ranks! Media images exacerbate these negative stereotypes by consistently presenting themes depicting what people with disabilities are like and defining the "experience" of people with disabilities. In the following section, a few of the images of people with disabilities are briefly summarized.

MEDIA IMAGES OF DISABILITY

One popular theme depicts "disability as transgression," something that individuals can somehow manage and control, a condition that can be cured or, failing that, minimized—if the person tries hard enough (Fleischer and Zames 2001). Like other minority groups, stories of people with disabilities frequently communicate myths of exaggeration, representations of individuals who, against all odds, "pull themselves up by the bootstraps." For people with disabilities, this image is realized through stories of cure brought about by the sheer willpower and strength of character of individuals with disabilities. Able-bodied people easily assimilate these fables into their already formed stereotypic representations of people with disabilities. The message is clear: Disability is curable, and those who are not cured are simply not trying hard enough. Such images not only provide the justification to blame people with disabilities who "fail" but also allow able-bodied people to assume that, if they were to enter the ranks of people with disabilities, they would successfully overcome their disability.

Another popular theme depicts people with disabilities as pitiable. He or she lives a life that is unfulfilling—a life too terrible to contemplate (Switzer 2003). Such stories portray disability as the sole identity of the individual, occupying a central position in any of the relationships or experiences of the individual's life. Virtually everything that happens to people with disabilities is connected to the disability. The contradictory attitudes Americans hold simultaneously toward people with disabilities—both pity at their tragic fate and admiration for living with a disability—are supported through survey findings. Other research demonstrates that a significant percentage of respondents agree that they would rather be "dead than disabled" (Fleischer and Zames 2001).

A third presentation of disability depicts people with disabilities as dependent on others. In these fictional accounts, people with disabilities require the help of others in coping with the psychological difficulties resulting from living with a disability. Stories that revolve around the failure of an individual with disabilities to adapt to the disabilities are resolved by the introduction of an able-bodied savior who rescues the individual, eventually solving these failures to adjust (Longmore 2003; Switzer 2003). The medical model supports this image by insinuations of people with disabilities as weak and dependent on able-bodied people for physical and psychological support. There is a rather obvious cognitive dissonance in these story lines; apparently, despite their limited exposure to disabled individuals and the lack of direct experience with disability, the able-bodied expert is perfectly capable of providing mentoring assistance. It is particularly impressive considering the popular conception of disability as a "fate worse than death." Silvers claims the dissonance between perceptions of people with disabilities as "other" and assumptions about self-predictions is easily resolved. What one supposes is that, were one in that situation, one would act in more honorable ways (Silvers 1998).

A PRESSING ISSUE: EUTHANASIA

One of the most critical issues confronting the disabled community is euthanasia. The vast majority of information that speaks to this issue, however, is couched in more palatable terms, such as death with dignity, the right to die, and other nonthreatening terminology. While many in the disabled community support issues of choice, the fear that the "right to die" will become the "duty to die" renders the issue more complicated and personal than it is for able-bodied people. There is already pressure on people with disabilities (Fleischer and Zames 2001). Under the capitalist system, people with disabilities are living in (or presumed to be living in) a body considered nonexploitable and therefore valueless. There is little hope that the public, holding attitudes regarding disability as "a fate worse than death" and supposing that living with a disability is a terrible existence, will lend support if (or when) cost/benefit analyses are applied to life-and-death choices about people with disabilities. There is a difference between choosing to take one's own life and a duty to die. What people with disabilities fear is that the able-bodied population, who are treated to images of themselves as superior to people with disabilities and who are inundated with media perceptions of their own expert status in their relationships to people with disabilities, will be all too eager to encourage death for people with disabilities. John Hockenberry states, "There is much more effort put into cure ... or discussing the legal issues involved in suicide for the severely disabled than there is into integrating disabled folks into society at large. Pray to be normal no matter how impossible it seems is the sentimental message. The alternative is too horrible to contemplate" (Hockenberry 1995, 204). Hockenberry suggests that people with disabilities are made to feel that if cure is not an option, they have a civic responsibility to die.

Evidence suggests that the lives of people with disabilities are not only seen as less worthy than the lives of able-bodied people (Fleischer and Zames 2001), but that these perceptions affect the likelihood of whether they will live or die. Timmermans (2001) found that hospital medical staff are likely to consider certain patients as socially dead—thus, although biologically alive, they are treated as if they are corpses. In resuscitation attempts and in the speed and vigor with which resuscitation attempts are pursued, hospital staff practice passive euthanasia, defining certain patients as socially dead. Not surprisingly, patients with disabilities are much more likely to be defined socially dead than are able-bodied patients. In interviews with medical staff, their attitudes toward the value of life reflected the same views about disability as those held by the public (Timmermans 2001).

Already a growing number of people are promoting suicide for people with disabilities. Using misleading figures about disability costs, their aim is to convince the public that the services and technology required to maintain people with disabilities result in an "inherently undignified lifestyle" (Coleman and Gill in Fleischer and Zames 2001, 245). Media coverage and groups who support the "duty to die" philosophy suggest that the funds used to support people with disabilities and the expensive accommodations being demanded under the ADA are extensive, although actual statistics reflect a vastly different scenario (Fleischer and Zames 2001).

Jack Kevorkian, one of the most vocal supporters of the "right to die" philosophy, is perceived by some in the able-bodied community as compassionate because of his appeals regarding death with dignity. Yet Kevorkian also believes that "voluntary self-elimination of individual and mortally diseased or crippled lives taken collectively can only enhance the preservation of public health and welfare" (Kevorkian quoted in Longmore 2003, 186).

If the potential for euthanasia becomes realized, people with disabilities will be at greater risk than others. The same discrimination that is applied in the delivery of health services to people with disabilities would certainly influence threats of euthanasia. Even within the disabled community, certain segments may be more adversely affected than others. Those who are less likely to be cured, suffer from more severe disabilities, or have fewer financial resources at their disposal will be more likely to be the victims of euthanasia policies. It is here that the interaction of minority status with other characteristics will be likely to further disadvantage some groups. Women, already socialized to believe their primary function is to nurture others, will no doubt be prone to concerns about being a burden to others. They may be more easily convinced—or convince themselves—to sacrifice their lives (Fleischer and Zames 2001).

CONCLUSION

How do people in the United States maintain their belief in their country as the defender of human rights, yet justify exclusion of people with disabilities from full participation in the opportunities afforded others? Why are we comfortable with charity approaches used to raise money for specific disabilities, but resentful of programs and policies that create a more accessible, inclusive environment? What does it say about our country that a group of people must be concerned not only about the lack of human dignity they are accorded, but fear whether this lack of respect might be translated into a death knell?

Citizens have a right to benefit from programs that reflect respect for human dignity and the worth and equality of all individuals (Russell 1998). In the United States resources for these ends must be wrested from the state, and those who are less able to compete are subjected to humiliating processes to be maintained at bare subsistence levels. Unfortunately, the drive for individual competition compels us to deny our sense of community and responsibility toward one another. Every program that is established to provide for some group or to redress previous and current grievances is met with resistance and resentment (Russell 1998). The disability rights movement has been no exception.

While there have been victories achieved by the disabled community, real changes require more than curb cuts and the illusion of change. In the United States, people with disabilities continue to confront discrimination in employment, education, health care, media coverage, and other institutions, all of which severely impacts the achievement of full social and economic participation. The disability movement, like all movements, needs external allies who value and support the efforts of its members. It is interesting that the disability rights movement gains such little attention and support, yet impacts the lives of almost all citizens, regardless of any other statuses they occupy.

REFERENCES

Blau, Judith, and Alberto Moncada. 2006. *Justice in the U.S.: Human Rights and the U.S. Constitution.* London: Rowman and Littlefield.

———. 2005. *Human Rights beyond the Liberal Vision.* New York: Rowman and Littlefield.

Colker, Ruth. 2005. *The Disability Pendulum: The First Decade of the Americans with Disabilities Act.* New York: New York University Press.

Erkulwater, Jennifer L. 2006. *Disability Rights and the American Social Safety Net.* Ithaca, NY: Cornell University Press.

Fleischer, Doris, and Frieda Zames. 2001. *The Disability Rights Movement from Charity to Confrontation.* Philadelphia: Temple University Press.

Hockenberry, John. 1995. *Moving Violations: War Zones, Wheelchairs, and Declarations of Independence.* New York: Hyperion.

Longmore, Paul K. 2003. *Why I Burned My Book and Other Essays on Disability.* Philadelphia: Temple University Press.

Russell, Marta. 1998. *Beyond Ramps: Disability at the End of the Social Contract.* Monroe, ME: Common Courage.

Silvers, Anita. 1998. "Introduction." Pp. 1–11 in *Disability, Difference, Discrimination: Perspectives on Justice in Bioethics and Public Policy,* edited by Anita Silvers, David Wasserman, and Mary B. Mahowald.. Lanham, MD: Rowman and Littlefield.

———. 1998. "Formal Justice." Pp. 13–145 in *Disability, Difference, Discrimination: Perspectives on Justice in Bioethics and Public Policy,* edited by Anita Silvers, David Wasserman, and Mary B. Mahowald. Lanham, MD: Rowman and Littlefield.

Switzer, Jacqueline Vaughn. 2003. *Disabled Rights: American Disability Policy and the Fight for Equality.* Washington, DC: Georgetown University Press.

Timmermans, Stefan. 2001. "Social Death as Self-Fulfilling Prophecy." Pp. 305–321 in *The Sociology of Health and Illness: Critical Perspectives,* edited by Peter Conrad. New York: Worth.

ADDITIONAL RESOURCES

Americans with Disabilities Act of 1990:
    http://www.dol.gov/esa/regs/statutes/ofccp/ada.htm.
Convention on the Rights of Persons with Disabilities:
    http://www.ohchr.org/english/law/disabilities-convention.htm.
Human Rights Web:
    http://www.hrweb.org.
National Council for Support of Disability Issues:
    http://www.ncsd.org/NCSD_files/NCSD_goals.htm.
New Freedom Initiative's online resources for Americans with Disabilities:
    http://www.disabilityinfo.gov/digov-public/public/DisplayPage.
    do?parentFolderId=500.
San Francisco State University Institute on Disability:
    http://bss.sfsu.edu/disability/dateline.html.
Society for Disability Studies:
    http://www.uic.edu/orgs/sds/generalinfo.html.
U.S. Dept. of Health and Human Services (Civil Rights on the Basis of Disability):
    http://www.hhs.gov/ocr/discrimdisab.html.

CHAPTER NINE

~

Rights of Indigenous Peoples

KERI E. IYALL SMITH

The reputation of the United States within indigenous communities is not positive. Within its own borders the United States stole lands, sought to assimilate tribes and then terminate tribes, and continues to weaken sovereignty through the federal courts. The fact that Indian Law is within the jurisdiction of the United States is evidence that tribes and the government do not share a nation-to-nation relationship. In this chapter I summarize the Indigenous and Tribal Peoples Convention (ITPC) (1989), which establishes the rights of indigenous peoples around the globe. I then explore contemporary violations of the human rights of indigenous peoples within the U.S. boarders and abroad.

THE TREATY

The ITPC (1989), also known as the International Labour Organization (ILO) Convention 169, was, and remains, a revolutionary document. This treaty updates the Indigenous and Tribal Populations Convention and Recommendation of 1957 and consists of forty-four articles dealing with general policies, land, recruitment and employment, vocational training, handicrafts and rural industries, social security and health, and education and means of communication. For space considerations I focus on the first nineteen articles here, which pertain to general policies and land. The preamble to the convention notes the importance of "the aspirations of these peoples to exercise control over their own institutions, ways of life and economic development and to maintain and develop their identities, languages and religions, within the framework of the States in which they live" (International Labour Organization 1989). It also recognizes "the distinctive contributions of indigenous and tribal peoples to the cultural diversity and social and ecological harmony of humankind and to international cooperation and understanding" (International Labour Organization 1989).

The first section focuses on application, defining terms, and establishing the rules for implementing the convention at the state level. Paraphrasing the definition, indigenous and tribal peoples are socially, culturally, and economically distinguished from others; partially or fully regulated by their customs or traditions; descended from populations who lived in the area at the time of conquest; and retain all or some of their own social, economic, cultural, and political institutions (International Labour Organization 1989). Self-identification is the fundamental criterion for determining a group's status as indigenous. States are protected in Article 1.3: "The use of the term 'peoples' in this Convention shall not be construed as having any implications as regards the rights which may attach to the term under international law" (International Labour Organization 1989). The ILO definition of indigenous and tribal peoples is important for the ways it empowers indigenous groups but also for the protection it affords states from secession (Article 2.1). Calling for human rights, gender equality, citizenship rights, protections from prejudice and discrimination, political and economic equality, and freedom for indigenous and tribal peoples, the ILO (1989) seeks to protect indigenous and tribal peoples from discrimination (Article 2.2). Indigenous and tribal peoples should be involved in the process of applying the provisions of the convention, with states responsible for establishing the institutions to support this cooperative process where necessary (International Labour Organization 1989).

The convention focuses on promoting cooperation between the government and indigenous and tribal peoples and respect for the cultures of indigenous peoples. Indigenous and tribal peoples are to be permitted to form institutions that reflect their values (Article 6), which the state should support, including customary legal structures (Article 9). Traditional methods of punishment are encouraged over prison (Article 10.2). Indigenous and tribal peoples are to be protected from abuse of their rights and freedoms, and provisions should be made so that they understand legal proceedings as necessary (Article 12).

In relation to land, the convention calls upon governments to respect the importance of land to the cultures of indigenous and tribal peoples (Article 13.1) and asserts that the term "land" refers to the "total environment" (Article 13.2). This holistic definition is intended to reflect the diverse conceptualizations of land among indigenous and tribal peoples instead of the legal definitions created by states. Article 14.1 protects the right of ownership of traditional lands or the rights to access, for example for nomadic peoples or shifting cultivators. Governments are also charged with the task of identifying traditional territory and protecting the rights of indigenous and tribal peoples' ownership and possession of traditional lands (Article 14.2). The states must also establish a legal system for processing land claims (Article 14.3). Indigenous and tribal peoples have the right to "participate in the use, management, and conservation of these resources" (International Labour Organization 1989, Article 15.1). Indigenous and tribal peoples are protected from forced removals (Article 16.1) and permitted a right of return to their traditional lands (Article 16.3). In the event that it is not possible to return (Article 16.4) or in the case of relocations (Article 16.5), indigenous and tribal peoples are to be compensated with lands of similar quality. Penalties for unauthorized trespassing or land use will be established (Article 18). Any national agrarian programs must be equally applied to indigenous and tribal peoples (Article 19).

It is important to include the full text of Article 15.2, as it relates directly to violations committed by the United States against indigenous and tribal peoples. It states:

> In cases in which the State retains the ownership of mineral or subsurface resources or rights to other resources pertaining to lands, governments shall establish or maintain procedures through which they shall consult these peoples, with a view to ascertaining whether and to what degree their interests would be prejudiced, before undertaking or permitting any programs for the exploration or exploitation of such resources pertaining to their lands. (International Labour Organization 1989)

This article creates the provisions for protecting indigenous interests when lands might be mined for resources (surface or subsurface).

HOW THE UNITED STATES VIOLATES THE RIGHTS OF AMERICAN INDIANS

The United States has a blighted history in its dealings with Native Americans. During the early years it sought to usurp land (1789–1815 Treaty Era, 1815–1845 Removal Era, 1845–1887 Reservation Era, and 1887–1934 Allotment Era). Then the United States began a concerted effort to assimilate tribes (1934–1945 Indian Reorganization Era and 1945–1960 Termination Era). In spite of a history of theft and coercion, Native Americans currently live in an era of self-determination (1960–present). They are becoming vocal about human rights violations committed against them by the United States. Key issues include sovereignty, criminal jurisdiction, violence against women, religious freedom, racial discrimination, loss of homelands, and pollution of the environment.

Sovereignty: Lack of Sovereignty Is a Violation of Articles 6 and 9

The Federal Acknowledgement Process (FAP) was developed in 1978 as a way for Indian tribes to gain access to federal protections and resources. Tribes that do not have a prior treaty-based relationship with the U.S. government can apply to the Branch of Acknowledgement and Research (BAR), now the Office of Federal Acknowledgement (OFA), for recognition by the U.S. government. Federal acknowledgement is also a form of sovereignty, allowing recognized tribes to self-govern and providing tribes with a land base. According to the Bureau of Indian Affairs (2006a), since 1978, 314 groups have sent letters of intent to apply for acknowledgement. Of these groups, only eighty-two have submitted full petitions. Out of the eighty-two petitions, forty-one were resolved by the BAR/OFA and were resolved by congressional action or other means (e.g., withdrawing from the process or merging with another petitioner). Of the resolved cases, only fifteen groups were acknowledged, while twenty-three tribes had their petitions denied (Bureau of Indian Affairs 2006b). The remaining three cases were "clarified by other means," one of which was clarified by legislation (Bureau of Indian Affairs 2006b). As of 2006, ten petitions were currently under active consideration, and another nine petitions were completed and waiting for active consideration. Two groups were in the postfinal decision appellate process within the OFA, and two others were in litigation in federal court (Bureau of Indian Affairs 2006a).

As described in 25 CFR Part 83.7, the petition for acknowledgement must provide evidence that:

> The petitioner has been identified as an American Indian entity on a substantially continuous basis since 1900.

1. A predominant portion of the petitioning group comprises a distinct community and has existed as a community from historical times until the present.
2. The petitioner has maintained political influence or authority over its members as an autonomous entity from historical times until the present.
3. A copy of the group's present governing document including its membership criteria. In the absence of a written document, the petitioner must provide a statement describing in full its membership criteria and current governing procedures.
4. The petitioner's membership consists of individuals who descend from a historical Indian tribe or from historical Indian tribes which combined and functioned as a single autonomous political entity.
5. The membership of the petitioning group is composed principally of persons who are not members of any acknowledged North American Indian tribe.
6. Neither the petitioner nor its members are the subject of congressional legislation that has expressly terminated or forbidden the Federal relationship (Bureau of Indian Affairs 1978.)

All criteria are mandatory. To prove points 1, 2, and 3, tribes often have to work with academic experts who gather evidence of the tribe's continuity, the distinctness of the tribal community, and its political structure. Evidence of descendants can also be a challenge to document, as the tribe must gather state-sanctioned evidence, such as birth and death certificates. A complete petition can take years to assemble and years to process and can be thousands of pages long. The OFA assesses applications by applying anthropological, genealogical, and historical research methods (Bureau of Indian Affairs 2006a). Tribes can appeal the OFA's decision, and it is also common for other acknowledged tribes to sue tribes that are applying for recognition, questioning the petitioning tribe's legitimacy. Taking into account the demanding nature of petitioning for recognition along with the Eurocentric nature of the application procedure, it is questionable whether the FAP constitutes a form of self-determination. While the few tribes that have successfully applied are now able to exercise a limited form of self-government, those tribes that are in the process of petitioning for acknowledgement are not yet experiencing sovereignty. It is nearly thirty years since the Department of the Interior developed this procedure, and yet more than 200 tribes remain unrecognized and are therefore not able to practice their sovereign rights as tribes or become eligible for assistance from the federal government.

The Native Hawaiians lack sovereignty as well. When Hawaii became a state, the U.S. government required the formation of the Office of Hawaiian Affairs to manage relations with the Native Hawaiians. The relationship between Hawaiians and the United States is an ongoing colonial relationship (Trask 1999).

Tribes that are acknowledged or reorganized also experience a lack of sovereignty. A Supreme Court decision (*Cherokee Nation v. Georgia*) deemed American Indians wards of the state in 1831. The nation-to-nation relationship that supposedly exists between tribes and the U.S. government is marred by this declaration. Sovereign immunity prohibits the U.S. federal government from being sued unless it waves this immunity or consents to the lawsuit. Sovereign immunity also protects states within the United States from lawsuits (as the Supreme Court found in *Blatchford v. Native Village of Noatak*, 501 U.S. 775 [1991]).

The Bureau of Indian Affairs (BIA) has a bad reputation for its dealings with American Indian tribes. In the case of *Cobell v. Kempthorne,* a member of the Blackfeet tribe is suing the U.S. secretary of the interior for breaking the trust with American Indians. The suit charges the Department of the Interior with mismanagement of the Individual Indian Money accounts and poor maintenance of financial records, resulting in losses suffered by individual account holders (Blackfeet Reservation Development Fund n.d. a). This case has been in litigation since 1996, and is still not resolved.

Criminal Jurisdiction: Lack of Criminal Jurisdiction Is a Violation of Article 2

Criminal jurisdiction in Indian Country (reservation and trust lands) is often referred to as a "web" for its confusing limitations. Although a tribe retains its power to punish offenders as a part of its sovereignty, tribes have criminal jurisdiction only if Congress has given them this power (Pevar 1992). Congress and U.S. courts have established limits for tribal criminal jurisdiction. The rules for criminal jurisdiction in Indian Country are as follows:

1. For non-Indians who commit crimes against Indians, the federal government has criminal jurisdiction.
2. When an Indian commits a crime against a non-Indian, the federal government has criminal jurisdiction. The tribe also has criminal jurisdiction.
3. Crimes committed by Indians against Indians on reservations are under the jurisdiction of the tribe.
4. If a treaty gives a tribe the right to prosecute certain crimes, then that is under the jurisdiction of the tribe.
5. If a nonmember Indian commits a crime on a reservation, the tribe has jurisdiction.
6. Congress has limited the punishments that tribal courts can impose to one year in jail and a $5,000 fine. (Richland and Deer 2004)

7. The federal government has criminal jurisdiction over all instances involving major crimes: murder, manslaughter, rape, assault with intent to kill, arson, burglary, larceny, kidnapping, incest, assault with a dangerous weapon, assault resulting in serious bodily injury, assault with intent to commit rape, robbery, and felonious sexual molestation of a minor. This jurisdiction applies regardless of the identity of the victim or criminal. Tribes can also prosecute Indians who commit major crimes, but they are subjected to the limits in "6" above.
8. States have jurisdiction over crimes committed on a reservation that are not written in federal statutes but *are* in a state statute.
9. States also have jurisdiction when a crime is committed on a reservation by a non-Indian against a non-Indian.
10. Indians can also be tried twice for the same offense: by the state and the tribe. This does not constitute double jeopardy because two different governments are prosecuting the criminal activity.
11. Under Public Law 280, certain states have criminal jurisdiction on reservations within their borders. These states are Alaska, California, Maine, Minnesota, Nebraska, New York, Oregon, and Wisconsin. Criminal jurisdiction of tribes in these states was terminated by this legislation.

Jurisdictional limits established by the U.S. government render tribes unable to implement their own systems of justice. Congress further limited tribes by placing limits on the punishments that tribes can exact. Tribal criminal legal statutes, in general, also look very similar to American criminal legal statutes. The Bureau of Indian Affairs and the Department of the Interior have worked to shape tribal courts so that they now mirror American courts instead of their traditional models. Tribes are creative in defining jurisdiction and have had to use this creativity to prosecute non-Indians. This may involve using civil codes, police power to arrest and remove, consent or stipulation, civil contempt, expulsion, and civil forfeiture (Garrow and Deer 2004).

Violence against Women: A Violation of Articles 2.1 and 2.2a

Citing data from the federal government, Amnesty International (2007) identified a problem: Native American and Alaskan native women are 2.5 times more likely to be raped or sexually assaulted than women in the United States in general. More than one in three American Indian women will be raped during their lifetime. Amnesty International finds that confusion over jurisdiction and reluctant federal prosecutors are allowing acts of sexual violence against American Indian women on Indian lands to go unpunished (Amnesty International 2007). Non–Native American men commit over half of these rapes, and they cannot be prosecuted for the crimes they commit by the tribal courts. Racism and cultural differences are barriers to American Indian women reporting the crimes. Amnesty International (2007) documents problems in policing, gathering forensic evidence, treatment for survivors, and support services as contributing to a failure to protect indigenous women in the United States from sexual violence. Forensic examinations to gather evidence are often not obtained due to racism of hospital staff or a lack of available facilities on or near reservations (Amnesty International 2007). Indian Health Services offices are reluctant to conduct forensic examinations, citing their policy to offer only medically related treatments.

Amnesty International urges U.S. government action, as a part of its trust responsibilities, to protect the human rights of indigenous women in the United States. Their recommendations require the support and action of both federal and state governments to develop comprehensive plans of action to stop violence against indigenous women, end discrimination on the basis of indigenous status and gender, ensure accountability, increase federal funding, end impunity for abusers, ensure appropriate and effective policing, ensure access to sexual assault forensic examinations, provide support services for survivors, ensure that prosecution and judicial practices deliver justice, and integrate a human rights perspective (Amnesty International 2007).

Religious Freedom: Lack of Religious Freedom Is a Violation of Articles 13, 15.1, 15.2, and 18

The religion of many Native American groups is deeply rooted in the environment and natural sites. Many Native Hawaiians practice various forms of Christianity, but others are returning to their traditional religion, *Ho'omana*. One island, Kaho'olawe, is an important island spiritually because it is the site of ceremonies honoring Lono, the god of fertility and agriculture. Kaho'olawe became a U.S. Navy bombing practice ground, which decimated the landscape further and littered it with unexploded ordnance (Hartwell 1996). This has left the island barren and the environment is severely damaged. Erosion is unchecked. In 1976 an organization called Protect Kaho'olawe 'Ohana formed, seeking to stop navy bombing and to regain the island for Native Hawaiian spiritual observances (Hartwell 1996).

Through protest and political action, 'Ohana first gained the right to have access to the island forty days per year, and then the navy returned the island to the state in 1989, which allows only traditional Hawaiian use (no commercial activity). Makahiki, a four-month celebration, is now celebrated at Kaho'olawe annually. Instead of following tradition precisely, celebrants must modify the schedule, avoiding conflict with access rights, modern responsibilities, and the desolate state of the environment on the island—chants promoting growth on the island have been added to ceremonies. Monies are allocated for the removal of the unexploded ordnance, but only small areas of the island are currently safe.

On the mainland two other tribal communities are seeking to have exclusive access to sacred sites for religious purposes. In California, the Wintu people seek to conduct renewal ceremonies at Mt. Shasta in Panther Meadows without interruption by New Age practitioners (McLeod 2001). The New Age practitioners dance naked in the meadows and leave crystals in the water, acts that the Wintu fear offend the mountain. Their foot traffic is also damaging natural springs, which are sacred sites for the Wintu people (McLeod 2001).

The Lakota regard Mato Tipila, the Lodge of the Bear, as a sacred site of renewal. This site is also known as Devils Tower, a popular climbing destination in Wyoming (McLeod 2001). Climbers at Devils Tower disturb the silence that is essential for

Lakota people and other local tribal groups who perform sun dances and vision quests in the areas surrounding the site (McLeod 2001). Climbing a sacred site, some Lakota people claim, violates their culture. The National Park Service is attempting to mediate by asking climbers not to climb in June, the most active ceremonial season (McLeod 2001). Mandatory climbing closures are in place to protect endangered species (the prairie falcon), but the June moratorium remains voluntary. Climbers are protesting the June moratorium in the courts, arguing that this policy is a violation of the constitutional separation of church and state (McLeod 2001). Climbers who do not respect the climbing moratorium in June are violating the religious freedom of Lakota people.

Racial Discrimination: A Violation of Articles 2.1, 2.2.a, 13, 15.1, and 15.2

The United States was recently sanctioned by the UN Committee on the Elimination of Racial Discrimination (CERD) for its actions on Western Shoshone lands in Nevada. The Western Shoshone initially sought assistance from the United Nations because they were concerned about the way the U.S. government was handling its ownership of their lands (the federal government asserts that it owns 90 percent of Western Shoshone lands), including use of the land for military testing, open pit cyanide heap leach gold mines, and nuclear waste disposal (Western Shoshone National Council 2006). The CERD responded to these concerns by issuing an Early Warning and Urgent Action Procedure Decision to the United States in March 2006. The CERD decision noted that U.S. actions fail to "respect and protect the human rights of the Western Shoshone peoples" and orders the United States to freeze its privatization of lands; "desist from all activities planned and/or conducted on Western Shoshone ancestral lands" and stop imposing grazing fees and restrictions on hunting, fishing, and gathering (Western Shoshone National Council 2006). A report issued in February 2007 provides evidence that the United States has not taken action as prescribed by CERD and is continuing to engage in discriminatory action. In it, the Western Shoshone note the continuing U.S. role in privatizing land, permitting open pit cyanide heap leach gold mining, appropriating water, constructing a coal-fired power plant near Western Shoshone lands, allowing grazing on Western Shoshone sacred lands, and conducting controlled burns in spite of tribal protest (Western Shoshone National Council et al. 2007).

Loss of Homelands: A Violation of Articles 13, 14.1, 14.3, 15.1, and 15.2

The Hawaiian Homes Commission Act of 1920 set aside 200,000 acres for Native Hawaiians (Dudley and Agard 1993, Hartwell 1996, Trask 1999). The lands set aside were the least desirable on the island—far from water and too rocky to farm easily (Hartwell 1996). When Hawaii became a state in 1959, the text of the act admitting Hawaii to the union required the state to hold the trust lands and the income from the lands (Getches, Wilkinson, and Williams 1993). The income from leased properties was to be used for education, to improve the conditions of the Native Hawaiians, to develop farm and home ownership, and to provide lands for public use (Getches, Wilkinson, and Williams 1993). Government agencies lease 29,000 acres, and 93,500 acres are leased to nonbeneficiaries for commercial, industrial, or other uses (Hartwell 1996). Almost 20 percent of the acreage is set aside for federal use, such as for military bases and parks (Dudley and Agard 1993). The income from these leases do not even cover the expenses of the Department of Hawaiian Homelands (Hartwell 1996; Trask 1994). The Office of Hawaiian Affairs, which was created during the state's constitutional convention to oversee the trust, continues to mismanage the funds and the land. This constitutes an abuse of Hawaiian Homelands trust lands.

More than 29,000 applications were on file for pastoral and residential lots in 1998 (Trask 1999). Yet more than 130,000 acres of trust lands were being used illegally (Hartwell 1996; Trask 1999). Only 40,400 of the total acres have been distributed to eligible Native Hawaiians (Hartwell 1996). Many Native Hawaiians still do not have lands that are due to them under the Hawaiian Homelands law. The wait for property to become available is long. Native Hawaiians cannot challenge the illegal use of lands in state or federal courts (Trask 1999). Adequate trust lands were not allocated early in statehood, and today the majority of Native Hawaiians are on a waiting list for homelands instead of enjoying their benefits.

In addition to the Native Hawaiians, American Indians have all lost their homelands to the U.S. government. This happened during the Treaty and Allotment Eras, as the settlers moved west demanding land and security from Indians. Alaska Natives lost their lands through the Alaskan Native Claims Settlement Act of 1971, which established village-based corporations and allotted lands by the size of the corporation. Villagers were compensated for lands they lost, but many corporations went bankrupt, losing their allotted lands.

Pollution of the Environment: A Violation of Articles 13, 15.1, 15.2, and 18

Many tribes are seeking to protect the environment on reservations and at sacred sites. A few examples are presented here. The Northern Cheyenne Nation seeks to stop the development of methane gas wells near their Cheyenne homelands, which they fear will pollute the water and damage the soils of the reservation (Grossman 2005). The Gwich'in people are working to stop oil drilling in the Alaskan National Wildlife Refuge. The porcupine caribou occupy proposed drilling sites. This animal is culturally important and a source of food for Gwich'in people (Grossman 2005). Waters polluted with dioxins by the paper companies surround the Penobscot Nation homelands. The state of Maine claims that the water is clean and refuses to take action against the polluters. The state will also not allow the Penobscot people to sanction the paper companies, nor will it allow the Penobscot people to monitor water quality in an official capacity (Grossman 2005). The Peabody Coal Company is conducting strip-mining operations on the Colorado Plateau, sacred lands to the Hopi people (McLeod 2001). The tribe initially leased the land under the guidance of an attorney working for both the tribe and Peabody Coal (McLeod 2001). Seven Hopi shrines on Woodruff Butte in Arizona have been destroyed by mining operations (McLeod 2001). The agreement makes it difficult for tribal members to protect their sacred sites (McLeod 2001). The U.S. government arguably had a duty to the Hopi tribe in this circumstance: It should have protected them from the actions of an unethical attorney.

HOW THE UNITED STATES VIOLATES THE
RIGHTS OF INDIGENOUS PEOPLES

There are two primary ways that the United States is presently violating the rights of indigenous peoples: (1) it opposes the United Nations draft Declaration on the Rights of Indigenous Peoples, and (2) it is the largest producer of greenhouse gases, contributing to global warming.

Opposition to the UN Draft Declaration on the Rights of Indigenous Peoples: A Violation of Articles 6 and 9

The UN draft Declaration on the Rights of Indigenous Peoples, which has been in the drafting stage for more than ten years and has the approval of the Commission on Human Rights, will not become a full declaration because of opposition to use of the term "peoples" in this document. International statements and doctrine pertaining to indigenous peoples use many terms to refer to these populations. The most common are "indigenous populations" or "indigenous peoples," while the ILO uses the phrase "indigenous and tribal populations" (Swepston 1989). States often contest the use of the term "peoples" because they fear it implies self-determination and secession (Swepston 1989). "Peoples" is not defined in international law (Muehlebach 2003), yet normatively it has applied to groups seeking the right to secede from existing states and form a new state body. It is this norm that causes states to reject the application of the term "peoples" to indigenous groups in the UN draft declaration.

States advocate the use of the term "people" instead, which both protects the state from secession and prohibits indigenous groups from the right to self-determination (Morgan 2004; Scott 1996). However, if "people" is substituted for "peoples" this denies indigenous groups collective rights. The collective nature of many of the rights and freedoms that indigenous groups seek, such as the right to culture and language, demands that a document supported by the United Nations recognizes a collective population instead of individuals. The United States was one of the most vocal opponents in this case. States fear that it will allow indigenous groups to seek and attain self-determination in the form of secession.

Unchecked Greenhouse Gas Emissions: A Violation of Articles 13.1, 13.2, 14.1, and 15.1

The Inuit Circumpolar Conference (ICC) composed a petition in 2005 documenting the violation of human rights due to global warming caused by the United States. The ICC petition includes a list of sixty-three signatories, individuals whose rights they argue have been violated by the United States, specifically their "property, physical well-being and cultural life are being adversely affected by acts and omissions described in this petition" (Watt-Cloutier and Inuit Circumpolar Conference 2005, 10). The petition details the damages wrought by global warming in the Inuit society: its impact on hunting and fishing, the economy, social and cultural life, the land, and climate. It also documents the U.S. contribution to CO_2 emissions to provide evidence of the results of its actions and inaction in contributing to global warming and the violation of the human rights of Inuit people (Watt-Cloutier and Inuit Circumpolar Conference 2005). In addition to extensive scientific data, the petition includes information submitted by each of the petitioners to provide evidence that the climate is changing due to human activity. They note profound changes that are impacting their local communities: Land is slumping due to melting permafrost; the cold season is shorter; animal populations are changing; ice is thinner; drier soil is causing a decrease in the quality of edible roots; meat is spoiling before it dries; more land is being lost due to erosion; beaches are narrower; polar bears are too thin to eat; and people are starting to experience sunburns (Watt-Cloutier and Inuit Circumpolar Conference 2005).

MOVING TOWARD COMPLIANCE

Although the United States has a woeful history of interaction with Native Americans and indigenous peoples around the globe, new models are emerging that might allow the United States to develop a better relationship with indigenous peoples in the future. The Working Group on Indigenous Peoples, which first met in 1982 (Dunbar-Ortiz 2006), is a model of inclusion of indigenous peoples in governance. Indigenous organizations are permitted to participate in the Working Group on Indigenous Peoples, regardless of their status as NGOs, although they must still apply to the Economic and Social Council (ECOSOC) prior to participation (Quesenberry 1997). They participate in the working group as equals with states. This working group is significant: It is establishing international standards for the recognition of indigenous peoples, promoting indigenous peoples' participation in international governance, providing an alternative source of protections of rights for indigenous peoples, establishing legal standards, and is global in scope (Quesenberry 1997). The Working Group on Indigenous Peoples encourages all governments to foster relationships that put indigenous groups on equal footing, perhaps even with the United States.

REFERENCES

Amnesty International. 2007. "Maze of Injustice: The Failure to Protect Indigenous Women from Sexual Violence in the USA," available at http://web.amnesty.org/library/print/ENGAMR510352007. (Accessed May 3, 2007.)

Blackfeet Reservation Development Fund. n.d. a. The Facts v. the Brochure: The Interior Department attempts to cover up incompetence and fraud in its handling of Individual Indian Money Accounts in a glossy new "progress report," available at http://www.indiantrust.com/_pdfs/IndianTrustBrochure.pdf. (Accessed July 3, 2007.)

———. n.d. b. Indian Trust: *Cobell v. Kempthorne* Case Chronology, available at http://indiantrust.com/index.cfm?FuseAction=Overview.Chronology. (Accessed July 3, 2007.)

Bureau of Indian Affairs. Department of the Interior. 2006a. Office of Federal Acknowledgement, available at http://www.doi.gov/bia/off_fed_acknowledg/brief_overview.pdf. (Accessed July 3, 2007.)

————. Department of the Interior. 2006b. Status Summary of Acknowledgement Cases, available at http://www.doi.gov/bia/off_fed_acknowledg/summary_status.pdf. (Accessed July 3, 2007.)

————. Department of the Interior. 1978. 25 CFR Part 83 Procedures for Establishing That an Indian Group Exists as an Indian Tribe, available at http://www.doi.gov/bia/off_fed_acknowledg/brief_25CFR_part83.pdf. (Accessed July 3, 2007.)

Cherokee Nation v. Georgia, 30 U.S. 1 (1831).

Cobell v. Kempthorne, Case No. 1:96CV01285 (D.D.C.).

Dudley, Michael Kioni, and Keoni Kealoha Agard. 1993. *A Call for Hawaiian Sovereignty.* Honolulu, HI: Nₑ Kₑne O Ka Malo Press.

Dunbar-Oritz, Roxanne. 2006. "The First Decade of Indigenous Peoples at the United Nations." *Peace and Change* 31: 58–74.

Garrow, Carrie E., and Sarah Deer. 2004. *Tribal Criminal Law and Procedure.* Lanham, MD: Altamira Press.

Getches, David H., Charles F. Wilkinson, and Robert A. Williams, Jr. 1993. *Federal Indian Law: Cases and Materials.* St. Paul, MN: West.

Grossman, Roberta, dir. 2005. *Homelands.* DVD. Produced by the Katahdin Foundation.

Hartwell, Jay. 1996. *Nₑ Mamo: Hawaiian People Today.* Honolulu, HI: 'Ai Pₑhaku Press.

Heckathorn, Bruce. 1998 [1988]. "The Native Hawaiian Nation: The Hottest Political Issue of the 1990s." Pp. 324–337 in *Hawaii Chronicles II: Contemporary Island History,* edited by Bob Dye. Honolulu: University of Hawaii Press.

International Labor Organization. General Conference. 1989. Indigenous and Tribal Peoples Convention, available at http://www.ohchr.org/english/law/indigenous.htm. (Accessed May 17, 2007.)

McLeod, Christopher. 2001. *In the Light of Reverence.* DVD. Produced by Christopher McLeod and Malinda Maynor.

Morgan, Rhiannon. 2004. "Advancing Indigenous Rights at the United Nations: Strategic Framing and Its Impact on the Normative Development of International Law." *Social Legal Studies* 13: 481–500.

Muehlebach, Andrea. 2003. "What Is Self-Determination? Notes from the Frontiers of Transnational Indigenous Activism." *Identities: Global Studies in Culture and Power* 10: 241–268.

Pevar, Stephen L. 1992. *The Rights of Indians and Tribes: The Basic ACLU Guide to Indian and Tribal Rights, Second Edition.* Carbondale: Southern Illinois University Press.

Quesenberry, Stephen V. 1997. "Recent United Nations Initiatives Concerning the Rights of Indigenous Peoples." *American Indian Culture and Research Journal* 21: 231–260.

Richland, Justin B., and Sarah Deer. 2004. *Introduction to Tribal Legal Studies.* Walnut Creek, CA: Altamira.

Scott, Craig. 1996. "Indigenous Self-Determination and Decolonization of the International Imagination: A Plea." *Human Rights Quarterly* 18: 814–820.

Swepston, Lee. 1989. "Indigenous and Tribal Peoples and International Law: Recent Developments." *Current Anthropology* 30: 259–264.

Trask, Haunani-Kay. 1994 [1992]. "Kupa'a 'Aina." Pp. 15–32 in *Hawaii: Return to Nationhood,* edited by Ulla Hasager and Jonathan Friedman. Copenhagen, Denmark: International Working Group for Indigenous Affairs.

————. 1999. *From a Native Daughter: Colonialism and Sovereignty in Hawai'i.* Honolulu: University of Hawaii Press.

Watt-Cloutier, Sheila, and Inuit Circumpolar Conference. 2005. Petition to the Inter-American Commission on Human Rights Seeking Relief from Violations Resulting from Global Warming Caused by Acts and Omissions of the United States, available at http://

inuitcircumpolar.com/files/uploads/icc-files/FINALPetitionICC.pdf. (Accessed July 5, 2007.)

Western Shoshone National Council. 2006. Press Release: Western Shoshone Victorious at United Nations: U.S. Found in Violation of Human Rights of Native Americans—Urged to Take Immediate Action, available at http://www.wsdp.org/un_cerd_wsdp.htm#gov0320. (Accessed July 3, 2007.)

Western Shoshone National Council, the Timibisha Shoshone Tribe, the Yomba Shoshone Tribe, the Wells Band of Western Shoshone, and the Te-Moak Tribe of Western Shoshone with the assistance of the University of Arizona Indigenous Peoples Law and Policy Program. 2007. Update to Committee on the Elimination of Racial Discrimination on the Early Warning and Urgent Action Procedure Decision 1 (68), available at http://www.wsdp.org/70th_Session_Update_Feb_07.pdf. (Accessed July 3, 2007.)

ADDITIONAL RESOURCES

Aboriginal Canada Portal:
   http://www.aboriginalcanada.gc.ca/acp/site.nsf/en/index.html.
Amnesty International Canada, The Rights of Indigenous Peoples:
   http://www.amnesty.ca/themes/indigenous_overview.php.
Center for Pacific Studies:
   http://www.hawaii.edu/cpis/psi/index.html.
Cultural Survival:
   http://www.culturalsurvival.org/home.cfm.
Eastern Navajo Dine Against Uranium Mining (ENDAUM):
   http://endaum.org/home.html.
Enlace Zapatista:
   http://enlacezapatista.ezln.org.mx/ (Spanish).
Indian Country Today:
   http://www.indiancountry.com/index.cfm.
Indian Law Research Center:
   http://www.indianlaw.org.
Indian Trust: Cobell v. Kempthorne:
   http://www.indiantrust.com.
Indianz.com:
   http://64.62.196.98/about.asp.
International Work Group for Indigenous Affairs:
   http://www.iwgia.org/sw153.asp.
Inuit Circumpolar Conference:
   http://inuitcircumpolar.com/index.php?ID=1&Lang=En.
Message Stick: Aboriginal and Torres Straight Islander Online:
   http://abc.net.au/message.
Native American Rights Fund:
   http://www.narf.org.
Researching Indigenous Peoples' Rights Under International Law:
   http://intelligent-internet.info/law/ipr2.html.
Resource Centre for the Rights of Indigenous Peoples:
   http://www.galdu.org/web.

Survival International:
       http://www.survival-international.org.
UNESCO Culture Section, Indigenous Peoples:
       http://portal.unesco.org/culture/admin/ev.php?URL_ID=2946&URL_DO=DO_
       TOPIC&URL_SECTION=201.
United Nations. Fact Sheet No. 9 (Rev. 1), The Rights of Indigenous Peoples:
       http://www.unhchr.ch/html/menu6/2/fs9.htm.
United Nations. Guide for Indigenous Peoples:
       http://www.ohchr.org/english/issues/indigenous/guide.htm.
United Nations. High Commissioner for Human Rights, Documents on Indigenous Peoples:
       http://www.ohchr.org/english/issues/indigenous/documents.htm.
United States. Office of Tribal Justice Homepage:
       http://www.usdoj.gov/otj.
UN Permanent Forum on Indigenous Issues:
       http://www.un.org/esa/socdev/unpfii.
Western Shoshone Defense Project:
       http://www.wsdp.org.

Chapter Ten

~

The Human Right to Sexual and Gender Self-Expression

Gerald F. Lackey

If all human beings can love and make love, why is this human right granted only to heterosexuals? Just as we labor and fall ill, so too do we fornicate and fall in love. We are as much sexual creatures as we are laboring ones, and as such we are invested with certain inalienable human rights, two of which are the rights to sexual and gender self-expression. All people are entitled to these rights solely by being human. Human rights do not depend on one's loyalty to a country or membership in a privileged group, but rather on a shared humanity.

What I term the rights to sexual and gender self-expression have also been called the rights to sexual orientation and gender identity (Norway Statement on Climate Change 2006), but regardless of the name, the tenets of the rights remain the same. These rights protect and affirm a person's sexual and gender dignity, autonomy, and self-determination in all civil, political, economic, social, and private realms. They avow that consenting adults have the right to engage in sexual relationships and to openly express their gender identity, without fear of recrimination and without curtailment of any other human right. They also affirm that all persons should be free from unwanted sexual contact, especially children. These rights are particularly important to recognize for lesbian, gay, bisexual, and transgender (LGBT) people because they are outside of the privileged heterosexual norm.

At first it might seem that these human rights already exist, but a closer examination shows that this is only true for heterosexuals. For heterosexuals these rights are recognized in laws such as the right to marry (Article 23 of the International Covenant on Civil and Political Rights), the right for people with disabilities to have children (Article 23A of the Convention on the Rights of Persons with Disabilities), the right for migrant families to remain together (Article 44 of the International Convention on the Protection of the Rights of All Migrant Workers), and the right to privacy (Article 17 of the International Covenant on Civil and Political Rights). For LGBT people, however, rights to sexual and gender self-expression are more an aspiration than an actuality.

Fortunately, progress toward more inclusive and explicit sexual expression and gender identity rights is being made. The discussions taking place within the UN Human Rights Committee and other regional human rights bodies (e.g., European Union Court of Human Rights) on the topic of sexual rights are at the forefront of the evolving concept of human rights. The purpose of this chapter is twofold: (1) to describe the evolving international framework surrounding the rights to sexual and gender self-expression; and (2) to demonstrate how the United States has removed itself from this evolving framework.

The United States has created a situation where it is both structurally and socially isolated from the majority of its contemporaries (i.e., other countries of similar political, social, and economic structures). Structurally, the United States has failed to ratify most of the human rights treaties and their optional protocols, meaning that its citizens cannot challenge its domestic laws on human rights grounds. This has segregated the United States outside of the legal structure that has been used to advance human rights for LGBT people around the world. This is what I term the structural isolation of the United States.

The social isolation of the United States comes from the country's refusal to enter into official discourse on the topic of sexual and gender human rights. Where there have been initiatives to formally codify human rights to sexual and gender self-expression, the United States has remained silent. It has preferred to abstain from voting and discussing these topics. That is, it has removed itself from the evolving discourse surrounding human rights. This is what I term the social isolation of the United States.

THE EXISTING LEGAL FRAMEWORK

Equal treatment of LGBT persons under U.S. domestic law is largely nonexistent. One of the more discriminatory federal policies is the "Don't ask, don't tell" compromise, which was passed in 1993. While this compromise policy prevents the military from directly asking about a service member's sexual orientation, it also permits that person to be discharged if he or she is suspected of having sexual relations with members of the same sex. The one major legal advance in the United States is the 2003 Supreme Court decision that legalized gay male sexual activity (*Lawrence v. Texas*). For its European contemporaries, however, this legal precedent is about two decades old (*Dudgeon v. United Kingdom* 1981; *Norris v. Ireland* 1988; *Modinos v. Cyprus* 1993). In fact, since about 1993 LGBT rights have continued to be advanced among European countries at a faster rate than in the United States. For instance, unequal age-of-consent laws were struck down in 1997 (*Sutherland v. United Kingdom*) and the ban on LGBT people in the military was lifted in 2000 (*Smith v. United Kingdom*), while in the United States both laws are still enforced against LGBT people.

Instead of adopting national laws to affirm the rights of LGBT people, the U.S. federal government has been deferring to individual states to decide their rights. Notably, this was the same approach used to defer the advancement of civil and political rights for African Americans in the United States. The end result is a pockmarked legal landscape for LGBT people, whereby persons are granted or denied rights based on their state of residence. In thirty states (60 percent of states) open discrimination against LGBT persons in housing and employment continues to be legal (National Gay and Lesbian Task Force 2007). In twenty-two states it is legally unclear whether a same-sex partner may become the second parent of a child, while in three states (Nebraska, Ohio, and Wisconsin) appellate courts have ruled that no such right exists (National Gay and Lesbian Task Force 2007). In six states (Florida, Michigan, Mississippi, Nebraska, North Dakota, and Utah) laws have been passed to prevent LGBT people from adopting children altogether (National Gay and Lesbian Task Force 2007).

The international framework on human rights is more uniform, although not necessarily equal, in its treatment of LGBT persons. When the member states of the United Nations passed the Universal Declaration of Human Rights in 1948, there was not yet open discussion of human rights for LGBT people. In fact, for most of the twentieth century, the issue of injustice against LGBT people was completely absent from the international discourse on human rights. These topics were considered a matter of moral judgment and as such were considered the sole purview of the nation-state (*Hertzberg et al. v. Finland* 1982). As a result, there is no explicit recognition of sexual orientation or gender identity rights in the Universal Declaration of Human Rights (1948) or in any of the global treaties on human rights that grew out of that declaration.

By the early 1990s, the increasing visibility of LGBT communities worldwide and a more accepting social environment within the United Nations created mounting pressure for them to take a stand in defense of these communities. In 1994, the Human Rights Committee overruled its 1982 decision in *Hertzberg v. Finland,* reversing an official policy of moral relativism with regard to sexual and gender self-expression. This ruling affirmed that arguments on moral grounds were not exclusively a domestic issue (*Toonen v. Australia* 1994). The ruling also affirmed that Article 2 of the Universal Declaration of Human Rights includes sexual orientation as a protected category subsumed under the term "sex." This is an important ruling because Article 2 is what proclaims the applicability of all other human rights to all people.

For the first time, the possibility that LGBT people had human rights was a legal reality. Since then, individuals have used this legal precedent to appeal their countries' discriminatory laws directly to the United Nations. In addition to the cases noted above, separate appeals have also been made to the UN High Commissioner for Refugees and the International Criminal Tribunal for Rwanda. In one case the UN High Commissioner for Refugees ruled that the term "social group" in the Convention Relating to the Status of Refugees does include lesbians and gay men (Tahmindjis and Graupner 2005). Similarly, in another case, the International Criminal Tribunal for Rwanda ruled that the term "group" in Article 2 of the Genocide Convention of 1948 could also include gays and lesbians (Tahmindjis and Graupner 2005).

Despite the advances made in support of human rights to sexual and gender self-expression, especially in Europe, there is much work to be done before all persons, including LGBT people, have these rights. A 2007 report sponsored by the International Lesbian and Gay Association says as much, citing that a full 85 percent of the UN member countries still criminalize same-sex action between adults (Ottosson 2007). Additionally, LGBT persons are universally denied access to the social institution of marriage. In the United States, the Defense of Marriage Act (1996) explicitly limits the definition of marriage to a man and a woman. This act also limits the legal recognition of any future state-granted same-sex union to the boundaries of that state. Between 1995 and 2004, a total of thirty-three states (66 percent of states) passed legislation to ban same-sex marriages, while eight states took the more restrictive step of passing constitutional amendments against same-sex marriage (National Gay and Lesbian Task Force 2007).

Although some European Union member states offer civil unions, this is not universal. Restrictive laws still exist in Europe, and the European Court of Human Rights has repeatedly interpreted marriage to be a human right available only for heterosexuals, even barring persons who have undergone gender reassignment from marriage to the opposite sex (*Cossey v. United Kingdom* 1990; *Sheffield and Horsham v. United Kingdom* 1998; *X, Y and Z v. United Kingdom* 1997). On the international stage, the UN Human Rights Committee has also ruled against LGBT people who have appealed for the right to marry under Article 23 of the International Covenant on Economic, Social and Cultural Rights (*Joslin et al. v. New Zealand* 2002).

AN EVOLVING DISCUSSION

The division among UN member states on the issue of sexual and gender human rights is most evident in the recent debates about whether or not to draft a separate treaty to explicitly recognize the human rights of LGBT individuals. In 2003, Brazil proposed such a resolution titled "Human Rights and Sexual Orientation." It had only six relatively modest propositions stating that the UN Human Rights Commission:

1. Expresses deep concern at the occurrence of violations of human rights in the world against persons on the grounds of their sexual orientation;
2. Stresses that human rights and fundamental freedoms are the birthright of all human beings, that the universal nature of these rights and freedoms is beyond question and that the enjoyment of such rights and freedoms should not be hindered in any way on the grounds of sexual orientation;
3. Calls upon all States to promote and protect the human rights of all persons regardless of their sexual orientation;
4. Notes the attention given to human rights violations on the grounds of sexual orientation by the special procedures in their reports to the Commission on Human Rights, as well as by the treaty monitoring bodies, and encourages all special procedures of the Commission, within their mandates, to give due attention to the subject;

5. Requests the United Nations High Commissioner for Human Rights to pay due attention to the violation of human rights on the grounds of sexual orientation;

6. Decides to continue consideration of the matter at its sixtieth session under the same agenda item. (Human Rights and Sexual Orientation 2003)

The Brazil proposal met with severe opposition by a coalition of Muslim countries including Saudi Arabia, Pakistan, Egypt, Libya, and Malaysia. Moreover, the resolution had only twenty-seven supporters, which were limited mainly to European Union nations but also included Australia and Canada. The proposal was tabled until 2004, but Brazil dropped its sponsorship of the bill due to lack of international support. The bill was eventually dropped altogether in 2005. While it is disappointing that specific countries opposed the proposal, they expressed these beliefs openly and in written form, thus advancing the dialogue about sexual and gender human rights. They made claims that extending human rights to LGBT people might infringe on the human right to practice religious beliefs (Article 18 of the International Covenant on Civil and Political Rights) and the right to maintain cultural values (Article 15 of the International Covenant of Economic, Social, and Cultural Rights). By presenting their concerns, they were able to engage in a discussion that ultimately shaped the evolution of human rights. The United States, however, chose to abstain from voting or giving an opinion on the matter.

The United States remained silent again in 2005 when New Zealand proposed a statement that raised awareness that the Brazil resolution was allowed to be permanently tabled. It also called on the UN Human Rights Committee to uphold the principle of nondiscrimination in regard to LGBT people. It was supported by thirty-two, mainly European, nations. As the New Zealand ambassador Tim Caughley put it: "Sexual orientation is a fundamental aspect of every individual's identity and an immutable part of self. It is contrary to human dignity to force an individual to change their sexual orientation, or to discriminate against them on this basis. And, it is repugnant for the State to tolerate violence against individuals" (Caughley 2005).

In a similar move in 2005 before the UN Human Rights Committee, the European Union president, José Manuel Barroso, called for an end to all discrimination. This came to be known as the Luxemburg Statement, and it was supported by thirty-four E.U. nations. It cautioned that "discrimination can take many forms, often insidious" and urged that the "E.U. would stress the unacceptability of any discrimination based on sexual orientation"(Luxemburg Statement 2005). Again, the United States had no comment on the matter.

The most recent statement in support of sexual rights, and also for the first time gender identity, was made by Norway in 2006. This statement urged the UN Human Rights Committee to take action on the issue of sexual and gender identity soon. It was supported by fifty-four countries, one of which was the United States. This is the only proposal on LGBT human rights that the United States has supported. The statement has three main points:

- At its recent session, the Human Rights Council received extensive evidence of human rights violations based on sexual orientation and gender identity, including deprivation of the rights to life, freedom from violence and torture.

- We commend the attention paid to these issues by the Special Procedures, treaty bodies and civil society. We call upon all Special Procedures and treaty bodies to continue to integrate consideration of human rights violations based on sexual orientation and gender identity within their relevant mandates.
- We express deep concern at these ongoing human rights violations. The principles of universality and nondiscrimination require that these issues be addressed. We therefore urge the Human Rights Council to pay due attention to human rights violations based on sexual orientation and gender identity, and request the President of the Council to provide an opportunity, at an appropriate future session of the Council, for a discussion of these important human rights issues. (Norway Statement 2007)

STRUCTURAL ISOLATION OF THE UNITED STATES

The ability for individual citizens to appeal to international and regional human rights bodies has been an important avenue for the advancement of human rights to sexual and gender self-expression. By arguing that existing human rights should apply to LGBT people, the legal framework already in place is being successfully used to advance rights for this group. Using the existing human rights framework in such a way is not possible for U.S. citizens because the United States has not ratified the necessary international treaties and optional protocols that make it possible for citizens to use the appeal option. This structural isolation protects the U.S. government from having to openly defend its violations of the human rights of LGBT people. It also limits the ability of U.S. citizens, especially LGBT citizens, to engage in shaping the emerging concept of human rights. Perhaps most important, however, it keeps a discussion of human rights out of the legal and social mainstream in the United States, which retards its growth and understanding among the U.S. populace.

Of the sixteen different UN human rights treaties and optional protocols that exist, the United States has only ratified five, which represents less than one-third of all possible proposals. Moreover, all five of the treaties the United States ratified are considered nonself-executing in the U.S. domestic legal framework. A nonself-executing treaty means that, although a nation has ratified the treaty, there needs to be specific domestic legislation that enacts the treaty within the signatory's legal framework; without such legislation the ratification is legally impotent. There is no such federal or state legislation. Of the five treaties, three are core human rights treaties—the International Convention on the Elimination of All Forms of Racial Discrimination (effective 1994), the International Covenant on Civil and Political Rights (effective 1992), and the Convention Against Torture and Other Cruel, Inhuman or Degrading Treatment or Punishment (effective 1994). The other two treaties are the Optional Protocol to the Convention on the Rights of the Child on the Involvement of Children in Armed Conflict (effective 2003) and the Optional Protocol to the Convention on the Rights of the Child on the Sale of Children, Child Prostitution and Child Pornography (effective 2003).

Comparing the United States to other countries presents a clearer picture of how structurally isolated it is. I created a table of all the UN member countries that have ratified at least one of the sixteen possible treaties or protocols. This results in a total of 161 countries. Using this table, I generated a series of univariate statistics to explore how the United States compares to other countries. The maximum number of treaties/protocols that have been ratified by any given country is twelve and only three countries have ratified that number (Costa Rica, Denmark, and Uruguay). The average number of treaties/protocols that have been ratified is five, but with a large deviation around that average of plus or minus three treaties/protocols. The United States appears to be about average, having ratified five treaties. However, these treaties were ratified as non-self-executing and therefore are not equal in terms of legal importance to the other countries' ratifications. There are also sixty countries (37 percent of the total) that have ratified more treaties/protocols than the United States. These countries include nations with an otherwise similar level of cultural and economic development as the United States, such as Canada, France, Ireland, Germany, Spain, the United Kingdom, Denmark, and Italy.

In addition to comparing the counts of treaties and protocols among countries, it is also telling to examine the number of shared treaties and protocols among countries. That is, which countries ratified the same treaties and how many did they ratify in common? Answering this question will give a sense of how similar countries are to one another. Those countries that ratified more treaties/protocols in the previous table will be in a more central position among all countries if these treaties/protocols are the most common ones. Oppositely, those countries that ratified only a few treaties/protocols or that ratified very uncommon ones will not be very central actors. To examine this I created an affiliation table by multiplying the previous table against its transpose. The newly generated table has countries listed across both rows and columns, where each cell now represents the number of shared treaties/protocols among countries.

Examining univariate statistics on this affiliation table shows that the United States shares none of its ratified treaties/protocols with countries that are not central actors (e.g., St. Vincent, Qatar, Fiji, South Korea) and all of its ratified treaties/protocols with those countries that are central actors (e.g., Australia, Israel, France). Nonetheless, on average the United States shares only two of its five ratified treaties/protocols with any other given country, while the average number shared by all other 161 countries is three. Comparatively, Australia, Israel, and France share a mean of four treaties/protocols with any other given country. This suggests that while the United States is connected in a loose way to the central actors, given that it shares some of the same ratified treaties/protocols, it is not very well connected to the majority of the UN member countries.

So which countries are central leaders in advancing the human rights framework that has been used to advocate for LGBT rights? Looking at a plot of just the most central actors (i.e., those countries that share ten or more ratified treaties/protocols) can help answer this question. In Figure 10.1, each dot is a country and the connections among the dots represent the number of commonly ratified treaties/protocols. The dark blue line between Uruguay, Costa Rica, and Denmark shows that they each ratified twelve treaties in common, the maximum number ratified. The darker red lines connect all the countries that have ratified at least eleven treaties/protocols in common, and the grey lines connect all the countries that share at least ten treaties/protocols in common.

Figure 10.1 shows a dense core of countries sharing a majority (eleven or twelve) of the existing treaties/protocols with each other (i.e., Uruguay, Costa Rica, Sweden, Denmark, Norway, Austria, Italy, and Venezuela). Outside this core are also a number of other countries sharing a large number (ten) of ratified treaties/protocols, but not always with every other country like the core countries do. It is also notable that this group of leading countries comprised a mix of European and developing nations. These developing nations include Uruguay, Costa Rica, Ukraine, Peru, Venezuela, Senegal, Columbia, and the Philippines. Thus, in addition to segregation from its European peers, the United States is also pushing itself away from many developing countries that are central actors in this evolving framework of human rights. It is structurally isolating itself.

Figure 10.1 Connections among Central Leaders in Treaty/Protocol Ratification

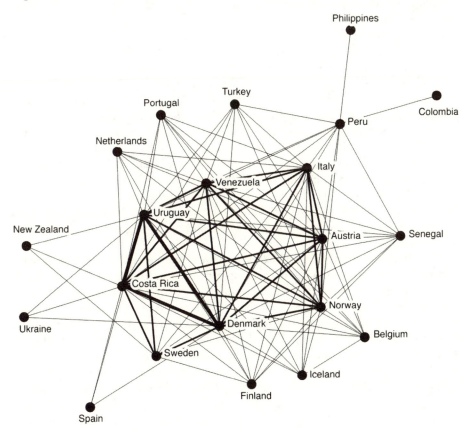

SOCIAL ISOLATION OF THE UNITED STATES

At the same time that the United States is structurally segregating itself from the international framework that is advancing LGBT rights, it is also withdrawing itself from discussions about LGBT rights. On an international level, the United States has supported some minor proposals such as the inclusion of the International Lesbian and Gay Association (ILGA) on certain UN committees. However, the United States has not supported or engaged in discussions surrounding many other human rights proposals on the rights to sexual and gender self-expression.

Specific proposals affirming LGBT rights have received little to no support from the United States. These proposals include the use of the term "sexual orientation" as a protected category in the Special Rapporteur on Extrajudicial Executions (2002), the Brazil Resolution for a treaty on the human right to sexual self-expression (2003), the New Zealand Statement on the human right to sexual self-expression (2005), and the Luxemburg Statement on the end to discrimination (2005). The exception to this rule is recent U.S. support for the Norway Statement on the need for action to protect sexual and gender identity (2006).

Concern over U.S. actions stems less from the fact that it does not support these particular human rights proposals, but that it has refused to present its arguments as to why. This self-imposed social isolation severely limits the ability of the United States to help shape the emerging notion of human rights to sexual and gender self-expression. It also serves to push the United States away from its contemporaries who largely support these and other human rights.

Comparing U.S. support for LGBT human rights issues against the support of other countries reveals how the United States has socially isolated itself. I created a table of all the countries that supported at least one sexual human rights issue as reported by Sanders (2005). This results in a total of seventy-six countries. The LGBT issues I include are all state-sponsored proposals such as the Special Rapporteur on Extrajudicial Executions, the Brazil Proposal, the New Zealand Statement, and the Norway Statement. I also include support for the initial ILGA UN accreditation, the second accreditation of the ILGA, the accreditation of the ILGA to the World Conference on Racism, the wording on lesbian rights at the Fourth World Conference on Women, and lesbian and gay rights at the meetings of the Organization for Security and Cooperation in Europe.

At first, the United States appears to be a strong supporter of LGBT human rights among the seventy-six countries in the sample, but a closer examination shows that its support has largely been outside the discussion of any of the four main proposals. Only Austria supports all nine issues, with five countries supporting a maximum of eight issues and six countries supporting a maximum of seven issues. The average number of issues supported is four. The United States supports a total of six issues, but this high number is a result of its support for the multiple attempts at accreditation by the ILGA (three proposals) and its support for minor wording adjustments to conferences (two). Not included in its total is support for any of the country-sponsored human rights propositions, with the exception of the most recent Norway Statement. However, the vast majority of the discourse that is shaping the evolving notion of human rights is taking place around the written arguments opposing and supporting these types of proposals. This means that the United States is isolating itself from where the real action is occurring.

In addition to comparing the raw counts of support for LGBT issues, it is also telling to examine the number of shared issues that countries support. The transformation from the original table to an affiliation table is done in the same manner as for the previous treaties/protocols table. Univariate statistics reveal that the average number of shared proposals is two. The United States also shares two proposals with the other countries; however, of its six supported issues, it shares all of these only with Austria and Australia. Yet both Austria and Australia support other LGBT issues that the United States does not. This suggests that the six issues the United States has chosen to support are not commonly supported among the seventy-six countries. Thus, the United States again appears to be outside of the central group of actors in its support of particular issues. This can be most easily seen by looking at a plot of all countries that have supported six or more LGBT issues and locating how the United States is connected versus how the other countries are connected to one another.

Figure 10.2 shows that the discourse surrounding sexual and gender human rights is being led by the dense connections among Sweden, the United Kingdom, Austria, France, Germany, and Canada, all of whom share eight issues in common including all of the country-sponsored proposals (Austria supports all nine issues). These countries would be considered the central leaders. These connections are indicated by the blue line among the countries. Also densely connected are those countries sharing seven issues in common with each other, which is indicated by the red line. Among these six countries the most commonly omitted issue was support for the third attempt at ILGA accreditation. This is an interesting but hardly agenda-setting item. Most interesting are the thin grey lines that indicate shared support for six of the proposals among different countries. Notice that most of the countries that support a maximum of six issues also share these issues in common with each other, thus the connections among them. That is, they are somewhat densely connected despite having supported only six proposals. The United States, however, is something of an outlier by sharing its six supported issues in common with only two countries. It is not strongly connected to other countries. It is socially isolating itself.

CONCLUSION

While the global framework of human rights legislation does not yet include the rights to sexual and gender self-expression, the momentum of the discussion seems to be progressing toward that goal. Countries within the European Union and developing countries appear to be leading the way toward this new conceptualization, while countries with strong religious traditions in the Middle East are reminding us that we need to balance the right to sexual self-expression with the right to espouse religious beliefs and the right to express one's cultural values. Only through discourse, sometimes very contentious discourse, can a resolution be worked out.

Figure 10.2 Connections among Countries Supporting Six or More LGBT Issues

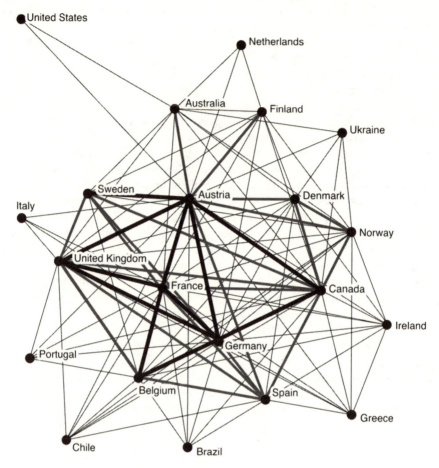

The position of the United States, however, has generally been not to argue for or against the rights to sexual and gender self-expression, but rather to remove itself from the global discourse and the international human rights framework that are advancing these issues. One way in which it does this is by refusing to ratify existing human rights treaties and protocols. In so doing it prevents its citizens from raising objections with the United Nations about discriminatory U.S. domestic laws. In a similar fashion, the United States has refused outright to support, and most often ignored, a number of LGBT-affirming actions on an international level. Whether or not this has disrupted the flow or progress of the discussion is unknown, but it clearly has left the United States with little to say on the matter. At this point, one can only wonder what position the United States and its citizens will find themselves in if they continue along the paths of structural and social isolationism regarding LGBT human rights.

REFERENCES

Caughley, Tim. 2005. Speech, available at http://www.ilga.org/news_results.asp?LanguageID=
1&FileCategory=61&FileID=533. (Accessed March 30, 2008.)

Cossey v. United Kingdom. 1990. (16/1989/176/232). European Court of Human Rights.

Dudgeon v. United Kingdom, Application 7525/76 (1981). European Court of Human
Rights.

Hertzberg et al. v. Finland, Communication No. 61/1979, UN Doc. CCPR/C/OP/1 at 124
(1985).

"Human Rights and Sexual Orientation." 2003. Available at http://www.thegully.com/essays/
gaymundo/030422_UN_res_lgbt_br.html. (Accessed March 30, 2008.)

Joslin et al. v. New Zealand. 1999. CCPR/C/75/D/902/1999.

Lawrence v. Texas, 539 U.S. 558 (2003).

"Luxemburg Statement." 2005, available at http://ilga.org/news_results.asp?LanguageID=
1&FileCategoryID=61&FileID=585&ZoneID=4. (Accessed March 30, 2008.)

Modinos v. Cyprus, Application 15070/89 (1993). European Court of Human Rights.

National Gay and Lesbian Task Force. 2007. Issue Maps, available at http://www.thetaskforce.
org/reports_and_research/issue_maps.

Norris v. Ireland, Application 10581/83 (1988). European Court of Human Rights.

"Norway Statement." 2007, available at: http://www.norway-un.org/NorwegianStatements/
OtherStatements/20070312_Johansen_MRr%C3%A5d_statement.htm. (Accessed
March 30, 2008.)

Ottosson, Daniel. 2007. "State-Sponsored Homophobia." International Lesbian and Gay
Association," available at http://www.ilga.org/statehomophobia/State_sponsored_
homophobia_ILGA_07.pdf. (Accessed March 30, 2008.)

Sanders, Douglas. 2005. "Human Rights and Sexual Orientation in International Law." International Lesbian and Gay Association, available at http://www.ilga.org/news_results.
asp?LanguageID=1&FileCategory=44&FileID=577. (Accessed February 12, 2008.)

Sheffield and Horsham v. United Kingdom. 1998. (31-32/1997/815-816/1018-1019). European
Court of Human Rights.

Smith v.United Kingdom, Application 33985/96. 1999. European Court of Human Rights.

Sutherland v. United Kingdom. 1994. European Court of Human Rights.

Tahmindjis, Phillip, and Helmut Graupner, eds. 2005. *Sexuality and Human Rights: A Global
Overview.* London: Hamilton Park Press.

Toonen v. Australia. 1994. UN Doc CCPR/C/50/D/488/1992.

X, Y & Z v. United Kingdom. 1997. (75/1995/581/667). European Court of Human Rights.

ADDITIONAL RESOURCES

International Gay and Lesbian Human Rights Commission:
        http://www.iglhrc.org/site/iglhrc.

International Human Rights Instruments:
        http://www.unhchr.ch/html/intlinst.htm.

International Lesbian and Gay Association:
        http://www.ilga.org.

Lesbian/Gay Law Notes. New York Law School:
        http://www.nyls.edu/pages/3876.asp.

Norway Statement on Climate Change:
    http://www.stakeholderforum.org/norway26oct06.html.
United Nations Treaty Information:
    http://www.unhchr.ch/tbs/doc.nsf/Statusfrset?OpenFrameSet.

CHAPTER ELEVEN

Language Rights
as Human Rights

TANYA GOLASH-BOZA AND DOUGLAS PARKER

From a human rights perspective, all people, regardless of where they live and whether they live in the country of their birth or elsewhere, share a common human dignity and inalienable rights. As Judith Blau and Alberto Moncada (2005) point out, these rights apply to all persons, not just to citizens of certain nation states. Human rights entail the recognition of the rights of others, and action on the part of states or other organizations to ensure that rights are upheld. In the case of language rights, there are many international conventions that stipulate that individuals should not be discriminated against on the basis of the language they speak. In addition, some international conventions specify one or more other rights, for example, that individuals have the right to use their mother tongue in public and private, that education should promote respect for each individual's cultural and linguistic identity, and that states have the responsibility to provide instruction to students in their mother tongues. The realization of these language rights is fundamental for achieving a society that respects human dignity.

In this paper, we argue that language rights are often not realized in the United States and identify three reasons for this. First, most international conventions and declarations do not have explicit statements about the linguistic rights that individuals have in educational and other institutions. Second, the United States has not ratified many of the international conventions involving language rights, and U.S. judicial and legislative practices have prevented individuals from litigating claims under the conventions that the United States has ratified. Third, U.S. laws do not specifically guarantee certain language rights, and the interpretations of these and other domestic laws by the judicial branch have made it difficult for individuals to obtain language rights.

We discuss language rights in terms of both *negative* and *positive* rights. Negative rights are realized when there is a secular authority that prevents an adversary (a state or some other party) from interfering with activities such as speaking, assembling and protesting, acquiring and owning property, and worshiping, alone or together with others. Positive rights are created when individuals receive entitlements such as medical care and social security and when social conditions promote the availability and access to such experiences as education, employment, rest and leisure, and a cultural life in the community. Negative rights generally involve freedom from intervention by some level or agency of the state or by another party. Conversely, positive rights often require the intervention or action of the state or some other party. In the United States, given our liberal tradition, negative rights are generally preferred over positive rights (Blau and Moncada 2005). A prominent negative linguistic right is the right to *not* face discrimination on the basis of language, while an important positive linguistic right is the right of students to attend schools that promote tolerance of their languages and cultures. This latter right requires that the state provide schools that promote tolerance and understanding.

POSITIVE AND NEGATIVE LINGUISTIC RIGHTS IN INTERNATIONAL CONVENTIONS AND DECLARATIONS

The negative right not to face discrimination is in many of the international conventions, including the International Covenant on Civil and Political Rights (ICCPR), signed by U.S. president Jimmy Carter in 1977 and ratified by the Senate in 1992. This is one of the few conventions that the United States has ratified. Article 26 of the ICCPR states: "All persons are equal before the law and are entitled without any discrimination to the equal protection of the law. In this respect, the law shall prohibit any discrimination and guarantee to all persons equal and effective protection against discrimination on any ground such as race, colour, sex, *language,* religion, political or other opinion, national or social origin, property, birth or other status" (our emphasis) (United Nations 2007d).

Another convention signed in 1977 by President Carter but not ratified by the Senate is the International Covenant on Economic, Social, and Cultural Rights (ICESCR), which is an embodiment of positive rights with a specification of how these rights are to be realized. Article 13 declares that primary, secondary, and higher education shall be made available and accessible to all individuals and that education shall "promote understanding, tolerance and friendship among all nations and all racial, ethnic or religious groups," and Article 2 stipulates that each state will take steps to fully realize the rights "by all appropriate means, including particularly the adoption of legislative measures" (United Nations 2007e). Indeed, the majority of the linguistic rights being discussed in this paper are positive rights in that they require states to provide instruction, protect and promote cultural expressions, and promote tolerance, which in part may explain why most of the international conventions have not been ratified by the United States given its historical suspicion of anything that would impede individual initiative and enterprise (another part of the explanation would be various contemporary U.S. hegemonic interests) (Blau and Moncada 2005).

Although a convention (or covenant) is legally binding and is generically synonymous with the term "treaty," a declaration may indicate only that the states that approved it want to declare certain aspirations and establish a common standard for achievement as was the case in 1948 when the General Assembly of the United Nations adopted the Universal Declaration of Human Rights. Such a declaration has no legally binding force unless it brings about general practices by states that are then accepted as part of the international law that is derived from custom (United Nations 2007f; 2007g). The declaration that is most relevant to language rights is the Declaration on the Rights of Persons Belonging to National or Ethnic, Religious and Linguistic Minorities, adopted by the UN General Assembly on December 18, 1992. This declaration emphasizes the importance of "the constant promotion and realization of rights of persons belonging to national or religious and linguistic minorities." The first two articles of this declaration stipulate that "States shall protect the existence and the national or ethnic, cultural, religious and linguistic identity of minorities within their respective territories" and that persons belonging to these minorities have the right "to use their own language, in private and in public without interference or any form of discrimination." The fourth article specifies that "States should take appropriate measures so that, whenever possible, persons belonging to minorities have adequate opportunities to learn their mother tongue or to have instruction in their mother tongue" (United Nations 2007c).

Two other conventions should be mentioned in this discussion of language rights. The first, the Convention against Discrimination in Education (1960), stipulates that educational institutions should not discriminate against individuals on the basis of language and that members of national minorities should have the right to carry on and maintain their own educational institutions insofar as this right does not prevent the integration of members of national minorities into the society. It also specifies that the standards of education should not be lower for members of linguistic minorities, and that attendance at educational institutions that are designed to meet the needs of linguistic minorities should be optional. This convention does not request state support for the maintenance of minority-operated schools (United Nations 2007a). The second, the Convention on the Protection and Promotion of the Diversity of Cultural Expressions (2005), holds that "linguistic diversity is a fundamental element of cultural diversity," and that education plays a fundamental role "in the protection and promotion of cultural expressions." The convention takes the position that "the protection and promotion of the diversity of cultural expressions presuppose the recognition of equal dignity of and respect for all cultures, including the cultures of persons belonging to minorities and indigenous peoples" (United Nations 2007b). This convention identifies a number of financial, regulatory, and other measures that can be taken by public, private, and states parties to implement the convention. As of August 2007, the United States had not yet ratified these conventions.

International human rights conventions thus do address linguistic rights. Nevertheless, linguistic human rights researchers and others have pointed out deficiencies in the international conventions and problems with their realization. These deficiencies include the omissions in nearly all of the conventions of explicit statements that individuals have the right to learn and use their own language in educational and other institutions, and the problems include the failure of some nations to provide legislative implementation of the rights and to facilitate judicial review of claims of linguistic rights violations. In the case of the United States, the problem is twofold. On the one hand, the United States has not signed and ratified most of the relevant conventions. On the other, it has been difficult, if not impossible, to implement and uphold those conventions that the United States has signed.

DEFICIENCIES AND PROBLEMS IN THE REALIZATION OF LINGUISTIC RIGHTS

Educational Institutions and Linguistic Rights

Schools are where children learn to become members of society. They learn how to speak, dress, and act in a socially acceptable manner. Schools are an important place for the realization of linguistic rights insofar as it is in schools that children learn whether or not their mother tongue is valued or devalued by society. Pierre Bourdieu and Jean-Claude Passeron (1990) argue that disciplinary sanctions by teachers signal to children, especially those from the lower classes and status groups, how little their languages and cultural attainments are valued. As Bourdieu and Passeron (1990, 28) put it, "These calls to order tend to produce in them, if not explicit recognition of the dominant culture, then at least an insidious awareness of the cultural unworthiness of their own acquirements." Some examples of this symbolic violence that has denigrated children for their manner of speaking are discussed later in this paper.

For language rights to be realized, it would helpful if international conventions required the promotion of linguistic rights in educational institutions. However, this is not generally the case. Tove Skutnabb-Kangas and Robert Phillipson (1994), in an analysis of language rights in education, note that most international conventions fail to require educational institutions to ensure linguistic human rights for all children. They contend that national constitutions and statutes, for example, those of Finland with respect to speakers of Swedish and Sámi, provide more protection for minority languages in education than many of the international covenants and declarations of the United Nations and other organizations (1994, 81).

Skutnabb-Kangas and Phillipson discuss five of the international conventions and declarations that do not provide for linguistic rights in education: (1) Articles of the United Nations Charter (1945) mention the freedom of language, but there is no specific article on education and thus the charter is silent about language in education; (2) the paragraph on education in the Universal Declaration of Human Rights (1948) does not refer to language; (3) the International Covenant on Economic, Social, and Cultural Rights (1966) omits any reference to language or linguistic groups in the educational article even though it does refer to "racial, ethnic or religious groups"; (4) articles in the International Covenant on Civilian and Political Rights (1966) stipulate that the law guarantees all persons equal and effective protection against discrimination on the basis of language and that "persons belonging to linguistic minorities shall not be denied the right, in community with other members of their group, to use their own language," but there is nothing about the use of their language in education; and (5) the UN Convention on the Rights of the Child does specify that there should be continuity in the child's linguistic background but only when the child is temporarily or permanently deprived of the family environment (1994, 81–83). Skutnabb-Kangas and Phillipson (1994, 83–84) contend that in these conventions "minorities are allowed to use their languages in private, but not in schools."

Skutnabb-Kangas and Phillipson acknowledge that the phrase "in public" in the Declaration on the Rights of Persons Belonging to National or Ethnic, Religious and Linguistic Minorities (discussed above) extends the space of appearance for linguistic rights from "in community with other members of their group" of the earlier ICCPR, but then they ask what constitutes "appropriate measures" and "adequate opportunities" for learning the mother tongue and how will the state determine what is "possible"? For these linguistic human rights researchers, "the alternatives permit a reluctant state to provide minimalist protection" (1994, 97). This certainly seems to play out in the case of the United States.

The Judicial Branch and International Conventions

The realization of linguistic rights in the United States has usually been blocked by the judicial branch of the national government. The U.S. judiciary has eliminated most of the possibilities for litigating claims under international law, and that accounts for part of the U.S. failure to advance and uphold linguistic rights.

Sandra Del Valle (2003, 303) indicates that there are two types of international law: customary and statutory. Customary law reflects international norms, and the norms with the highest status are called *jus cogens,* which are binding on all nations. Examples of *jus cogens* norms that are generally accepted include prohibitions against torture, extrajudicial killing, genocide, and slavery. Statutory law, on the other hand, involves rights and obligations found in written documents such as treaties that are formal agreements between independent nations concerning the public welfare. For the United States, the Supremacy Clause of the U.S. Constitution (Article VI, Paragraph 2) specifies that the Constitution, all federal statutes, and "all treaties made, or which shall be made, under the authority of the United States, shall be the supreme Law of the land" (Wikipedia 2007).

In response to civil rights complaints that included allegations of violations of the UN Charter and the Universal Declaration of Human Rights, U.S. courts invented two doctrines to obstruct lawsuits based in part on international law. The first makes a distinction between "self-executing" and "non-self-executing" treaties. A treaty is self-executing if it confers rights in the absence of implementing legislation; it becomes part of U.S. federal law upon ratification by the Congress. If the U.S. government took steps to ratify and thereby elevate the Declaration on the Rights of Persons Belonging to National or Ethnic, Religious and Linguistic Minorities to the status of a treaty, it would be a non-self-executing treaty because it requires the intervention of the state to provide the means to implement it as specified in its first and fourth articles; it would not become part of U.S. federal law upon ratification. The ICCPR was ratified by the United States but with the reservations, understandings, and declarations that were attached by Congress; U.S. obligations under the covenant were largely restricted to those already protected under domestic law. More important, Congress did not pass implementing legislation so that the ratification became subject to a judicial declaration that it is "non-self-executing." The second doctrine that the courts created to avoid dealing with international law is the argument that they need to maintain "a separation of powers" between the executive and legislative branches and its own judicial incompetence in foreign affairs that might embarrass the executive branch. In *Banco Nacional de Cuba v. Sabbatino,* a case involving the Cuban government's nationalization of private companies in violation of international law, the Supreme Court established a precedent for federal court inactivity by refusing to use international law to invalidate the Cuban expropriation (Del Valle 2003, 331–333).

Recently Stephen Vladeck (2004) addressed the issue of non-self-executing treaties, which constitutes the main obstacle to judicial review of claims alleging violations of international law. Vladeck first discusses a footnote (fn. 22) in *Ogbudimkpa v. Ashcroft.* This was a case brought by a Nigerian national who applied for relief under the Convention Against Torture and Other Cruel, Inhuman or Degrading Treatment or Punishment (CAT) from the Immigration and Naturalization Service, which was holding him in custody and previously had ordered his deportation to Nigeria. The executive branch of the government contended that federal courts were barred from judicial review by the legislative measure that implemented the CAT, but the U.S. Court of Appeals for the Third Circuit ruled that federal courts can exercise jurisdiction over petitions alleging violations of the CAT or its implementing legislation because the Congress did not speak with sufficient clarity to deprive the courts of that jurisdiction (*Ogbudimkpa* 2003).

In the *Ogbudimkpa* footnote, the Third Circuit distinguishes between ratification that purports to define a treaty as non-self-executing and "a cause of action," which is a claim that an individual has suffered a wrong and should be provided a remedy or relief in the form of a court order. Vladeck comments that "contrary to the Third Circuit, most courts assume that non-self-execution is a bar to the enforcement of treaty rights in any form. Yet it is possible that the non-self-executing nature of a treaty is not fatal to an assertion of jurisdiction under it, provided that the cause of action over which jurisdiction is asserted exists in some other statute—as is the case for habeas petitions." Vladeck points out that "the private cause of action for habeas, the court argued, is guaranteed by other provisions of federal law; a treaty need only provide jurisdiction for the courts to hear such a claim" (Vladeck 2004, 2011–2012). A ratified treaty, in short, can provide at least the jurisdiction, and a separate federal statute can provide the basis for a cause of action or claim for judicial relief.

Vladeck advances a separate argument based on the Supremacy Clause of the U.S. Constitution. He notes that the Supreme Court has never suggested "that self-executing treaties are the supreme law of the land, but non-self-executing treaties are not" and that "the plain text of the Supremacy Clause, encompassing 'all treaties,' implies the opposite" (Vladeck 2004, 2012). Vladeck (2004, 2013) then argues that "whether a treaty is self-executing or not dictates whether it gives rise to independent remedies;

that a treaty is ratified by the Senate in the first place is all the Constitution requires for the Supremacy Clause to attach." Vladeck (2004, 2014) recommends that the Supreme Court address these arguments soon, because currently nearly all of the most important covenants in international humanitarian law, including the International Covenant on Civil and Political Rights and the Geneva Conventions, are regarded as entirely or partially non-self-executing and thus to be unenforceable.

The Judicial Branch and U.S. Domestic Law

The extremely conservative interpretations of U.S. laws by the judiciary during the past several decades also account for part of the U.S. failure to advance and uphold linguistic rights. The U.S. laws that were the national basis for many of the claims that linguistic minorities have made to obtain and realize their rights have included the Fourteenth Amendment to the U.S. Constitution with its Due Process and Equal Protection Clauses (1868), the U.S. Civil Rights Act with its Titles VI and VII (1964), and the Equal Educational Opportunities Act (1974).

A few years after World War I, during which there was considerable propaganda that demonized Germans including the 7 million who had migrated to the United States from 1820 to 1920, many states passed legislation that prohibited the teaching of German in schools. In 1923, the U.S. Supreme Court, in *Meyer v. Nebraska,* found that the legislation in Nebraska and other states that eliminated the teaching of German in schools violated the Fourteenth Amendment that ensures due process. The Supreme Court asserted that although "the state may do much, go very far, indeed, in order to improve the quality of its citizens, physically, mentally and morally, is clear; but the individual has certain fundamental rights which must be respected. The protection of the constitution extends to all—to those who speak other languages as well as to those born with English on the tongue" (quoted in Del Valle 2003, 37). However, in 1973, in *San Antonio Independent School District v. Rodriguez,* the Supreme Court found that there was not a fundamental right to an education guaranteed by the Constitution. Poor minority students had brought a claim to the state of Texas that there was inadequate funding for their schools in comparison to wealthy white school districts, but the Supreme Court ruled that these students would have to turn to their state constitution for a right to an education (Del Valle 2003, 234).

In 1974, in *Lau v. Nichols,* the Supreme Court, though not basing its decision concerning the educational rights of language minorities on the U.S. Constitution, did invoke Title VI of the 1964 Civil Rights Act, which makes it illegal for any entity that receives federal funding to discriminate against someone on the basis of race, color, or national origin. The Court pointed out that the federal department providing funding for education has the authority to promulgate regulations prohibiting discrimination in federally assisted school systems, and the department had done so by requiring these school systems to rectify English-language deficiencies. Noting also that California state law requires compulsory full-time educational attendance between the ages of six and sixteen years, the Court declared that "there is no equality of treatment merely by providing students with the same facilities, textbooks, teachers, and curriculum; for students who do not understand English are effectively foreclosed from any meaningful education," and the Court directed a lower court to fashion appropriate relief (*Lau* 1974, 566).

Although *Lau v. Nichols* in 1974 did not endorse bilingual education, the same year Congress passed the Equal Educational Opportunity Act (EEOA), and section 1703(f) of the act stipulated that "no state shall deny equal educational opportunity to an individual on account of his or her race, color, sex, or national origin, by ... (f) the failure by an educational agency to take appropriate action to overcome language barriers that impede equal participation by its students in its instructional programs" (quoted in Del Valle 2003, 243). Earlier testimony to Congress by a cabinet member from the executive branch that had prepared the legislation indicated that the intent of section 1703(f) of the EEOA was to establish a right to receive bilingual education (ibid.).

But judicial and congressional support for linguistic rights of minorities faded in the years that followed. In 1981, in *Castañeda v. Pickard*, the Fifth Circuit Court of Appeals claimed that Congress "did not specify that a state must provide a program of 'bilingual education' to all limited English speaking students" (*Castañeda* 1981, 1009). The court then devised a three-part test for ascertaining whether a school district was in violation of section 1703(f) of the EEOA: (1) There must be an examination of the evidence concerning the soundness of the educational theory upon which the challenged program is based; (2) there must be an inquiry into whether the resources and personnel necessary are provided "to transform theory into reality"; and (3) there must be a determination of whether the school's program, after a trial period, produces "results indicating that the language barriers confronting students are actually being overcome" (*Castañeda* 1981, 1009–1010). As Del Valle (2003) notes, the trial period and the subsequent assessment means that the three-part test stipulated by the court requires a number of years to determine whether a violation of law has occurred. As others would say, justice delayed is justice denied.

Bilingual education is based partly on the hypothesis that second-language competence is associated with the level of competence already achieved in the first language. Longitudinal research in the 1990s on bilingual education programs for linguistic minority students indicated that students in late-exit programs did better than those in early-exit or English immersion programs (Del Valle 2003). But in the 1990s, there was increasing intolerance of minorities, and support for bilingual education rapidly declined. In 1997, for example, Proposition 227, the "English for the Children" initiative, an attempt to place all children in English-language classrooms and thereby eliminate bilingual education in the state of California, was passed by the electorate.

Del Valle (2003) suggests that periods of linguistic intolerance in the United States could have been challenged on the basis of international conventions and that recent efforts to reduce or eliminate bilingual education and advance and pass English-only laws should be viewed from an international law paradigm in order to situate the U.S. struggle within the world struggles for minority linguistic rights. However, international conventions cannot be used in most litigation in the United States, given the current doctrines and practices adopted and promoted by the judicial and legislative branches of the federal government. The United States has deliberately not made itself subject to the international conventions that might be used to contest violations of linguistic rights.

PUNISHED FOR SPEAKING IN THE MOTHER TONGUE

Skutnabb-Kangas and Phillipson (1994) contend that as racism based on biological "characteristics" such as skin color and skull form became untenable in modern societies, it was necessary to establish other criteria to legitimate the unequal division of power and resources. A new sophisticated form of racism appeared, which Skutnabb-Kangas and Phillipson call "linguicism," that is, the hierarchical organization of groups in societies based on language whereby the dominant groups ensure through their control of institutions such as education that the languages and cultures of other groups are deprived of resources and a reasonable chance to survive. As a kind of social Darwinist result, the majority languages and cultures become the "fittest survivors," which then are "used as proof of their being the fittest" (1994, 104). However, Eduardo Hernández-Chávez (1994, 156) argues that "throughout U.S. history, the drive for Anglo-American hegemony has demanded the suppression and elimination of non-English cultures." Initially the English slaveholders participated in the separation of Africans from their tribes and children from their parents, which destroyed their languages, and later English-American settlers engaged in a similar practice with Native American schoolchildren (Del Valle, 2003; Hernández-Chávez, 1994).

The United States has a disturbing history with regard to the protection of linguistic rights in educational institutions. Many school officials in the United States enforced a strict English-only policy well into the twentieth century. Students who spoke Cherokee, Lakota, Italian, German, Spanish, and other languages at home quickly learned that those languages were not acceptable at school. Students were punished for speaking languages other than English in the classroom, with their friends, or even on the playground (MacGregor-Mendoza 2000). For example, MacGregor-Mendoza conducted a study that involved oral histories with Spanish-speaking New Mexicans who had attended school in New Mexico in the 1970s. Her informants reported being physically abused by teachers, being sent to detention, having their mouths washed out with soap, and other punishments for speaking Spanish, and sometimes even for speaking English with a Spanish accent. As a result, many of these children learned to forget Spanish (MacGregor-Mendoza 2000).

Children from American Indian communities report similar forms of abuse at Indian schools. In 1963, One Star, a monolingual Lakota speaker, was sent off to a Bureau of Indian Affairs Indian school, where he and the other children would be spanked on their bare buttocks with a wooden paddle for speaking Lakota (Waxman 2003). Indeed, it was a widespread practice to forbid the speaking of indigenous languages at these Indian schools, as they were designed to assimilate the Indians into majority culture and society. While Indian schools have been abolished, reports of punishment for speaking indigenous languages continue to crop up. In a South Dakota prison, prisoners were abused by guards for speaking Lakota up until 2001, when the policy that prohibited speaking Lakota was finally repealed (Secours 2007).

Even more recently, in December 2005, a teenager was suspended from school for speaking Spanish in a Kansas City high school. Zach Rubio, a sixteen-year-old high school junior was asked by his friend: "*¿Me prestas un dólar?* [Will you lend me a dollar?]" Zach responded, "*No problema.*" A teacher overheard the hallway conversation and sent the boys to the principal's office. The principal decided to suspend Zach for a day and a half because, according to her disciplinary referral, this was not the first time Zach had been asked not to speak Spanish at school. Amidst public criticism, the suspension was overturned, and Zach's father, Lorenzo Rubio, filed a federal lawsuit. Zach's response was that "I know it would be, like, disruptive if I answered in Spanish in the classroom. I totally don't do that" (Reid 2005, A3). Once this case came to light, two other parents came forward and reported that their children had also been sent home for speaking Spanish at school (Burke 2005).

In another recent incident in Mt. Prospect, Illinois, in December 2006, Latino students received a letter designed to put a stop to bullying. The letter said: "Comments made in Spanish will be assumed to be bullying," and indicated that students would be suspended for such behavior. As in the Rubio case, the superintendent apologized and rescinded the letter once parents challenged the issue (Long 2006).

Lest we think that this is limited to the Midwest, we will briefly discuss a case in Oregon. In December 2005, parents of children at Irrigon Junior-Senior High School in Irrigon, Oregon, reported that their children were sent home for speaking Spanish at school. The principal, Ron Anthony, denied the parents' claims that children were not allowed to speak Spanish at school. Nevertheless, fifty parents showed up at the Morrow County School District board meeting to complain about this and other forms of discrimination against their children.

We certainly have come a long way in that school officials can be convinced that it is not acceptable to ban languages other than English in educational institutions. This can be seen in the fact that in the cases in Kansas City and Mt. Prospect, the superintendents revoked the previous decisions, and the principal at Irrigon told reporters after the school district board meeting that they have not had a policy of forbidding Spanish at schools for over a decade. However, these three recent cases from 2005 and 2006 show that there is still work to be done in terms of promoting a climate of tolerance and an acceptance of linguistic diversity in all of our schools.

According to the ICCPR, which the United States has ratified, students have a right not to be discriminated against on the basis of their language; and according to the ICESR, which the United States has not ratified, students have the right to an education free from discrimination. If we put these two conventions together, we can say that students should have the right to attend educational institutions where they do not face differential treatment on the basis of the language that they speak. In the Rubio case, Zach Rubio was punished for speaking a language other than English. This amounts to discrimination on the basis of language. In the Mt. Prospect case, students were told that speaking in Spanish would get them in trouble. This is also discrimination on the basis of language. The case in Irrigon is similar—students faced differential treatment on the basis of the language they spoke. Nevertheless, in each of these cases, school officials and administrators were able to see that the students do have the right to not face discrimination on the basis of language and took action to ensure that students would not face discrimination.

The right to not face discrimination, however, is just one of the rights included in international conventions and is a negative right. The question then becomes: How does the United States hold up in terms of the other rights set forth in international conventions, particularly in terms of positive rights? Do students have the right to speak their languages in public and private? Are schools promoting tolerance and understanding of linguistic diversity? Are schools providing education in students' mother tongues?

The cases discussed above indicate that students are chastised for speaking their language in public. In the Zach Rubio case, the teacher commented that she had asked Zach not to speak Spanish a few times before. This indicates that there is not a climate at that school in which the students' right to express themselves is ensured. These cases also indicate that some schools are not promoting tolerance and understanding of linguistic diversity. If school officials are equating speaking Spanish with bullying, this is not indicative of a climate of tolerance. If children are asked not to speak their native tongues in school, this is not promoting an understanding of linguistic diversity.

According to the Convention on the Rights of the Child, schools should promote respect for children's parents and their cultural identities. Language, especially the mother tongue, is a fundamental part of our cultural identity. When teachers and administrators tell children that they should not speak their mother tongues in school, this constitutes symbolic violence. When the teacher, an authority figure, tells students that schools, the place for learning how to become a member of society, are not the appropriate place to speak a child's mother tongue, the teacher is in effect telling the child that his or her cultural traditions and identity must be shed in order to become a member of society. In addition, the teacher is telling the child that the language that his or her parents speak is not a language that is valued by the school. When a child hears this, he or she may resist and reject the ideals of the school, or he or she may accept these ideas and reject the cultural identity of his or her parents. Either response is bound to have negative consequences. For these and other reasons, prohibitions on speaking languages other than English in the school setting constitute violations of human rights, and claims need to be filed with and recognized by domestic courts and possibly international courts as well.

In order to achieve a society in which all persons are ensured the recognition of their linguistic rights, it is imperative that we respect the international norms that exist and take positive steps towards implementing these norms. Our current system of laws does not do enough to protect linguistic rights, nor does it allow for the implementation of widely accepted international conventions. This creates a situation in which linguistic rights are not upheld in the United States today.

REFERENCES

Banco National de Cuba v. Sabbatino, 376 U.S. 398 (1964).

Blau, Judith, and Alberto Moncada. 2005. *Human Rights: Beyond the Liberal Vision.* Lanham, MD: Rowman and Littlefield.

Bourdieu, Pierre, and Jean-Claude Passeron. 1990. *Reproduction in Education. Society and Culture.* 2d ed. London: Sage.

Burke, G. 2005. "Suspension for Speaking Spanish Draws New Student Plaintiffs." *Wichita (KS) Eagle,* December 14, 2005.

Castañeda v. Pickard, 648 F 2d 989 (5th Cir. 1981).

Del Valle, Sandra. 2003. *Language Rights and the Law in the U.S.: Finding Our Voices.* Clevedon, UK: Multilingual Matters.

Hernández-Chávez, Eduardo. 1994. "Language Policy in the U.S.: A History of Cultural Genocide." Pp. 141–158 in *Linguistic Human Rights: Overcoming Linguistic Discrimination,* edited by Tove Skutnabb-Kangas and Robert Phillipson, in collaboration with Mart Rannut. Berlin: Mouton de Gruyer.

Lau v. Nichols, 414 U.S. 563 (1974).

Long, Jeff. 2006. "'Bully' Contract Leads to Apology. District 26 Denies Spanish Speakers Were Targeted." *Chicago Tribune.* December 13.

MacGregor-Mendoza, Patricia. 2000. "*Aquí No Se Habla Español*: Stories of Linguistic Repression in Southwest Schools." *Bilingual Research Journal* 24, no. 4: 355–367.

Meyer v. Nebraska, 262 U.S. 390 (1923).

Ogbudimkpa v. Ashcroft, 342 F.3d 207 (3d Cir. 2003).

Reid, T. R. 2005. "Spanish at School Translates to Suspension." *Washington Post.* December 9, A3.

San Antonio Independent School District v. Rodriguez, 411 U.S. 1 (1973).

Secours, Molly. 2007. "Minority and Disenfranchised Youth in Juvenile Justice: A Dominant Majority Problem—Reframing and Renaming the Issues," available at http://louisville.edu/journal/workplace/issue6p1/secours.html. (Accessed February 12, 2008.)

Skutnabb-Kangas, Tove, and Robert Phillipson. 1994. "Linguistic Human Rights, Past and Present." Pp. 71–110 in *Linguistic Human Rights: Overcoming Linguistic Discrimination,* edited by Tove Skutnabb-Kangas and Robert Phillipson, in collaboration with Mart Rannut. Berlin: Mouton de Gruyer.

United Nations. 2007a. Convention Against Discrimination in Education, available at http://www.unhchr.ch/html/menu3/b/d_c_educ.htm. (Accessed February 12, 2008.)

———. 2007b. Convention on the Protection and Promotion of the Diversity of Cultural Expressions, available at http://Unesdoc.Unesco.Org/Images/0014/001429/142919e.pdf. (Accessed March 30, 2008.)

———. 2007c. Declaration on the Rights of Persons Belonging to National or Ethnic, Religious, or Linguistic Minorities, available at http://www.unhchr.ch/html/menu3/b/d_minori.htm. (Accessed February 12, 2008.)

———. 2007d. International Covenant on Civil and Political Rights, available at http://www.unhchr.ch/html/menu3/b/a_ccpr.htm. (Accessed March 30, 2008.)

———. 2007e. International Covenant on Economic, Social, and Cultural Rights, available at http://www.unhchr.ch/html/menu3/b/a_cescr.htm. (Accessed February 12, 2008.)

———. 2007f. International Law, available at http://www.ohchr.org/EN/ProfessionalInterest/Pages/InternationalLaw.aspx. (Accessed March 30, 2008.)

———. 2007g. UN Treaty Collection, available at http://untreaty.un.org/ENGLISH/guide.asp. (Accessed February 12, 2008).

Vladeck, Stephen. 2004. "Non-Self-Executing Treaties and the Suspension Clause after St. Cyr." *Yale Law Journal,* 114, no. 8: 2007–2014.

Waxman, Sharon. 2003. "Abuse Charges Hit Reservation Church-Run Schools Cited in Wide-Ranging Lawsuit." *Washington Post,* June 2, A1.

Wikipedia. 2007. Supremacy Clause, available at http://en.wikipedia.org/wiki/Supremacy_Clause. (Accessed February 12, 2008.)

ADDITIONAL RESOURCES

UNESCO website for linguistic rights:
  http://www.unesco.org/most/ln2lin.htm.
Universal Declaration of Linguistic Rights:
  http://www.linguistic-declaration.org/index-gb.htm.

CHAPTER TWELVE

∼

Cultural Rights

RODNEY D. COATES

Corruption and hypocrisy ought not to be inevitable products of democracy, as they undoubtedly are today.

—Mahatma Gandhi

Hitler's concept of concentration camps as well as the practicality of genocide owed much, so he claimed, to his studies of English and U.S. history. He admired the camps for Boer prisoners in South Africa and for the Indians in the Wild West; and often praised to his inner circle the efficiency of America's extermination—by starvation and uneven combat—of the red savages who could not be tamed by captivity.

—Toland 1976, 202

The United States is a modern nation in that the state bureaucracy concentrates power through which it controls society.[1] As a modern nation, it has also wielded this bureaucracy to either implicitly or explicitly control social, political, cultural, gendered, and racial groups. As the nation has gained both political and economic superiority, it has expanded its sphere of control internationally. Ideologically, the United States has a long and distinguished history of advocating freedom, democracy, and justice both domestically and abroad. Realistically, U.S. history has been tainted by genocide, racism, exploitation, discrimination, imperialism, and corruption. These ends have been facilitated through the use of state-sponsored and/or sanctioned assassination, terrorism, war, bribery, and conspiracy. These alternative views, a form of dissonance, have often been viewed and manipulated through U.S. cultural institutions. At the very least, these cultural institutions have served to minimize the dissonance, at the extreme they have served as conspirators in what some have described as cultural[2] genocide. The primary purpose of this paper is to explore how these cultural institutions have functioned to legitimate, obfuscate, and often perpetuate cultural genocide at both the national and international levels.

DEFINING CULTURAL GENOCIDE

Article 7 of the United Nations Draft Declaration on the Rights of Indigenous Peoples (August 26, 1994) defines "cultural genocide":

> Indigenous peoples have the collective and individual right not to be subjected to ethnocide and cultural genocide, including prevention of and redress for:
>
> a. Any action which has the aim or effect of depriving them of their integrity as distinct peoples, or of their cultural values or ethnic identities;
> b. Any action which has the aim or effect of dispossessing them of their lands, territories or resources;
> c. Any form of population transfer which has the aim or effect of violating or undermining any of their rights;
> d. Any form of assimilation or integration by other cultures or ways of life imposed on them by legislative, administrative or other measures;
> e. Any form of propaganda directed against them.

If culture, cultural diversity, and cultural identity are both values and rights that affirm racial, ethnic, religious, and indigenous diversity, then systems and processes that would deny these rights and values deny racial, ethnic, religious, and indigenous diversity. Regrettably, while physical genocide is quite apparent and obvious, cultural genocide is less obvious, subtle, and often obscured. Furthermore, while physical genocide leads to the extermination of peoples and groups, cultural genocide leads to the destruction of culture, ways of life, and belief systems. With the loss of cultural moorings, the individuals and groups become controlled, if not docile, receptacles into which dominant cultural biases and distortions find little resistance. While we may identify different forms of cultural genocide, the motivations appear to be remarkably the same. Specifically, while the genocide may be situationally specific, the primary motivations seem to fall within seven distinctive areas: gain, glory, fear, revenge, ideology, power, and terror (Freeman 1995, 213–214). Any particular form of genocide may utilize any one or combination of motivations to achieve its particular end. The motivations may indeed be the means by which another motivation is obtained, or they may be ends unto themselves. Cultural genocide may appear as stages or cycles, natural or imposed, sequential or chaotic. Cultural genocide may be clothed in ideologies[3] of progress or civilization, democracy or divinity, capitalism or socialism, evil or good, or science or religion. The most effective strategies for cultural genocide utilize multiple interacting and intersecting sets of ideologies. Unfortunately, while some are doing their best to create programs and policies that would limit cultural genocide, others are doing their best to delegitimize these very same programs and policies.

Since the inception of the United Nations, the official U.S. policy regarding the Charter and Declaration on Human Rights has been clear: "[The U.S.] government has made it clear in the course of the development of the declaration that it does not consider that the economic and social and cultural rights stated in the declaration imply an obligation on governments to assure the enjoyment of these rights by direct governmental action" (Roosevelt 1949–50). From that time to the present, the United

States has consistently either refused or severely limited its support of UN declarations and international laws regarding human rights and cultural genocide. It would be easy to compile a long list of treaties that the United States has either failed to endorse or, when it has endorsed them, has seriously limited their enforcement. Some of the most blatant ones are:

- The Kyoto Protocol of 1997 for controlling global warming was declared "dead" by President Bush in March 2001. In November 2001, the Bush administration shunned negotiations in Marrakech (Morocco) to revise the accord, mainly by watering it down in a vain attempt to gain U.S. approval.
- The Comprehensive [Nuclear] Test Ban Treaty was signed by 164 nations and ratified by 89, including France, Great Britain, and Russia, and was signed by President Clinton in 1996 but rejected by the Senate in 1999. The United States is one of 13 nonratifiers among countries that have nuclear weapons or nuclear power programs. In November 2001, the United States forced a vote in the UN Committee on Disarmament and Security to demonstrate its opposition to the Test Ban Treaty.
- The Optional Protocol, 1989, to the UN International Covenant on Civil and Political Rights was aimed at abolition of the death penalty and contained a provision banning the execution of those under the age of eighteen. The United States has neither signed nor ratified, and specifically exempts itself from the latter provision, making it one of five countries that still execute juveniles (with Saudi Arabia, the Democratic Republic of Congo, Iran, and Nigeria). China abolished the practice in 1997, Pakistan in 2000.
- The only countries that have signed but not ratified the 1979 UN Convention on the Elimination of All Forms of Discrimination Against Women are the United States, Afghanistan, and Sao Tome and Principe.
- The United States finally ratified in 1988 the UN Convention on the Prevention and Punishment of the Crime of Genocide, 1948, adding several "reservations" to the effect that the U.S. Constitution and the "advice and consent" of the Senate are required to judge whether any "acts in the course of armed conflict" constitute genocide. The reservations are rejected by Britain, Italy, Denmark, the Netherlands, Spain, Greece, Mexico, Estonia, and others. (Du Boff 2001)

U.S. HISTORICAL REALITIES

Long before Europeans ventured into this hemisphere an estimated 150 to 1,000 different cultural and language groups were identifiable (Grosjean 1982; Sherzer 1992). Cultural diversity notwithstanding, the founding fathers envisioned a country exclusively dominated by European peoples and culture. And thus, from the first settlements, Europeans systematically and with deliberation began the wholesale genocide of both the indigenous cultures and the peoples. Long after any physical threat to European hegemony was present, the cultural genocide of Native Americans went unabated. The cultural genocide, originally targeting Native Americans, soon encompassed other groups both nationally and internationally.

Toward an Understanding of Cultural Hegemony and Genocide

In the past, the United States and much of the Western World have utilized priests as the advanced guard of our imperialist efforts. These priests, armed with their cultural hegemonic values wrapped up in the "god concept," dutifully plied their crafts upon unsuspecting peoples. Once these peoples were convinced of the superiority of their "magic" and "god concept," the door was open for military exploitation. Military control over resources, both mental and material, allowed for the imposition of an economic system aimed at maximizing the extraction of resources. Over time, these exploitative systems were recodified into explanations again packaged into cultural hegemonic garb. These cultural hegemonic garbs or tropes are then preserved, maintained, and sustained by institutions such as the church, school, and state. Normative patterns and ideologies, now assumed as legitimate and permanent, serve to justify the hyperexploitation of resources, the cultural subordination of indigenous peoples, and the creation of a racial hierarchy.

In the more recent past, it was anthropologists who took on the role of missionaries, helping poor, backward people come to grips with their cultural inadequacies. They then took on the task of overseeing the inculcation of the new, cultural hegemony that, in turn, allowed for the process of political and economic hegemony to come into being. The net result, again, was the hyperexploitation of resources, the cultural subordination of the people, and the creation of a racialized hierarchy. Elsewhere I argue that this cultural subordination, taking the guise of democracy, serves to not only create but also maintain these racial hierarchies. Specifically:

> The political ideology of democracy suggests that the exogenous elite will choose to rule indirectly. That is to say, they will align themselves with particular indigenous elite to which and with which they will rule. Such indirect rule, often described as "enlightened colonial powers," provides the illusion of democracy. Under such regimes, we note the colonizing power may establish economic structures, educational, religious, political and administrative institutions. The primary purposes of the latter (starting with educational institutions) are to assure the proper training, leadership, and system integrity to maximize exploitative operations. The whole structure, under the ruse of democratic or enlightened colonial systems, produces the illusion of freedom while maximizing the exploitative capacities of the colonial situation. (Coates 2006)

Many of the founders of disciplines such as psychology (Billig 1978), sociology (Hayes 1973), history, and economics served in this role. Thus cultural hegemony, tied to Western imperialism, has been promulgated around the globe, often hiding behind such terms as "culture of poverty," "ghetto-specific behavior," "human capital," and "cultural deficiency." More recently, more virulent academic racism has been found in education and social policy (Herrnstein and Murray 1994), genetics, and medicine.

In 1937, textile heir Wickliffe Draper created the Pioneer Fund to keep eugenics alive. The fund, spending more than $10 million over the last thirty years, gives racist and anti-immigrant policies not only a platform, but capital to lend respectability to racist and eugenic solutions. Racial betterment, uplift, and inclusion of Eastern Europeans are promoted while all others are denigrated.

Western entertainment has been the most useful tool for the transmission of cultural hegemony in the modern world. Thus, from Disney to Hollywood, from the tabloids to CNN, from country and western to gospel and blues, from rock to hip-hop, Western cultural hegemony has been preached to the masses of the world. It is through these modern mediums and their messages of consumption and exploitation and sexual manipulation and racialization that the new cultural hegemony has been promoted and promulgated.

The cultural hegemony of the United States does not lead to the complete destruction of other cultural systems. No cultural hegemony is more subtle. What happens is the devaluing of other cultural systems. Mignola critically discusses the globalization by which this hegemonic culture has developed:

> Thus, the globalization of "culture" was always there, since "culture" (in whatever technology of the time was available) is the material aspect in which the history of capitalism and of global designs (Christianity, Civilizing Mission, Development and Modernization, Marketization) evolved. Technology today allows "culture," and financial markets, to move faster. However, I would not say that there is a globalization of culture. I would rather say that planetary communication and the coloniality of power move faster and, like in the sixteenth century, in one direction. The force with which Inca's and Aymara's "cultures" entered and modified Castilian's was less significant than the reverse. That is, Castilian knowledge and attitude toward life did not change as much as knowledge and attitude toward life among Aymara and Inca people. The same today: Bolivia's music players and restaurants in the United States or Europe are less relevant (aren't they?), than European television and popular music in Bolivia. In La Paz, for example, there is a "German Channel" that provides the state of the weather in Germany and in Europe for the Bolivian audience. I am not aware of a "Bolivian Channel" in Germany that does the same. (Cited in Delgado and Romero 2001, 8)

It is important to note the distinction that Mignola is making when he asserts that it is not really *a* "globalization of culture" but rather *the* globalization of a particular cultural form that serves to destroy or distort other cultural forms. As one considers the globalization of culture represented by entertainment and sports, academia and science, religion and science, technology and art—the totality of cultural devaluation or devolution is astounding. When one further considers the considerable U.S. influence on the World Bank, the United Nations, international trade, and geopolitical systems, the possibilities for cultural dominance are endless.

The most obvious manifestation of globalization is cultural dominance. Cultural domination has been greatly facilitated by the speed of communication, information, travel, and products. The mass production of these modes, the very essence of modernity, has for the past fifty years defined the United States. This dominance has been facilitated by the U.S. creation and control for much of this period of the major cultural means of production to include technology associated with TV (in all forms, but especially news, soaps, and advertising), cinema, music, and information. These cultural means of production—and their celebration of consumerism and consumption and racial and sexual exploitation—serve to indoctrinate and sublimate cultural groups both domestically and abroad.

Control the News, Control the Views

> *I know of no country in which there is so little independence of mind and real freedom of discussion as in America.*
> —Alexis de Tocqueville

Ideologically and constitutionally, the United States advocates freedom of speech and a free press. In reality, both have yet to be achieved. While one might conceivably understand how the news media becomes the chief instrument of propaganda, one is hard-pressed to account for the almost daily assault upon truth found masquerading as news. While the current policies of George Bush have served to aggravate and accelerate anti-Americanism, these feelings run deep and are historic. The aggressive militarism, consumerism, and exploitative history of the United States underlie many of these feelings. Many throughout the world concur with the assessment reached by the Council on Hemispheric Affairs in 1982, which concluded:

> Basic civil liberties including the right to life, liberty and the freedom of personal and political expression, suffered a drastic setback in 1981. In more than a dozen regional nations, even the most fundamental rights—life and the inviolability of the person—were transgressed by the government-condoned practice of harassing, torturing and murdering political opponents of those in power.... These reverses can be linked to policies adopted by the Reagan administration ... [which] has allied the United States with the most violent regimes in the hemisphere. He [Reagan] has sanctioned atrocities and human rights abuses by providing those governments with essentially unconditioned U.S. support. ("Media Control and Censorship" 2007)

While many know of the abuse of the press that regularly went on during the McCarthy era and the cold war, currently we are documenting similar abuses associated with the Iraq war:

> In his recent book *The Assault on Reason,* former vice president Al Gore describes how "the potential for manipulating mass opinions and feelings initially discovered by commercial advertisers is now being even more aggressively exploited by a new generation of media Machiavellis." The concentration of broadcast media ownership is indeed a real threat to democracy, as we learned the hard way when more than 70 percent of Americans were convinced, falsely, that Saddam Hussein was involved in the attacks of September 11—thus enabling the launch of a disastrous and unnecessary war in Iraq. (Weisbert 2007)

An overwhelming majority (82 percent) of Americans receive their news from TV, and less than half from print sources. While these figures have remained constant for the last decade, the percentage of those who rate these news sources as credible has consistently declined.

Based upon the most recent PEW study, even journalists concede that they are under constant pressure to satisfy corporate clients and refrain from reporting those items or issues that might affect the bottom line. Hence they are more likely to:

> worry about growing financial pressure that the media is paying too little attention to complex stories. In addition, the belief that the twenty-four-hour news cycle is weakening journalism is much more prevalent among this group than among news people who do not view financial pressure as a big problem, and a majority says news reports are increasingly full of factual errors and sloppy reporting. And most journalists who worry about declining quality due to bottom-line pressures say that the press is "too timid" these days. (PEW 2007)

If this were not bad enough, in 2004, both the *New York Times* and the *Washington Post* declared that they had indeed been duped into believing that an invasion of and war with Iraq were justified. The *Times* admitted that they had misled the public regarding weapons of mass destruction and acknowledged:

> Editors at several levels who should have been challenging reporters and pressing for more skepticism were perhaps too intent on rushing scoops into the paper.... Accounts of Iraqi defectors were not always weighed against their strong desire to have Saddam Hussein ousted. Articles based on dire claims about Iraq tended to get prominent display, while follow-up articles that called the original ones into question were sometimes buried. In some cases, there was no follow-up at all. (Editors, 2004)[4]

Further, as observed by Massing (2004): "One of the most entrenched and disturbing features of American journalism [is] its pack mentality. Editors and journalists don't like to diverge too sharply from what everyone else is writing." It is clear that the United States is perceived as being one of the leading sources of instability in the world among Europeans, with 53 percent of the E.U. public agreeing that the United States represents a "threat to world peace." As one considers the totality of U.S. cultural hegemony, these fears take on more meaning. The cultural values of consumerism, sexual objectification, xenophobia, militarism, and violence are explicitly and implicitly transmitted in the wide assortment of cultural products exported.

SEX, DRUGS, HIP-HOP, AND ROCK

One of the central features of any culture is its ability to create artful representations of reality. The cultural hegemony of the United States in art has served to replace, manipulate, transform, or dictate the course of art development throughout the world. Again, it should be stressed that cultural hegemony is not always direct, but often indirect and subtle. Consider the malaise that many German intellectuals have experienced as they have tried to come to grips with what some might label their "postmodern identity crises."

> In all the pedantic and apologetic answers to this question about the failure of European culture to be central to our concerns, it is all the more striking to see that it is "Hollywood"—the image of what Europeans felt made them superior—that has taken over the intellectuals' main theme: coming to terms with the past. This has shaken our cultural certainties, perhaps no less than the other shocks to the pride and credibility of the intellectuals who play so much larger a role in Europe than their American counterparts occupy in the United States. (Schirrmacher 1994)

Particularly since World War II, much of world culture has been dominated by U.S. pop culture. The United States spent more than $23 million through programs such as the Marshall Plan to encourage both economic and cultural expansion.[5] Postwar youth, both domestically and internationally, discovered modernity through the gyrating hips of Elvis and the sultry lyrics of the Supremes. The 1960s music, reflecting the social and political unrest, became an instrument of protest and complaint. Many others learned of sex, drugs, and violence from the smooth Motown of the Temptations to the jarring rock 'n roll of Mick Jagger. Youth, through their music, drugged up, dropped out, or plugged into the movement and the moment. Music corporations, catering to these needs, soon monopolized the "new" talents and thus dictated the course of the new music. Thus transformed, American pop culture became the vehicle of modernity. Current youth—mesmerized by the "def" lyrics of Lauren Hill or 50 Cent, or the ballads by the Dixie Chicks and Garth Brooks—are no less being inundated by similar messages. Regardless of period, music and cultural expressions that started out as protest against both American prudishness and conservative values were soon replaced by the consumer-oriented messages promoting sex, drugs, mindless violence, and rock and roll. If one considers the almost monopolistic control of the industry by a relatively few corporations, the ease of these transformations is not that hard to understand.

> Universal Music Group (UMG) leads the music industry in global sales with an estimated worldwide market share in 2005 of 25.6 percent. Its global operations encompass the development, marketing, sales and distribution of recorded music through a network of subsidiaries, joint ventures and licensees in seventy-seven countries, representing approximately 98 percent of the music market. UMG is the No. 1 company in countries which together represent more than 50 percent of the global music market sales, including the United States and the U.K. UMG's business also includes music publishing.[6] (http://new.umusic.com/overview.aspx)

The Lone Ranger and Tonto, the Cisco Kid, Superman and Batman, Captain America and Pocahontas, and Robin Hood and Cinderella all reflect the same culturally sexist, racist, and classist themes: a white male from the upper echelons of society whose task it is to save the world. Rarely, if ever, does one find a hero, much less heroine, who rises from the marginalized segments of society. If one even considers the stories of

Cinderella or Pocahontas, one notes that it takes a white male from the aristocracy to not only rescue them, but deem them worthy of love and marriage. The hypocrisy of this becomes more blatantly clear when one sees how the true story of Pocahontas being raped and kidnapped by Sir Walter Raleigh gets totally retold under the banner of Disney. She becomes yet another damsel in distress. Perhaps the most revealing story, again from Disney, demonstrating these trends is that of *The Little Mermaid*. In this story, in order to attract and be seduced into marriage by the white male, Ariel had to both become dumb and grow legs. Thus, the message, if a woman wants to attract the "right" man, is that she must become silent and lose the unique qualities that make her a woman.

Minstrels in black face entertained postbellum America. These caricatures of blackness ridiculed and dehumanized a whole race. Similar racial parodies in red, yellow, and brown added inclusion to the racism of the day. As white America and the rest of the Western world laughed, colored America writhed in ghettoes and slums. With radio, while a few "authentic" persons of color found their place, their scripts were all too often racist. With movie theaters and TV, the viewing public called for more and more authenticity. Thus, a whole slew of Aunt Jemima's, Lightning, Buckwheat, Mr. Bojangles, and Amos and Andy stepped up to fill our racist appetite for amusement. It took a whole movement and racial enlightenment to demonstrate that such caricatures were not only dehumanizing but also racist.

Now, the minstrel show has returned in the likes of hip-hop. Hip-hop, originating in the mid-1970s, by the mid-1980s was a central feature of American culture. This modern form of music coupled deft poetry with not-so-subtle social commentary. Hip-hop, overnight, became the voice of urban America. In the earlier versions, social uplift was tied to positive images of black, urban identity. Women and men, from these communities, were often displayed as defiant and bold as they confronted police brutality, extreme poverty, and societal neglect. The commercialization of hip-hop brought this new medium to the mostly white youth culture in suburban America. As the consumer base for hip-hop moved from the urban centers to the suburban rings, the messages also shifted. The new messages dominating the mainstream hip-hop, catering to the voyeuristic urges of prepubescent male mentalities, now stressed black sexuality, violence, and drugs. Social and political protest was replaced with crude, often vulgar misogynistic images of both black males and females.

The shift also reflects the continual devaluation of women in general and black women in particular, who are more likely to be abused, dismissed, and demeaned. In our society, the black woman is more likely to work longer for less, get more grief, more ridicule, and less respect than men. Given the negatives associated with being female, the message that she often gets is that the only way to get attention is to "shake her money maker." Males, particularly black males, are also sexualized and objectified and told that their only claim to fame is tied to their ability to produce babies, commit random acts of violence, and spend large sums of money.

HOLLYWOOD: MOVIES, SOAPS, SITCOMS

The U.S. motion picture industry produces much of the world's feature films and many of its recorded television programs. The industry is dominated by several large studios, based mostly in Hollywood. However, with the increasing popularity and worldwide availability of cable television, digital video recorders, computer graphics and editing software, and the Internet, many small and medium-sized independent filmmaking companies have sprung up to fill the growing demand. In addition to producing feature films and filmed television programs, the industry produces made-for-television movies, music videos, and commercials. Establishments engaged primarily in operating motion picture theaters and exhibiting motion pictures or videos at film festivals also are included in this industry. Other establishments provide postproduction services to the motion picture industry, such as editing, film and tape transfers, titling and subtitling, credits, closed captioning, computer-produced graphics, and animation and special effects. (U.S. Department of Labor 2006)

Hollywood's cultural dominance was nearly complete in Europe as early as 1923 (Gomery 1980). Through its dominance of Europe, Hollywood has similarly influenced cinema and television in Asia and India (Morcom 2001), Africa, and the Middle East.

America exported $10.48 billion worth of film and television in 2004. The world's favorite TV show is the soap opera *The Bold and the Beautiful*. Every day, in almost every corner of the globe, people stream to movies made in the United States. They watch Halle Berry conjure up a storm with her eyes, Johnny Depp swashbuckle his way through the Caribbean, and Keanu Reeves swoon and mope in the company of Sandra Bullock. (Sorry about that last one, world!). But, in Uzbekistan, those same movie fans are denied the rights of free speech and assembly, while President Islam Karimov tightens his grip on power with an array of arms made in the USA. In the Philippines, they watch the country's debt skyrocket as President Gloria Macapagal Arroyo gobbles up American weaponry at startling prices and an alarming rate.

Like American entertainment, American arms are a multibillion-dollar industry that leans heavily on foreign sales. In fact, the United States exported $18.55 billion in fighter planes, attack helicopters, tanks, battleships, and other weaponry in 2005. All signs point to 2006 being another banner export year. Just as in the movie, TV, and music businesses, we dwarf the competition. Russia is the next largest arms exporter with a measly $4 billion in yearly sales. In fact, U.S. arms exports accounted for more than half of total global arms deliveries—$34.8 billion—in 2004, and we export more of them ourselves than the next six largest exporters combined. (Englehardt 2006)

SUBALTERN CULTURE: UNPLUGGED AND UNDERGROUND

Your freedoms are most precious to me.

—Jean-Paul Sartre

You are different from me and we celebrate those differences.

—Hannah Arendt

All too often, we assume that mere membership in broadly defined groups provides some basis of legitimacy. But as in the case of Clarence Thomas, Barack Obama, or Hillary Clinton, one must question if the subaltern message is being muted, diffused, or confused. Having a black, or tan, or gendered appearance does not necessitate legitimacy or accuracy. Listening goes farther than being open but also having access to the subaltern. It further, as my mother would say, requires us to "hear," which entails much more then listening, but understanding. Such understanding cannot come from formalized "texts" but the social *texts* constructed and translated by the subaltern themselves.

We are embedded in our culture, regardless of how we define that culture. As we envision another universe, we must realize that our envisioning is culturally specific. In this cultural dimension, the political, the social, and even reality take on meaning. The problem is that any reenvisioning must by necessity take into consideration this reality. W. I. Thomas once remarked that "a situation that is perceived as real is real in its consequences." How we are trained to perceive reality or how we come to perceive that reality is conditioned by the cultures that we have been taught to appreciate or disdain.

Many of our conversations about changing the world, regardless of how "valued" it may be, come with a particular set of cultural biases or cultural valuations. Another example might be in order—some years ago, an American Afro-centrist decided that what was needed was a new set of Afro-centrist holidays and developed what we now know as Kwanza. Modeling this new holiday after the Jewish notion of Hanukkah, seven days with seven candles, with seven key phrases to denote meaning, a new holiday season was born. While Kwanza was a recognition that many Africans in America longed for a stronger connection with Africa, what was designed resulted in a strange sort of Western-imposed imperial set of ideas. Rather than going back to any of the indigenous cultures in Africa, the originator simply "invented" a culturally relevant set that had nothing to do with any specific African cultural system or group. This form of Western imperialism, which would define externally some specific cultural value system and then attempt to impose this upon a cultural group, is at the heart of why we must understand cultural differences.

These cultural differences and cultural aspects of imperialism recognize that often cultural hegemonic structures hide the reality of blatant power and how these dynamics serve to structure how we view the world. Cultural hegemony serves to legitimate political, social, and economic hegemonies. At the heart of any effort to change must be an understanding of how cultural hegemonic structures operate, manipulate, and transform our viewpoint.

We, who have survived the almost revolutionary period of the 1960s—and its attendant calls for black, feminist, gay, brown, tan, yellow, and international rights—have heard an endless call to arms. We have shouted from the belfries and marched from the cathedrals; we have sat in and cried out to those with power. We have striven to give the subaltern a voice while seeking to hear that voice from the back rooms, the back streets, and the back alleys of our dimly lit portals into reality. But the question yet remains, can the subaltern speak? If so, what is being said and who is listening? No cultural system, regardless of how strong, has successfully destroyed all alternative systems or silenced all voices. Perhaps, the most successful illusion of cultural hegemonic structures is that it is "the only game in town." In reality, there have been and continue to be alternatives. The subaltern voices, both within and external to the United States, continue a long and distinguished tradition of reflecting different realities and possibilities. Spivak (1988) was correct when she asserted that postmodernism critique often and paradoxically serves to disenfranchise, exploit, and marginalize the already marginalized. Postmodernity, and other so-called progressive critiques, themselves products of Western cultural hegemony, often obscure, deny, or nullify the cultural other. "Epistemic violence" causes distortion because its interpretive lens filters culture through that of the dominant culture. Even efforts to relocate or reestablish this voice produce further distortion, as invariably they either (1) assume or attempt to impose cultural homogeneity among a culturally heterogeneous people, or (2) embody the implicit or explicit assumption that only Western intellectuals have legitimacy to discuss, evaluate, or research.

Listening to the voices from the bottom of the well reveals both vibrancy and hope. A poetics of liberation has long been heard from the subaltern valleys. Such voices, coming at times from disparate places, have served to not only challenge complacency but to bodaciously point to vistas of hope. These voices are found in the Dixie Chicks' challenge of a president and "I'm not ready to make nice," and by Lauren Hill, who argues that "hip-hop started out in the heart, now everybody trying to chart," which challenges hip-hop to go back to its anti-imperialist roots. Zonas Marginal, a radical hip-hop artist, spoke power to the darkness, challenging England to keep its hands off Venezuela. The Internet has served as the fulcrum of change as grassroots communities, NGOs, and political education have linked people across racial, gender, sexual, class, and national acts of protests. The winds of change are blowing, the songs of wonder are being heard, and the poetics of liberation are being rehearsed all around us. These forces, voices, and movements are the logical response of the subalterns to the rogue state and cultural genocide.

NOTES

1. Much of this chapter deals with the destructive consequences of U.S. cultural hegemony. I recognize that a significant alternative argument to this hegemony has been offered. I recognize the import of this argument to be that while U.S. cultural dominance is real, it nevertheless reflects the cultural melting pot that defines the United States. Whether the United States is a cultural melting pot, a smorgasbord, or something in between is beyond the scope of the current paper. There exists a long list of U.S. minimalists or apologists. A good example of this perspective was recently presented by Richard Pells (April 2002) in "American Culture Goes Global, or Does It?" in the *Chronicle of Higher Education*. The chapter concludes by assessing less dominant cultural forms both within the United States and internationally.

2. Culture refers to the meanings, values, and ideas we assign to physical, spiritual, and social reality. As such, culture also refers to the ways in which we manipulate, communicate, and record our individual and collective representations. Finally, it refers to the values, mores, customs, and beliefs that serve to structure and regulate our behavior with respect to each other, and the spiritual and physical universe.

3. Karl Mannheim (1936, 36) explains ideology as instruments utilized by the ruling elite to maintain and manipulate power, social institutions, and subordinates. Ideologies are

skillfully created myths and illusions, Mannheim continues, and should not be confused with reality.

    4.   For a detailed assessment of *New York Times* complicity in this regard, see Anthony Loewenstein (2004) "The *New York Times*' Role in Promoting War on Iraq." *Sidney Morning Herald,* May 23, 2004, http://www.smh.com.au/articles/2004/03/23/1079939624187.html. (Accessed February 1, 2008.)

    5.   Historian Geir Lundestatd referred to this as "empire by invitation." Quoted in Dina M. Smith, "Global Cinderella: *Sabrina* (1954), Hollywood, and Postwar Internationalism," *Cinema Journal* 41, no. 4: 27–51.

    6.   UMG's strength and legacy of music flows from a diverse family of record labels that include: Barclay, Interscope Geffen A&M, Geffen Records, Island Def Jam Music Group, Machete Music, Mercury Records, Polydor Records, Universal Motown Records Group, Universal Music Classics Group (which includes Decca, Deutsche Gramophone, Philips and ECM), Universal Music Latino, Universal Music Group Nashville (which includes Lost Highway, MCA Nashville, and Mercury Nashville), Universal Records South, and Verve Music Group (from their website).

REFERENCES

Billig, Michael. 1978. *Fascists: A Social Psychological View of the National Front.* New York: Harcourt, Brace, Jovanovich.

Coates, Rodney D. 2006. "Toward a Simple Typology of Racial Hegemonies." *Societies Without Borders* 1, no. 1: 69–91.

Delgado, L. Elena, and Rolando J. Romero. 2001. "Local Histories and Global Designs: An Interview with Walter Mignolo." *Discourse* 22, no. 3: 7–33.

Du Boff, Christopher 2001. "Rogue Nation," available at http://www.zmag.org/sustainers/content/2001-12/21duboff.cfm. (Accessed July 20, 2007.)

Editors, 2004. "The Times and Iraq." *New York Times,* May 26, available at http://www.commondreams.org/headlines04/0526-15.htm. (Accessed July 25, 2007.)

Englehardt, Tom 2006. "Frida Berrigan on the Weapons Trade as Entertainment," *Tomdispatch,* available at http://www.tomdispatch.com/post/106939/frida_berrigan_on_the_weapons_trade_as_entertainment. (Accessed July 25, 2007.)

Freeman, Michael. 1995. "Genocide, Civilization and Modernity." *British Journal of Sociology* 46, no. 2 (June): 207–223.

Gomery, Douglass. 1980. "Economic Struggle and Hollywood Imperialism: Europe Converts to Sound." *Cinema/Sound* 60: 80–93.

Grosjean, Francois. 1982. *Life with Two Languages: An Introduction to Bilingualism.* Cambridge, MA: Harvard University Press.

Hayes, James, R. 1973. "Sociology and Racism: An Analysis of the First Era of American Sociology." Phylon 34, no. 4: 330–341.

Herrnstein, Richard, and Charles Murray. 1994. *The Bell Curve: Intelligence and Class Structure in American Live.* New York: Free Press.

Mannheim, Karl. 1936. *Ideology and Utopia,* L. Wirth and E. Shills, translators. New York: Harcourt Brace.

Massing, Michael. 2004. "Now They Tell Us." *New York Review of Books* 53, no. 3 (February 26), available at http://www.nybooks.com/articles/article-preview?article_id=16922. (Accessed July 25, 2007.)

"Media Control and Censorship." *Third World Traveler,* available at http://www.thirdworldtraveler.com/Media/MediaCensorship.html. (Accessed July 25, 2007.)

Morcom, Anna. 2001. "An Understanding between Bollywood and Hollywood? The Meaning of Hollywood-Style Music in Hindi Film." *British Journal of Ethnomusicology* 10, no. 1: 63–84.

PEW 2007. "Press Going Too Easy on Bush: Bottom-Line Pressures Now Hurting Coverage, Say Journalists," Pew Research Center for the People and the Press, available at http://www.stateofthemedia.org/2007/journalist_survey_prc.asp. (Accessed July 25, 2007.)

Roosevelt, Eleanor. 1949–1950. Cited in "International Law Statute Which Prohibits Aliens Who Are Ineligible to Become Citizens from Owning Land Held Unenforceable as against the Charter of the United Nations and the Declaration of Human Rights." *Virginia Law Review* 36, no. 4 (October): 804–806.

Schirrmacher, Frank. 1994. "'Hollywood Hegemony' at Issue as Germans Again Debate Identity," *International Herald Tribune,* May 30, available at http://www.iht.com/articles/1994/05/30/schirr.php. (Accessed July 31, 2007.)

Sherzer, J. 1992. A Richness of Voices. Pp. 251–275 in *America in 1492: The World of the Indian Peoples before the Arrival of Columbus,* edited by. A. M. Josephy, Jr. New York: Alfred A. Knopf.

Spivak, Gayatri Chakravorty. 1988. "Can the Subaltern Speak?" Pp. 271–313 in *Marxism and the Interpretation of Culture,* edited by Cary Nelson and Lawrence Grossberg. London: Macmillan.

Toland, John. 1976. *Adolph Hitler.* New York: Doubleday.

U.S. Department of Labor. 2006. "Motion Pictures and Video Industries," available at http://www.bls.gov/oco/cg/cgs038.htm. (Accessed July 31, 2007.)

Weisbert, Mark. 2007. "Correa's War," *Guardian,* July 26, available at http://commentisfree.guardian.co.uk/mark_weisbrot/2007/07/democracy_in_ecuador.html. (Accessed July 28, 2007.)

ADDITIONAL RESOURCES

Declaration on Cultural Diversity:
> http://www.ohchr.org/english/law/diversity.htm.

Gayatri Spivak contributions to postmodernism, feminism, and subaltern studies:
> http://www.english.emory.edu/Bahri/Spivak.html.

And her turn toward ethics and human rights:
> http://en.wikipedia.org/wiki.

Gayatri_Chakravorty_Spivak:
> http://www.lib.virginia.edu/area-studies/SouthAsia/Ideas/subalternBib.html.

Making Democracy Sustainable:
> http://www.aidemocracy.org.

Chapter Thirteen

~

Rights to Water, Food, and Development

JENNIFFER M. SANTOS-HERNÁNDEZ
AND JOHN BARNSHAW

In 1943, psychologist Abraham Maslow developed a hierarchy of needs that included physiological needs such as food and water as the most essential requisites for the survival of humanity. Conversely, development is a process of change that could have positive and negative impacts on the distribution of water, food, and other resources, particularly when nonsustainable strategies are employed and their results are not monitored. If successfully implemented, as argued by Sen (1999), development has the potential of enabling freedoms or bringing about a variety of choices for individuals. Despite the widespread acknowledgement that food and water are essential for life and development; access to them was not considered a human right until the late twentieth century. This chapter outlines the positions of the United States as it relates to water, food, and development and how these policies reflect or diverge from the emerging international framework on human rights, most notably through actions, resolutions, declarations, and goals established by the United Nations. It is important to note that although water, food, and development are treated in successive sections, they are interrelated, and the break is done to facilitate the discussion. Indeed, access to clean drinking water is essential for humans and societies as well as for plants and animals that serve as the basis for food and ultimately contribute to development. Thus, any discussion of water, food, or development must necessarily treat all three as intersecting rights rather than independent social phenomena.

Following this exploration, we offer policy suggestions and implications that may assist in facilitating access to water, food, and development to those who throughout history have had limited access to these essential resources and ultimately human rights. Although the United States may bear some of the economic costs in a policy shift from the current framework to a broader and more inclusive rights framework, the social and political benefits of leading the international community in securing rights to food, water, and development for all citizens may far outweigh the economic consequences. Throughout the world, from Argentina to India to Uganda, many developed and developing nations have united to form an expanding majority of parties that designate the physiological needs of food and water as human rights through domestic and international frameworks such as the United Nations. Within this context, we now explore the cornerstone of human rights: the right to water and food for development.

WATER AS A RESOURCE

Water is the most abundant resource on Earth and is literally the source of life, as 70 percent of the human body is water, and humans begin to feel thirst after a loss of 1 percent of body fluids and risk death at a water loss of 10 percent (Gleick 1996). Although some 70 percent of the Earth's surface is water, most of this is salty oceanic water, while only 3 percent of all water is fresh. Furthermore, of the 3 percent that is freshwater, only 1 percent is easily accessible surface freshwater, as 99 percent of freshwater is found in ice caps and groundwater (Gleick 1996). Over the past 2,000 years, the world's population has increased by more than 2,000 times, yet there is no more water on earth now than there was then (Population Information Program 1998). In addition, in much of the world, readily accessible drinking water is polluted due to improper waste disposal and poor water management. In 2003, the World Health Organization (WHO) estimated that 2.6 billion people lived without access to proper waste disposal and 1.1 billion people lived without readily accessible clean drinking water. To put this in perspective, a lack of access to clean water yearly kills more than 2 million people, nearly the number of people who die from HIV/AIDS annually (Davidson, Myers, and Chakraborty 1992; U.S. Aid for International Development 1990; World Health Organization 2003). Despite these considerable challenges, relatively little has been done in the way of establishing a right to water in a national or international human rights framework until recently.

FROM "WATER RIGHTS" TO "WATER RIGHTS"

Although the U.S. Constitution and the UN Universal Declaration of Human Rights acknowledge life as essential for liberty, there was no acknowledgement that water is essential for life until Article 24 of the Convention on the Rights of the Child. The explicit exclusion of water from those statements does not necessarily mean that water was not considered fundamental to life until later, it simply means that its inclusion, like air, was thought unnecessary. Furthermore, since neither document was intended to serve as the final compendium of human rights, it was understood that future constitutions, amendments, declarations, and laws would expand upon these initially enumerated rights. As such, it is important to explore the U.S. framework for dealing with water and then expand upon this with an exploration of the UN international framework to help us arrive at an understanding of how both intersect and diverge from one another.

At present, three main doctrines have been utilized to establish water rights throughout the world. These doctrines of water rights are *riparian, prior appropriation,* and *Ottoman law. Riparian* comes from the Latin word meaning "riverbank" and has its origins in English common law. Riparian essentially means that whoever owns the land adjacent to a body of surface water has the right to use that water, and all those bordering the same body of water have equal rights to the water for natural purposes (Kazmann 1972). *Prior appropriation* means that whoever is first to use surface water has the highest priority rights, and users who draw on the same water source thereafter have proportional rights based on the order in which they arrived and began drawing upon that water (Hussein 2001). *Ottoman law* has it origin in the Ottoman Empire of the Near East. With Ottoman law, the state controls all surface water, and individual property owners own up to the water surface and receive allocations of water by the state (Laster 2000). Although still practiced in the state of Israel, Ottoman law is less common than prior appropriation and riparian systems, which are practiced throughout the world, sometimes even in the same nation, as is the case in the United States.

The United States has a hybrid practice of riparian and prior appropriation water rights depending upon the geography of the country. In the northern and eastern United States, which had abundant sources of water, the Western European colonials brought with them the riparian water rights doctrine of adjacent riverbank water use. As Americans migrated west of the Mississippi River, where surface water was somewhat less abundant, the settlers adopted the doctrine of prior appropriation to establish water rights. However, the utilization of prior appropriation became somewhat problematic for the predominantly white settlers, as Native Americans often held historic first claims to water resources. In 1908, the U.S. Supreme Court supported Native Americans in the doctrine of prior appropriation when it ruled in *Winters v. United States* (207 U.S. 564) that federally established lands such as reservations could reserve water for future use in amounts that would fulfill the purpose of the reservation. Although the *Winters* decision marked the first time the federal government had deviated from the established contention that water was a states' rights issue, the power of the federal government to mediate water rights was significantly undercut by the McCarren Amendment of 1952 (43 U.S.C. § 666), which required the federal government to waive its sovereign immunity, thereby empowering states to adjudicate water rights throughout the United States (Bureau of Land Management 2007). Since the McCarren Amendment, the federal government has been further limited in water rights cases and has adopted a policy of negotiating rather than litigating conflicts over Native American water rights (McCool 1993). Thus, the United States has developed a piecemeal and limited water rights framework of riparian and prior appropriation or some combination of the two that often varies from state to state or even municipality to municipality. Under such limiting conditions, it has been difficult to for U.S. policymakers to establish and embrace a broad-based legal framework that recognizes water as a human right as has been the thrust of international governing organizations such as the United Nations.

Within the UN framework, water has always been recognized as fundamental for human survival even if not explicitly stated. Water has been implicitly acknowledged as a right with the constitution of the World Health Organization (1946, 2), which states that "the enjoyment of the highest attainable standard of health is one of the fundamental rights of every human being." Thus, it was reasoned, though not explicitly stated, that clean water was essential for every human being to attain a minimum standard of health and, therefore, any "higher standard of health" would necessarily include a framework for clean water. For the second half of the twentieth century and beyond, UN declarations such as the Universal Declaration of Human Rights (1948) and the International Covenant on Economic, Social, and Cultural Rights (ICESR) (1976) have continued to recognize and stress that water is not only a human right but that is also directly linked to other rights such as the right to food and the right to health. Furthermore, the Convention on the Rights of the Child (CRC) (1989) specifically included a provision for clean drinking water that enumerated water within the human rights framework. Since the CRC, the United Nations and a majority of its states parties have established a commitment to water as a human right. Perhaps nowhere is this commitment better evidenced than in the Committee on Economic, Social and Cultural Rights (2002) General Comment 15, which states that "the human right to water is indispensable for leading a life in human dignity. It is a prerequisite for the realization of human rights." Thus, the United Nations has committed to establishing water as an essential right, even if the United States has been reluctant to do so.

THE UNITED STATES IN THE INTERNATIONAL WATER FRAMEWORK

Since the inception of the United Nations in 1945, of which the United States was a charter member, there have been five major declarations or statements regarding the right to water. Of these five declarations (ICESCR 1976; Protocol II Additional to the Geneva Conventions 1977; Declaration on the Elimination of All Forms of Discrimination against Women [DEADW] 1981; Declaration on the Rights of the Child [DRC] 1989; Kyoto Protocol to the UN Framework Convention on Climate Change [KPUNFCC] 2006) the United States has not ratified any, signed four, and not ratified one (Table 13.1). It is important to note that only ratification legally binds a national party to the document, signing a declaration is merely a gesture of endorsement without legal implications. Since the United States, at present, has not ratified any of these declarations, it is without a comprehensive framework for human water rights. As Table 13.1 illustrates, each of the four more recent declarations have more than 150 international parties and include such nations as China, Cuba, Iran, Iraq (under Hussein), and North Korea, which are frequent targets of some U.S. politicians for having poor records on human rights. These declarations are not ceremonial resolutions, but each has genuine policy implications as they offer specific rights, including protection of water for prisoners, providing water for sustainable

Table 13.1 U.S. Position on Major International Declarations on Water and Food

Declaration	Year	Parties	U.S. Status
International Covenant on Economic, Social, and Cultural Rights	1976	151	Signed
Protocol II Additional to the Geneva Conventions	1977	163	Signed
Declaration on the Elimination of All Forms of Discrimination Against Women	1981	174	Signed
Declaration on the Rights of the Child	1989	191	Signed
Millennium Development Goals (MDGs)	2000	189	Endorsed
Kyoto Protocol to the UN Framework Convention on Climate Change	2006	172	Not Ratified

development and vulnerable populations, as well as a framework for clean drinking water free from industrial pollution. However, we must not misunderstand U.S. actions as completely negative. While resistance to ratifying international declarations has been a pattern, the United States has contributed to international efforts to facilitate access to clean and safe water through programs such as the joint U.S.-Japan Clean Water Initiative (2001), though their extent and relative contribution are very small. The decision not to ratify each of these UN declarations is not without benefit or consequences, as the United States has some of the highest levels of water usage domestically and internationally.

Within the water resources literature, water usage was formerly measured by the amount of water withdrawal in the domestic, agricultural, and industrial sectors (Gleick 1993; Shiklomanov 2000). More recently, however, researchers have begun to measure water usage through a *water footprint* (Hoekstra and Chapagain 2007). A water footprint is a measure of the volume of water usage in relation to consumption and can be calibrated by an internal water footprint and an external water footprint so that the volume of water used by other countries within a country can be assessed. On average, the national global footprint is 1,240 cubic meters per capita per year (Hoekstra and Chapagain 2007). However, eight countries (India, China, the United States, the Russian Federation, Indonesia, Nigeria, Brazil, and Pakistan) contribute 50 percent of the total global water footprint. The United States has the largest global footprint of 2,480 cubic meters per capita per year and represents 9 percent of all water resources (Hoekstra and Chapagain 2007). Of the U.S. global footprint of water, 32 percent is accounted for by the consumption of industrial goods, which is again the highest internationally (Hoekstra and Chapagain 2007). The United States has developed into the largest economic power, due in large part to access to available resources such as water. Any political action that may call for greater conservation of such resources has been seen as detrimental to development. Thus, the tremendous reliance on water by the U.S. economy for sustainability, coupled with a piecemeal doctrine of water appropriation, has fostered a political and economic context that is largely inhospitable to international claims of water as a fundamental human right.

Evaluating the past performance of the United States on the recognition of water as a fundamental human right is a difficult task, since its involvement to ensure access to clean water has been limited and not salient throughout the twentieth century. This is due in part to a weak federal policy of domestic water rights, expanding global capitalist interests that rely upon water at various stages of production, and a long tradition of nonintervention in international issues that do not offer substantial benefits to the United States. As such, what can be evaluated is that, as of yet, the United States has not made concerted or sustained efforts to match the international community in placing the right to water as a core issue on the international agenda.

Although current U.S. policies may provide substantial economic benefits, ensuring that access to clean drinking water is a human right is important from a public policy perspective for at least five reasons. First, the establishment of water as a human right affirms that freshwater is a legal entitlement and not a commodity or service provided on a charitable basis. Second, by emphasizing water as a right, governments must take tangible steps toward fulfilling and protecting the right to water of all people within their jurisdiction. Often, this involves the reformation or rearticulation of policies that provide more equitable access for all citizens and producing additional funding for the maintenance and protection of freshwater resources (United Nations 2003). Third, the establishment of water rights may raise both public awareness and involvement in water policy in such a manner that extreme interests such as those of large corporations do not exceed the will of the majority. In this instance, large multinational corporations and agricultural businesses that require high levels of water consumption would draw unwanted public attention that may be detrimental to their short-term economic interests. Fourth, defining water as a human right ensures that the least served are not marginalized by market forces or piecemeal policies that do not explicitly take their vulnerability into account. Although the United Nations lists the United States among the highest for development of accessible clean water, shortages and a lack of routine maintenance often leave the U.S. water supply vulnerable for rural and underserved populations such as Native Americans. Fifth and finally, the establishment of water as a human right allows for the UN human rights system to monitor the progress of states parties and provides a framework and a place for the recognition of grievances not currently established. By participating in such a framework, the United States could serve as a model for water rights and development and be better able to serve developing nations in Central America, Africa, and Asia where improper waste disposal and poor water management cause serious public health problems such as malaria, cholera, typhoid, and famine that kill millions of people each year.

While lack of access to clean and safe water kills millions of people every year, hunger and malnutrition are also major causes of death around the world. Moreover, water as an essential part of the human diet is also linked to the right to food (Kent 2005). Highlighting the importance of the interconnections between human rights, development, and other sociodemographic and health indicators, we now turn our discussion to explore issues related to food as a human right.

DEVELOPMENT, INEQUALITY, AND FOOD

In 1798, Thomas Robert Malthus stated that food was necessary to human existence. Malthus argued that while the population was multiplying itself or growing geometrically, the capacity to subsist was increasing arithmetically. Given the imbalance in the population and resources equation, he predicted that a portion of the population was condemned to poverty. Malthus argued that food was the ultimate means of subsistence and that the uncontrollable population growth would inevitably lead to poverty. Further, Malthus's comments opposed the idea of welfare, as he believed that when individuals are held responsible for the subsistence of their families their sexual behavior is more prudent. Today we know that throughout history the Malthusian perspective has been highly critiqued and proved wrong.

Industrialization and the mechanization of agriculture have dramatically contributed to the massive production of one of the fundamental human needs: food. The truth is that while food production fell in 2005 (mainly because of a decline in crops in developed countries) it had continuously increased since the 1970s. In other words, dramatic improvements in food production have helped to balance the equation by increasing our ability to fulfill this basic human need. Nevertheless, the world currently encounters a global food crisis that has led to violence in countries such as Haiti, Cameroon, Indonesia, Egypt, and many other sub-Saharan and South Asian countries. Inadequate development and consumption patterns have also led to global warming, and it is expected to affect food availability, the stability of food supplies, access to food, and food utilization (see Intergovernmental Panel on Climate Change Fourth Assessment Report on Impacts, Adaption, and Vulnerability 2007). Moreover, climate change will exacerbate the problem of food distribution, increasing agricultural land in North America and the Russian Federation and presenting additional challenges to the already poverty-stricken regions of sub-Saharan Africa and South Asia. However, it is very important to highlight that people dying of hunger are not doing so because of a shortage of food. People are being killed by hunger because their economic and political situations are such that they lack the money to buy provisions, they are landless, and they lack the resources to produce food (Worldwatch Institute 2005).

THE UNITED STATES IN THE INTERNATIONAL
FOOD FRAMEWORK

Throughout the twentieth century, the international community has mobilized to address the global issue of hunger. The International Covenant on Economic, Social, and Cultural Rights (ICESCR) was completed and adopted by the General Assembly of the United Nations in 1966. Since then, the United Nations has accepted the endorsement and ratification of ICESCR from all of its member states. More than forty years later, all countries participating in this effort have signed and ratified the treaty, with the exception of the United States, Belgium, Pakistan, and South Africa. While U.S. president Jimmy Carter signed the ICESCR in 1977, the treaty has awaited ratification from the U.S. Senate for thirty years.

Somewhat similar to the ICESCR but with a greater focus on suitable indicators and adequate development measurements, the Millennium Development Goals (MDGs) were unanimously adopted in September 2000 by the UN General Assembly. The overarching goal of the MDGs is eradicating poverty and improving the quality of life of all human beings by 2015. While the United States adopted the MDGs, Samir Amin (2006) and many other scholars and activists are critical of the MDGs, arguing that while the declaration presents very worthwhile hopes, it does not show the commitment of any of the member states.

Seven years after the adoption of the Millennium Development Goals it has been argued by many, including the former UN secretary general, Kofi Annan, that even when progress is tangible it is not enough to accomplish the goals by 2015. But what has the United States done in regard to the existing international framework that, among many other things, attempts to ensure the fundamental right to adequate food? The truth is, not too much or at least not as much as is expected by the international community. For instance, throughout the years, many countries, mostly from the developing world, have complained about the lack of commitment of the United States in reducing trade barriers (Parliamentary Network on the World Bank 2004). Furthermore, the U.S. position at the World Food Summit in 2002 was astounding precisely because of its moral indifference toward the developing world. The U.S. representatives stated that they would not assent or sign any declaration that referred to food as a human right. While according to the Food and Agricultural Organization (FAO), a child dies of hunger every five minutes as a result of the economic and political situation in which he or she lives, the United States claims that food is a right to the extent that it guarantees access to food but not the capacity to acquire it. In other words, a right to food gives the citizens of all countries access to food, but does not ensure their capacity to buy it or secure the means to produce it (Rosset 2002).

The U.S. position in regard to food as a right is that national governments should be responsible for their citizens and not the international community. They argue for more trade liberalization and for the assignation of a primary role to genetically modified foods in solving the global issues of hunger. In fact, the United States supports the distribution of genetically modified rice, also known as "golden rice" because of its color resulting from the high concentration of Vitamin A in it, as a solution to the issues of malnutrition and hunger in developing countries. The main problem with this proposition is that, beyond the moral issues and the indifference in regard to the symbolic and cultural value of food, instead of helping to alleviate the issues of malnutrition and hunger by assisting national governments to assure their citizens access to balanced nutrition and an overall better quality of life, it just provides them with a strategy to stay alive. In other words, the United States presents a coping mechanism while it ignores the root causes of the incapacity of millions to secure food.

CONCLUSION

Amartya Sen (1999) argues that rights require correlated duties and that if there are not assigned duties, they are just heartwarming but incoherent thoughts. If duties to eradicate hunger and promote access to clean water are assigned, we can develop a concrete agenda of goals to fulfill; otherwise, we have agreeable arguments about a right that all individuals do not and will not have. In that sense, the U.S. commitment to development and its position in relation to the international human rights framework is very problematic and full of twists and turns. It is imperative to address the historical discrepancies between the speech and actions of the United States.

In an increasingly globalized world, it is necessary to attend to social problems and to seek solutions as a global community. If the U.S. economy increasingly benefits from the resources of the global community, it is important to assure that our own quest for development does not hinder the rights of others to access all resources and also the capacity to secure the means necessary for their subsistence. Further, it is very important that we ensure that the quality of living of all world citizens is improved continually. It is following that premise that we can extend the promise of freedom and enhanced living offered by development to all humankind.

REFERENCES

Amin, Samir. 2006. "The Millennium Development Goals: A Critique from the South." *Monthly Review* 57: 10.

Bureau of Land Management. 2007. "Federal Reserved Water Rights," available at http://www.blm.gov/nstc/WaterLaws/pdf/FedResWaterRights.pdf. (Accessed September 15, 2007.)

Davidson, Joan, Dorothy Myers, and Manab Chakraborty. 1992. *No Time to Waste: Poverty and the Global Environment.* Oxford, UK: Oxfam.

Easterling, W. E., et al. 2007. "Food, Fibre, and Forest Products." *Climate Change 2007: Impacts, Adaptation, and Vulnerability: Contribution of Working Group II to the Fourth Assessment Report of the Intergovernmental Panel on Climate Change,* edited by M. L. Parry, O. F. Canziani, J. P. Palutikof, P. J. van der Linden, and C. E. Hanson. Cambridge, UK: Cambridge University Press, 273–313.

Gleick, Peter. 1996. "Basic Water Requirements for Human Activities: Meeting Basic Needs." *International Water* 21: 83–92.

———. 1993. *Water in Crisis: A Guide to the World's Fresh Water Resources.* New York: Oxford University Press.

Hoekstra, Arjen, and Ashok Chapagain. 2007. "Water Footprints of Nations: Water Use by People as a Function of Their Consumption Pattern." *Water Resources Management* 21: 35–48.

Hussein, Mohammed. 2001. "Groundwater Rights and Legislation for Sustainable Development in Arid Regions: The Case of Saudi Arabia." *Water Resources Development* 17: 227–235.

Kazmann, Raphael. 1972. *Modern Hydrology.* New York: Harper and Row.

Kent, George. 2005. *Freedom from Want: The Human Right to Adequate Food.* Washington, DC: Georgetown University Press.

Laster, Richard. 2000. "Catchment Basin Management of Water." *Water, Air, and Soil Pollution* 123: 437–446.

Maslow, Abraham. 1943. "A Theory of Human Motivation." *Psychological Review* 50: 370–396.

McCool, Daniel. 1993. "Intergovernmental Conflict and Indian Water Rights: An Assessment of Negotiated Settlements." *Publius* 23: 85–101.

Parliamentary Network on the World Bank. 2004. "Background on Trade and the Millennium Development Goals," available at http://siteresources.worldbank.org/EXTPARLIAMENTARIANS/Resources/trade_intelligence_brief.pdf. (Accessed September 15, 2007.)

Population Information Program. 1998. "Solutions for a Water-Short World." *Population Reports* 26: 1–31.

Rosset, Peter. 2002. "U.S. Opposes Right to Food at World Summit." *World Editorial & International Law,* available at http://www.foodfirst.org/media/opeds/2002/usopposes.html. (Accessed September 15, 2007.)

Sen, Amartya. 1999. *Development as Freedom.* New York: Anchor Books.

Shiklomanov, Igor. 2000. "Appraisal and Assessment of World Water Resources." *Water International* 25: 11–32.

UN Food and Agriculture Organization. 2006. *The State of Food and Agriculture.* Rome: Sales and Marketing Group.

United Nations. 2002. Committee on Economic, Social, and Cultural Rights General Comment Number 15, available at: http://www.unhchr.ch/html/menu2/6/gc15.doc. (Accessed September 15, 2007.)

———. 1989. Convention on the Rights of the Child, available at: http://www.ohchr.org/english/law/pdf/crc.pdf. (Accessed September 15, 2007.)

———. 1981. Declaration on the Elimination of All Forms of Discrimination against Women, available at: http://www.unhchr.ch/html/menu3/b/21.htm. (Accessed September 15, 2007.)

———. 1976. International Covenant on Economic, Social, and Cultural Rights, available at: http://www.unhchr.ch/html/menu3/b/a_cescr.htm. (Accessed September 15, 2007.)

———. 2003. *International Year of Freshwater: 2003.* New York: UN Press.

———. 2006. Kyoto Protocol to the United Nations Framework Convention on Climate Change, available at: http://www.unhchr.ch/html/menu3/b/21.htm. (Accessed September 15, 2007.)

———. 1977. Protocol Additional to the Geneva Conventions of 12 August 1949, and Relating to the Protection of Victims of Non-International Armed Conflicts (Protocol II), available at http://www.unhchr.ch/html/menu3/b/94.htm. (Accessed September 15, 2007.)

———. 1948. Universal Declaration of Human Rights, available at http://www.un.org/Overview/rights.html. (Accessed September 15, 2007.)

U.S. Aid for International Development. 1990. *Strategies for Linking Water and Sanitation Programs to Child Survival.* Washington, DC: U.S. Aid for International Development.

U.S. Code. McCarren Amendment, 43 USC § 666 (1952).

Winters v. United States, 207 U.S. 564 (1908).

World Health Organization. 1946. Constitution of the World Health Organization, available at http://www.searo.who.int/LinkFiles/About_SEARO_const.pdf. (Accessed September 15, 2007.)

World Health Organization. 2003. *The Right to Water.* Geneva: World Health Organization Press.

Worldwatch Institute. 2005. *Vital Signs 2005.* New York: W. W. Norton.

ADDITIONAL RESOURCES

CARE: World Hunger Campaign:
    http://www.care.org/campaigns/world-hunger.

Declaration on the Elimination of All Forms of Discrimination against Women:
http://www.unhchr.ch/html/menu3/b/21.htm.

Declaration on the Rights of the Child:
http://www.ohchr.org/english/law/pdf/crc.pdf.

Food and Agriculture Organization of the United Nations:
http://www.fao.org.

International Covenant on Economic, Social and Cultural Rights:
http://www.unhchr.ch/html/menu3/b/a_cescr.htm.

Kyoto Protocol to the United Nations Framework Convention on Climate Change:
http://www.un.org/millennium/law/xxvii-23.htm.

Millennium Development Goals:
http://www.un.org/millenniumgoals.

Protocol II Additional to the Geneva Conventions:
http://www.unhchr.ch/html/menu3/b/94.htm.

2006 Global Hunger Index:
http://www.ifpri.org/pubs/ib/ib47.pdf.

United Nations World Food Programme:
http://www.wfp.org/english.

UN World Food Programme End Child Hunger by 2015:
http://www.fighthunger.org.

CHAPTER FOURTEEN

~

Environmental Rights

DAMAYANTI BANERJEE

At the 2002 World Summit on Sustainable Development in Johannesburg, Mary Robinson, the UN high commissioner for human rights, called for a new environmental agenda. Drawing upon commonalities in human rights and environmental rights frameworks, she argued that human rights cannot (and should not) focus on rights of individuals and groups to human dignity without paying equal attention to the environmental degradation that often results from the pursuit of the former. As she points out, "human rights are not by nature environmentally unfriendly. The right to safe drinking water is not the right to waste drinking water. The right to housing does not support the destruction of forests essential in both ecological and human health terms. The goals of protecting the earth for future generations and of ensuring the dignity of those living at the present time are inextricably entwined" (Robinson 2002).

Robinson's call for more attention to environmental preservation as a human right is by no means singular. Ever since the Brundtland Commission declaration in 1997 called for the pursuit of sustainable development amidst growing concerns for global environmental deterioration, activists and scholars working on environmental preservation have liked to see themselves as taking responsibility for our common future. Policymakers and activists have defined environmental rights as similar to other civil rights like rights to nourishment, health, housing, and livelihood, all of which are central to the International Covenant on Economic, Social, and Cultural Rights.[1] Further, UN Development Programme (UNDP) reports as early as 1998 called for inclusion of environmental rights into human rights agendas, especially since a large section of the world's population directly depends on our natural resources for their sustenance and attainment of human dignity. In fact, in recent years, international organizations, both in the state and nongovernmental sectors, have been enthusiastic in linking quests for environmental rights with human rights, especially in the aftermath of global environmental concerns ranging from global warming to the transfer of toxic wastes to developing nations—what Hugh Marbury (1995) calls "garbage imperialism."

Yet, while calls for a human rights approach to the environment have grown internationally, there remains a decided lack of attention to human rights concerns in the academic and policy discourses on environment within the United States. This is clearly evident in the history of the environmental justice movement, one of the premier environmental rights movements in the latter half of the twentieth century in the United States.

In particular, there has emerged a growing disconnect in the framing of the environmental justice movement. While the earlier framework drew its intellectual rigor from the civil rights movement in the United States, the recent internationalization of environmental concern requires a new framing of the movement based on an international human rights tradition. I argue that this disconnect is not a result of any limitation in either framework. In fact, much of the human rights scholarship in recent years draws upon principles of the civil rights movement, just as the civil rights paradigm emerged from concerns over social inequality and struggle for basic human rights. Instead, the disconnect rests in the long-standing apathy toward human rights concerns in the United States, which has traditionally dissociated itself from international human rights activism. I argue that a remedy lies in drawing better linkages between environmental justice and human rights.

Hence, I suggest that we expand the notion of justice as it pertains to environmental justice and reframe it as *environmental rights*. Justice, after all, is essentially a matter of *human rights* that include rights to racial, class, caste, gender, age, and environmental equality among others. A concise definition of justice needs to examine it as a question of rights. I begin with a brief exploration of the existing environmental justice framework, followed by an examination of the need for a human rights approach to the environment, especially in the post–Kyoto Protocol world. I end my discussion by outlining some of the components of this new environmental rights framework.

ENVIRONMENT AS A CIVIL RIGHTS CONCERN: ENVIRONMENTAL JUSTICE IN THE UNITED STATES.

In a seminal article exploring the ideological foundations of the environmental justice movement, Taylor (2000) argues that the success of the environmental justice movement lies in the effective alignment of two ideological frameworks—the civil rights movement and the environmental movement. As she postulates, one of the defining issues in examining social impacts of environmental degradation over the past few decades, the environmental justice movement in the United States has sought to bring civil rights and broader social justice concerns to the forefront of environmental debates. The movement's challenge to traditional environmentalism has led to a paradigmatic shift from exclusive attention to nature conservation to a study of race, class, and distributive inequities in environmental contexts—concerns highly relevant to the civil rights movement.

Early environmental justice literature in the United States sought to draw upon these linkages. Three studies, considered the precursors to the American environmental justice movement, have emphasized the importance of unequal distribution in creating and sustaining environmental injustices. To begin with, the General Accounting Office report (1983), studying hazardous waste locations, raised an important concern—three out of four landfills are located in predominantly African American communities. This report was followed by a second landmark study in 1987 conducted by the United Church of Christ (UCC). Using zip code analysis, the UCC study found that 37.6 percent of landfills are located in African American neighborhoods in the United States, a finding that lent support to earlier reports. A final scholarly analysis by Robert Bullard (1983) in the Houston area found that twenty-one out of twenty-five waste facilities are located in the vicinity of minority communities. The three studies underscored the social bases of environmental inequities leading environmentalists to call for an expansion of the civil rights framework to include environmental concerns.

These pathbreaking studies were followed by a succession of scholarly writings on what came to be known as *environmental racism.* Simply stated, environmental racism refers to environmental policies and regulation that affect communities differently on racial grounds (Bryant and Mohai 1992; Bullard 1993). Studies of environmental racism witnessed a further transformation in the mid-1990s with a shift in academic focus from power disparities in environmental decisionmaking to analyses of institutional mechanisms that shape these decisions. Writing under the aegis of *environmental justice,* environmental scholars proposed a more theoretically sophisticated analysis of ideologies of unequal distribution and examined sociohistorical or procedural analysis of environmental justice (Capek 1993; Pellow 2004; Szasz and Meuser 1997).

In one of the prominent studies in this tradition, Szasz and Meuser (1998) explore environmental inequities in Santa Clara County in San Jose, California, a county with twenty-three toxic sites listed on the EPA National Priorities List. The study compares median income in the area with pounds of toxic release inventory (TRI) emissions. Findings suggest a clear pattern of environmental discrimination in Latino neighborhoods. The authors suggest that such studies effectively showcase the embedded nature of racial discrimination in the historical experiences of minorities in the United States.

Others have presented theoretical analysis along similar lines. Introducing the notion of "Environmental Inequality Formation" (EIF), Pellow (2000) examines the processes by which environmental inequalities are created, reproduced, and challenged. Pellow's EIF explores four dimensions of environmental inequality, including the historical context within which environmental "bads" are produced, the role of multiple actors in the production process, the pervasive role of institutional racism in siting decisions, and finally the role of agency in using gaps in the political process to augment resistance movements. Others, including Capek (1993) and Epstein (1997), explore institutional processes contributing to environmental injustices. By examining institutional inequalities in decisionmaking, a phenomenon reminiscent of the civil rights movement, environmental justice scholars were seeking to rebuild the organizational networks of the earlier movement to help in their struggle against unequal distribution of both environmental "goods" (for example, better quality of life) and environmental "bads" (hazardous waste sitings).

Environmental justice research and activism have been very successful in mainstreaming environmental inequality concerns—so much so that even the Sierra Club has an active section on environmental justice on their website.[2] There is no doubt that environmental justice has played a remarkable role in the growing internationalizing of struggle against environmental inequities around the world. At the same time, there have been calls for a broadening of the framework to lend effectiveness in the face of global environmental ills. While there has been a very limited response in academic discourses in the United States, international environmental activists have been actively examining linkages between environmental justice and human rights discourses. In the next section, I wish to briefly consider the contours of the emerging international environmental justice paradigm in an attempt to bridge the disconnect in conceptualizing environmental justice between U.S. and international scholarly traditions.

INTERNATIONALIZING THE ENVIRONMENTAL JUSTICE FRAMEWORK: HUMAN RIGHTS, THE ENVIRONMENT, AND SHIFTING PARADIGMS

In one of his letters smuggled from jail, Ken Saro Wiwa, the late Nigerian activist, writer, and Ogoni leader, said that the "environment is man's first right. Without a safe environment, man cannot exist to claim other rights be they social, political, or economic."[3] For him, environmental rights refer to rights to self-determination so that affected communities can be responsible for their own resources and their own environment. Saro Wiwa was referring to the important role that human rights play in adding a sense of moral obligation to struggles against environmental injustices. Sachs (1997) suggests that environmentalists and human rights activists have adopted Saro Wiwa's message by forging coalitions as a strategy against environmental inequities. Multiple examples of human rights violations in environmental disasters bear testimony to the need for such coalitions.

In a 1997 report published in the Sierra Club magazine, Sachs documents the horrific story of human rights violations in Burma by a California-based oil corporation, Unocal, which was not only instrumental in destruction of tropical forests, wetlands, and mangrove swamps but also benefited from massive human rights abuses including genocide, slavery, rape, and murder in the hands of Burma's State Law and Order Restoration Council, the state partner of Unocal. In a court case filed in the United States on behalf of Burmese citizens, EarthRights International and the Center for Constitutional Rights called for the necessity to hold corporations responsible in the United States for their egregious violations abroad. The Burmese citizens won in 2005 in a landmark ruling that set an important precedent for prosecuting multinationals on U.S. soil for actions in other countries that violate international human rights agreements.

While the case above has witnessed effective coalition between environmental activists and human rights groups, the story of impending environmental health disaster in the shipbreaking industry bears testimony to the lack of such coalitions. Alang in western India boasts the largest shipbreaking yards in the world. Shipbreaking is one of the most hazardous jobs in the world, where workers (mostly nonunionized temporary workers) manually dismantle old ships that travel to the shipyard from all over the world. Their jobs feed their families but also contribute to a range of environmental health concerns that contribute to high rates of mortality among workers. In spite of high death rates associated with working in one of the most hazardous occupations, Alang has been constructed only as an "environmental issue" with little effort toward building viable coalitions with human rights groups. Yet, Alang and its workers are examples of the impact of economic inequality amidst great national gains, creating an economic underclass subject to grave environmental injustices and violations of rights and dignity of humans. An effective alignment may begin to address these egregious violations of both environmental and human rights.

These are only a few among many such instances where environmental rights violations and human rights atrocities have overlapped. Cases like the Save Narmada movement in India, the Ogoni tragedy in Nigeria, the Chernobyl and the Bhopal cases, and so on, highlight the importance of adopting human rights language in dealing with environmental disasters. Some have been addressed more effectively than others, but all of them highlight the possibilities embedded in approaching environmental injustices using a rights framework.

Environmental rights have also found a niche position in both U.S. and international academic discourses. Sachs (2003) suggests the need to broaden the definition of justice to include principles of fairness and equitable distribution (civil rights concerns) *and* human dignity (a human rights issue). He identifies some conceptual markers in environmental policy that can be completed with principles of human rights necessary for the emerging world society. Dorothy Thomas (2000) examines the causes behind inattentions to human rights in social movement discourses in the United States and American insularity as a result of long-standing government policies that have consistently sidelined human rights concerns to safeguard vested interests. Still others have explored the nature of international environmental politics in shaping environmental rights discourses (Hurrell and Kingsbury 1992), the role of NGOs in shaping human rights discourses in environmental debates (Raustiala 1997), and the emergence of a global civil society–based environmental rights network (Rohrschneider and Dalton 2002). Despite growing interest in the study of environmental rights in political science, philosophy, and international law, sociological literature on environmental justice in the United States is surprisingly silent in addressing these global environmental rights violations. Such inattention to environmental rights was also successful in resistance to engaging in environmental protection plans, including the Kyoto Protocol. In the post-Kyoto years, we have seen only lukewarm efforts to successfully engage in global environmental protection policies, though the United Nations has highlighted it as a significant issue for our common future as recently as 2008.

Hence, an environmental rights framework that conceptualizes the right to a clean environment, a human rights concern, is essential for garnering broad-based coalitions. But how do we construct a theoretical framework to initiate this process? Can we consider an environmental rights framework a viable theoretical framework for addressing global environmental justice concerns? Does linking environmental rights with human rights provide an effective platform for better environmental policies? International environmental scholarship certainly agrees. However, to better answer these questions, we need to explore some of the important components of an environmental rights framework and identify possible directions for future research linking environmental concerns with human rights.

FROM JUSTICE TO RIGHTS: TOWARD A HUMAN RIGHTS APPROACH TO THE ENVIRONMENT

"Justice" involves the creation of a set of institutions that directly or indirectly allocates liberties, rights, and other material and nonmaterial resources to their members (Miller 1999, 52). In political philosophy, justice is conceived as the "fairness principle," whereas in the civil rights literature it is defined as a quest for distributive equality. Both refer to the idea that an existing political community has equal access to the resources available to them. Environmental justice scholars and activists in the United States have drawn upon these definitions to examine justice as it pertains to environmental inequalities.

Yet, justice refers to something more. It involves the *right to human dignity*. In his work *Development as Freedom* (1999), Amartya Sen, the noted economist and philosopher, points out that distributive equity remains ineffective unless accompanied by the *right* to choose which resources we want depending on our cultural and social contexts, which is essential for a life of dignity. This is especially true when we work with international environmental concerns where distributive questions are precluded by the necessity for creating effective social arrangements. Further, an international environmental struggle may find a more effective reference point in human rights language than a U.S.-specific framework of environmental justice.

A human rights framework may even be worthwhile for addressing environmental concerns in the United States. As Thomas (2000) points out, the fact that U.S. groups rarely resort to human rights is hardly surprising. Using the case of the women's movement in the United States, Thomas suggests that "successive U.S. administrations have done everything in their power, in the fifty-plus years since the adoption of the Universal Declaration of Human Rights in 1948, to insulate the country from international scrutiny and to prevent its residents from meaningfully invoking their international human rights" (Thomas 2000, 2). This is evident in cases of environmental rights as well. In the aftermath of multiple cases of environmental litigation, like the example of Unocal discussed earlier, there have been growing calls for setting international standards for corporations that conduct business in developing nations. To that end, the United Nations is engaged in drafting a resolution that has already been challenged by the U.S. government (*Nation* 2005). Hence, calls for a human rights approach in the United States, both in the academic and activist dictum, are important for ensuring enforceability of international laws and regulations, calls that are not at odds with the principles of the civil rights movement. So what would an environmental rights framework look like? I identify some of the possible dimensions for a theory of environmental rights. These components are evolving in nature and underscore some of the possible future research agendas for our purposes.

First, the universality of the notion of human rights makes it a particularly effective construct to address environmental questions. The idea of human rights is a political idea with moral foundations (Henkin 1989, 11). The universality and cultural receptivity of these moral foundations makes human rights in general and environmental rights in particular an appealing and effective choice when effectively broadened to include *both* individual and communitarian rights to natural resources.

Second, an environmental rights framework moves us beyond the distributive questions to address issues of human entitlement and dignity. As Sachs (2003) points out, a human rights approach to the environment helps us move from a needs-based approach to a rights-based approach. The notion of entitlements is evocative of the social choice arguments of Sen (1999), who argues that poverty is not just a matter of lack of resources, it is also about limited *capacity* to access resources. For Sen, this limited capacity reflects a person's *functionings* (or what a person can succeed in doing or being), which in turn is indicative of her well-being. Well-being for Sen is determined not by effective distribution of goods or commodities, rather it is dependent on a person's *capacity* to transform those goods into functionings (or successful use of resources). Sen goes on to examine the nature and degree of social choice a person possesses to achieve those functionings, which is indicative of satisfaction of principles of human dignity. A rights framework asks deeper questions and allows us to broaden the definition of justice to include not only distributive issues (a civil rights concern) but also questions of capability formation and entitlement.

Third, an environmental rights approach helps us examine the ebb and flow of global capitalism and its impact on environmental justice concerns. In recent years environmental scholars have examined this issue. For example, Pellow (2004) explored the political economy of globalization in the case of the construction of a toxic incinerator in an African American neighborhood in Robbins, Illinois. Drawing our attention to the fact that the community itself was actively recruiting an incinerator, the authors argue that to view this as a case of environmental racism, we need to examine the role of global capitalism as an important predictor in economic decisions that will help us in understanding the political economy of globalization in contributing to transfer of toxic industries to poorer neighborhoods and developing nations.

Finally, a prominent argument against international environmental rights laws was that the cumulative impact of such laws would undermine state sovereignty. Litfin (1997) argues that if we define sovereignty as a mix of authority, control, and legitimacy, we witness a significantly different picture emerging in the last few decades whereby states have been able to achieve *more* sovereignty in some areas (gain in international legitimacy for example) and less in others (sharing of some authority and control with nonstate actors and international agencies). This reconfiguring of sovereignty, says Litfin, is especially important to a conceptualization of a rights approach as environmental concerns increasingly occupy center stage in the world politics of the twenty-first century, and as the political and economic effects of such developments as massive species extinction, climate change, international toxic trade and waste generation, and globalization of Western modes of consumption become critical social concerns (Litfin 1997, 198).

In short, an environmental rights framework helps us conceptualize a greening of civil society that allows space for the nuances of civil and cultural specificities without ignoring social inequality concerns. Above all, it helps us visualize a healthy environment as a right for all of us and an entitlement for our future generations.

NOTES

1. http://www.unhchr.ch/html/menu3/b/a_cescr.htm.
2. http://www.sierraclub.org/environmental_justice.
3. Complete Statement by Ken Saro-Wiwa to Ogoni Civil Disturbances Tribunal, available at http://www.ratical.org/corporations/KSWstmt.html. (Accessed February 13, 2008.)

REFERENCES

Bryant, Bunyan, and Paul Mohai, eds. 1992. *Race and the Incidence of Environmental Hazards: A Time for Discourse.* Boulder, CO: Westview.

Bullard, Robert D. 1983. "Solid Waste Sites and the Houston Black Community." *Sociological Inquiry* 53 (Spring): 273–288.

Bullard, Robert D., ed. 1993. *Confronting Environmental Racism: Voices from the Grassroots.* Boston: South End.

Capek, Stella M. 1993. "The 'Environmental Justice' Frame: A Conceptual Discussion and an Application." *Social Problems* 40: 5–24.

Epstein, Barbara. 1997. "The Environmental Toxics Movement: Politics of Race and Gender." *Capitalism, Nature, Socialism* 8: 63–87.

Henkin, Louis. 1989. "The Universality of the Concept of Human Rights." *Annals of the American Academy of Political and Social Science* 506: 10–16.

Hurrell, Andrew, and Benedict Kingsbury. 1992. *The International Politics of the Environment.* Oxford, UK: Oxford University Press.

Litfin, Karen, T. 1997. "Sovereignty in World Ecopolitics." *Mershon International Studies Review* 41, no. 2: 167–204.

Marbury, Hugh J. 1995. "Hazardous Waste Exportation: The Global Manifestation of Environmental Racism." *Vanderbilt Journal of Transnational Law* 28: 1225–1237.

Miller, David. 1999. "Social Justice and Environmental Goods." Pp. 151–172 in *Fairness and Futurity: Essays on Environmental Sustainability and Social Justice,* edited by Andrew Dobson. New York: Oxford University Press.

Nation. 2005. May 9.

Pellow, David N. 2004. "The Politics of Illegal Dumping: An Environmental Justice Framework." *Qualitative Sociology* 27, no. 4: 511–525.

———. 2000. "Environmental Inequality Formation: Toward a Theory of Environmental Injustice." *American Behavioral Scientist* 43: 581–601.

Raustiala, Kal. 1997. "States, NGOs, and International Environmental Institutions." *International Studies Quarterly* 41, no. 4: 719–740.

Robinson, Mary. 2002. "Civil Society Workshop on Human Rights, Sustainable Development and Environmental Protection." *World Summit on Sustainable Development,* available at http://www.unhchr.ch/huricane/huricane.nsf/0/A551686D4B5905D0C1256C280 02BF3D6?opendocument.

Rohrschneider, Robert, and Russell J. Dalton. 2002. "A Global Network: Transnational Cooperation among Environmental Groups." *Journal of Politics* 64, no. 2: 510–533.

Sachs, Aaron. 1997. "A Planet Unfree: What Do Human Rights Have to Do with Environmental Protection? Everything." *Sierra Magazine,* available at http://www.sierraclub. org/sierra/199711/humanrights.asp.

Sachs, Wolfgang. 2003. "Environment and Human Rights," available at http://www.wupperinst. org/globalisierung/pdf_global/human_rights.pdf.

Sen, Amartya K. 1999. *Development as Freedom.* New York: Anchor Books.

Szasz, Andrew, and Michael Meuser. 1998. "Unintended, Inexorable: The Production of Environmental Inequalities in Santa Clara County, California." *American Behavioral Scientist* 43: 602–632.

———. 1997. "Environmental Inequalities: Literature Review and Proposals for New Directions in Research and Theory." *Current Sociology* 45, no. 3: 99–120.

Taylor, Dorceta. 2000. "The Rise of the Environmental Justice Paradigm: Injustice Framing and the Social Construction of Environmental Discourses." *American Behavioral Scientist* 43, no. 4: 508–580.

Thomas, Dorothy, Q. 2000. "We Are Not the World: U.S. Activism and Human Rights in the Twenty-First Century." *Signs* 25, no. 4: 1121–1124.

United Church of Christ. 1987. *Toxic Wastes and Race in the U.S.* New York: United Church of Christ Commission for Racial Justice.

U.S. General Accounting Office. 1983. "Siting of Hazardous Waste Landfills and Their Correlation with Racial and Economic Status of Surrounding Communities." *GAO/ RCED-83-168.* Washington, DC: Government Printing Office.

ADDITIONAL RESOURCES

American Association for the Advancement of Science (this website has a link to a large collection of nongovernmental organization working at the intersection of environmental and human rights):
http://shr.aaas.org/hrenv/sources.php?st_id=5.

American Association for Advancement of Science research paper on "Environmental Protection, Public Health, and Human Rights":
http://shr.aaas.org/hrenv/docs/ahmed.pdf.

Asian Development Bank (website highlights sustainability concerns in Asia and its global impacts):
http://www.adb.org/Environment/default.asp.

Boston Research Center for the 21st Century (works on global citizenship and environment):
http://www.brc21.org/home.html.

Center for International Environmental Law (examines threats of oil drillings in Amazonia and is engaged in civil society participation in fighting for environmental rights):
http://www.ciel.org/index.html.

Intergovernmental Panel on Climate Change (examines scientific, technical, and socioeconomic information relevant for the understanding of climate change, its

potential impacts, and options for adaptation and mitigation):
　　http://www.ipcc.ch/index.html.
Kyoto Protocol, 1997:
　　http://unfccc.int/kyoto_protocol/items/2830.php.
Montreal Protocol on Substances That Deplete the Ozone Layer, 1997:
　　http://ozone.unep.org/pdfs/Montreal-Protocol2000.pdf.
Vienna Convention for the protection of the Ozone layer, 1985:
　　http://ozone.unep.org/Treaties_and_Ratification/2A_vienna_convention.shtml.

CHAPTER FIFTEEN

~

Rights of Prisoners

ANGELA HATTERY AND EARL SMITH

The U.S. State Department issued its annual review of human rights around the world last week rating each nation on its performances in a number of categories. Only one country escaped scrutiny: the United States itself.

—Elsner 2004

On this eightieth anniversary of Buck, let us not foolishly believe that victims of eugenics are an artifact of history. So long as we speak in terms of good genes and bad genes, recognize a life with a disability as an injury, and allow health policies to value some lives over others, we continue to create human rights violations every day.

—Imparto and Sommers 2007[1]

The role of incarceration in the United States is increasing in both reach (the number of individuals incarcerated) and power.[2] Today there are 2,269,780 million Americans incarcerated[3] (or 0.7 percent of the U.S. population) in nearly 1,700 state, federal, and private prisons, with many more under other forms of custodial supervision, including probation and parole (Harrison and Beck 2005).

Furthermore, despite the fact that we think of certain other countries as being dominated by incarceration, compared to other countries, the United States incarcerates a higher proportion of its population than all other developed countries and many in the developing world (Mauer 2003). Specifically, we note that in the United States a significantly higher proportion of citizens are incarcerated than in nation-states such as China, whose incarceration practices are frequently the target of investigations and reports by human rights watch groups such as Amnesty International (Amnesty International 2005).

Moreover, while much of the focus of American citizens and "watch dog" groups has addressed abuses in international prisons, many of the techniques applied in such

174

Figure 15.1 Number of Prison and Jail Inmates, 1900–2001

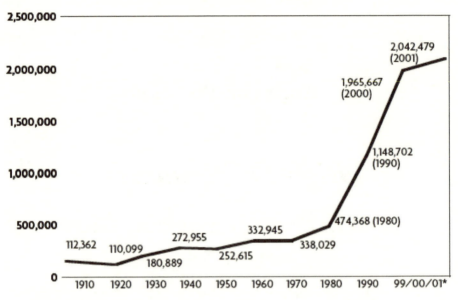

Source: Justice Policy Institute analysis of U.S. Department of Justice data.

Figure 15.2 Incarceration Rates by Country

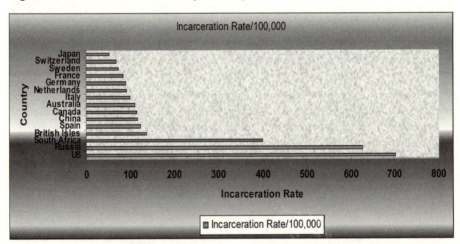

Source: Mauer (2003, 2).

jails as Abu Ghraib and Guantanamo Bay were developed and routinely used in state and federal prisons right here in the United States (Elsner 2004). In this chapter, we examine human rights violations, including torture and the death penalty, in the U.S. system of incarceration. We argue that though the United States demands that other countries uphold the basic human rights of their incarcerees, the United States does not abide by these principles itself and engages in the routine torture of both American and international citizens behind the bars of our own prisons.[4]

REVIEW OF RELEVANT TREATIES

For the purposes of this chapter, there are two relevant treaties that must be considered. The first is the UN Convention Against Torture and Other Cruel, Inhuman or Degrading Treatment or Punishment (CAT), which was presented for signature and ratification by the UN secretary general on February 4, 1985.[5] Of its many articles, two are of particular importance with regard to the United States. First, Article 1 defines torture as follows:

> For the purposes of this Convention, torture means any act by which severe pain or suffering, whether physical or mental, is intentionally inflicted on a person for such purposes as obtaining from him or a third person information or a confession, punishing him for an act he or a third person has committed or is suspected of having committed, or intimidating or coercing him or a third person, or for any reason based on discrimination of any kind, when such pain or suffering is inflicted by or at the instigation of or with the consent or acquiescence of a public official or other person acting in an official capacity. It does not include pain or suffering arising only from, inherent in or incidental to lawful sanctions.

Point 1 from Article 1 clearly states that torture is defined as any act that results in severe pain or suffering, either mental or physical. Torture that is inflicted for purposes ranging from interrogation to punishment violates the UN Convention on Torture. As we will demonstrate in the next section, prisoners in the United States are routinely subjected to abuse that qualifies as torture under the UN convention.

Second, Article 3 of CAT speaks directly to the practice of transporting prisoners and detainees from countries that have signed the convention to those that have not in order to conduct anctioned torture:

1. No State Party shall expel, return (*refouler*) or extradite a person to another State where there are substantial grounds for believing that he would be in danger of being subjected to torture.
2. For the purpose of determining whether there are such grounds, the competent authorities shall take into account all relevant considerations including, where applicable, the existence in the State concerned of a consistent pattern of gross, flagrant or mass violations of human rights.

As we will demonstrate later in this chapter, there is strong and compelling evidence that the United States engages in this practice of transferring prisoners and detainees into the custody of countries, such as Syria, that have not signed or ratified the treaty and that have records of gross, flagrant, or mass violations of human rights. This practice, as we will demonstrate, allows the United States to maintain a lean record on human rights while engaging in the torture of prisoners, mostly in the name of the war on terror.

Finally, we note that the UN convention lists the United States as one of the states that has signed but not yet ratified the Convention Against Torture. (The CAT can be accessed at http://www.hrweb.org/legal/cat.html.)

The second relevant treaty that we must review with regard to the rights of prisoners is the second Optional Protocol to the International Covenant on Civil and Political Rights (ICCPR), which is aimed at the abolition of the death penalty. It was adopted and proclaimed by UN General Assembly resolution 44/128 on December 15, 1989. Based on Article 3 of the Universal Declaration of Human Rights, adopted on December 10, 1948, and Article 6 of the International Covenant on Civil and Political Rights, adopted on December 16, 1966, this protocol stipulates in Article 1 that no person shall be executed and that all measures must be taken to abolish the death penalty. It is clear that the United States, as a whole, has not abolished the death penalty and instead leaves the decision to execute citizens up to the individual states. In this chapter, we demonstrate two key problems with the death penalty in the United States: (1) the incarceration and executions of innocent individuals; and (2) examples of specific executions that meet the standards of cruel and inhumane. (The ICCPR can be accessed at: http://www.hrweb.org/legal/cpr.html.)

THE UNITED STATES AS A ROGUE STATE

In this section we argue that the United States is a rogue state, by which we mean that the United States is undisciplined and non-normative with regard to the treatment of prisoners both within its own borders and inside the borders of other geopolitical states. First, we begin by comparing the United States to the international community. It is common in many things to compare oneself with one neighbors. Individuals may decide to buy an item because their neighbors have bought the item (keeping up with the Joneses). Industries set prices and standards by comparing their practices to their competitors; think of both the airline price wars and gasoline price wars. Even colleges and universities determine everything from standards for admission to tuition based on what their competitor campuses are doing; for example, the Ivies have a covenant that requires that they make major changes in tandem. Therefore, we begin by examining the neighborhood in which the United States lives with regard to (1) torture and (2) the death penalty. The following is the list of nation-states that have signed but not ratified the CAT: Belgium, Bolivia, Costa Rica, Cuba, Dominican Republic, Gabon, Gambia, Iceland, Indonesia, Morocco, Nicaragua, Nigeria, Sierra Leone, Sudan, and the United States of America. For the most part, this collective is not filled with nation-states with which we normally compare ourselves. These countries do not comprise our major economic or political peers. Rather, the majority of these countries are well known for their gross violations of human rights.

Second, when we consider the countries that have abolished (or not) the death penalty, again, the trend is in the direction of abolishing the death penalty.[6] According to Amnesty International, 128 countries have abolished the death penalty, while 69 retain it. Beginning in 2006, membership in the European Union *required* the abolition of the death penalty. This immediately sets the United States apart from its European counterparts (the group to which we routinely compare ourselves). Furthermore, Amnesty International estimates that: the United States, China, Iran, and Saudi Arabia account for over 80 percent of the executions recorded by Amnesty International (http://www.amnestyusa.org/abolish/worldwide.html). Thus, not only is the United States a rogue state by retaining the death penalty, but it also uses the death penalty routinely. In terms of the number of executions performed each year, the presence of the United States in the top four, alongside China, Iran, and Saudi Arabia, puts the United States in the company of countries that are widely criticized for their human rights violations.

The data on both torture and the death penalty recall for us the epigram that opens this chapter. According to Elsner, the United States is happy to police the world in terms of human rights, but we are not willing to look inward and engage in self-reflection on our own record on human rights, especially with regard to the rights of prisoners.

TORTURE IN U.S. PRISONS

The use of torture that violates international law (CAT), as well as our own sensibilities, is well documented. For example, we note the work of Deborah Davies, an investigative reporter, who produced the report *Torture Inc., American Brutal Prisons,* which aired in March 2005. In this documentary, available at http://www.informationclearinghouse.info/article8451.htm, she details several cases of torture, including some that ended in the death of the inmate. Among other things, the documentary shows footage of inmates being sprayed with mace and pepper spray that resulted in second-degree chemical burns on their bodies. In other footage inmates are shown being beaten and stomped on.

At its extreme, the torture of prison inmates sometimes results in their death. Davies's report examines the case of Frank Valdes, an inmate in the Florida State Penitentiary in Stark, Florida. Frank Valdes was on death row for killing a prison guard. Valdes wrote a series of letters and commentaries about the torture of prisoners inside the penitentiary for the local newspaper. The newspaper published accounts Valdes submitted in which he detailed his own experiences with torture as well as those of other inmates. The guards in the penitentiary demanded that Valdes stop airing the dirty laundry of the prison, and when he did not, they showed up in his cell one night and beat him to death. Frank Valdes was found dead in his cell in the Florida State Penitentiary at Stark, Florida, on July 17, 1999.

Several guards were tried for the murder of Frank Valdes. According to the testimony at the trial, Valdes was beaten so severely that all but two of his ribs were broken; they were described as splinters. His face was badly bruised. Prison officials maintained that Valdes was not murdered, despite the fact that death row inmates are housed in single cells and have no physical contact with anyone other than the guards. At the conclusion of the trial, the guards were acquitted. Davies notes that the trial was held in the local community, and the jury included former guards at the penitentiary in Stark. Furthermore, in interviews with jurors, they revealed that they all agreed that Valdes had been murdered; they just were not sure which of the guards had actually killed him. Many might argue that Valdes got what he deserved; after all he was a convicted murderer who had been sentenced to death anyway. Yet, according to CAT, even though a prisoner loses his or her rights to freedom of person, to work, to vote, etc., he or she does not give up the right of security of person. No one, regardless of his or her status as a prisoner, should be subjected to torture.

Though prison beatings have undoubtedly occurred since the first prison was developed, one of the more recent and controversial forms of torture is the restraint chair. Restraint chairs are marketed in the corrections community as a way to restrain inmates who are unruly as a result of intoxication, untreated mental illness, or general belligerence. E.R.C., Inc, a company that markets the restraint chairs, advertises them this way:

- Safely restrains a combative or self-destructive person
- Allows for safe transportation to court/hospital
- Does not restrict normal breathing
- Secures an individual without injury
- Protects your staff and the person being restrained (http://www.restraintchair. com)

As a result of advertisements such as these, as well as demonstrations at national corrections conventions, restraint chairs have become the latest tool in the corrections toolbox. Yet restraint chairs are described by many as a tool for torture. There are countless tales of inmates being restrained for hours and hours without being offered the chance to use the restroom or receive even the smallest amount of water. Inmates and staff report that inmates were left in their own urine and feces. Inmates with physical or mental health disorders have been left to suffer seizures in restraint chairs. And Davies reports that her research identified more than twenty cases of prisoners who have died in the past few years after being held in a restraint chair. The following is from the transcript of Davies documentary:

> Two of the deaths we investigated were in the same county jail in Phoenix, Arizona, which is run by a man who revels in the title of America's Toughest Sheriff. His name is Joe Arpaio. He positively welcomes TV crews and we were promised "unfettered access." It was a reassuring turn of phrase—you don't want to be fettered in one of Sheriff Joe's jails. We uncovered two videotapes from surveillance cameras showing how his tough stance can end in tragedy. The first tape, from 2001, shows a man named Charles Agster dragged in by police, handcuffed at the wrists and ankles. Agster is mentally disturbed and a drug user. He was arrested for causing a disturbance in a

late-night grocery store. The police handed him over to the Sheriff's deputies in the jail. Agster is a tiny man, weighing no more than nine stone, but he struggling. The tape shows nine deputies manhandling him into the restraint chair. One of them kneels on Agster stomach; pushing his head forward on to his knees and pulling his arms back to strap his wrists into the chair. Bending someone double for any length of time is dangerous; the manuals on the use of the restraint chair warn of the dangers of "positional asphyxia." Fifteen minutes later, a nurse notices Agster is unconscious. The cameras show frantic efforts to resuscitate him, but he's already brain dead. He died three days later in hospital. Agster's family is currently suing Arizona County.

Again, like the case of Frank Valdes, the use of restraint chairs, though necessary in a small number of cases, seems more often than not to be a tool for torture; whether they are used to restrain an inmate so that the guards can beat him or her more effectively or whether they are used as a tool of humiliation by leaving prisoners to defecate and urinate on themselves. These stories sound remarkably similar to those we heard coming out of Abu Ghraib where Iraqi detainees report similar forms of humiliation. Again, we point to CAT, which makes it clear that prisoners are not to be kept in these kinds of conditions.

We turn now to a tactic that the U.S. government uses to avoid being labeled as a violator of human rights: rendition. Rendition practices involve the detaining and transporting of individuals by the U.S. government to countries with poor records on human rights that refuse to sign in any manner the UN Convention on Torture. This rendition practice essentially allows the United States to torture detainees on foreign soil and thus not sully its own record on human rights.

RENDITION

Bob Herbert of the *New York Times* first broke the story of Canadian citizen Maher Arar who was detained by the United States for more than a year in Syria.

> Arar was detained at New York's John F. Kennedy Airport in 2002 during a stopover on his way home to Canada from a vacation with his family in Tunisia. He said he was chained and shackled by U.S. authorities for eleven days during interrogation and then flown to Syria, where he was tortured and forced to make false confessions. He was released ten months later, with Syrian officials saying they had no reason to hold him further. (CNN 2007)

Arar's case, with the help of *New York Times* op-ed contributor Bob Herbert (2005), brought widespread attention to a longtime practice engaged in by the CIA: rendition. Furthermore, though the CIA has been in the business of international detainment for decades, Amnesty International (2006) reports that these rendition practices have changed and increased since September 11. "Since September 11 the focus of rendition practice has shifted emphatically; the aim now is to ensure that suspects are not brought to stand trial, but are handed over to foreign governments for an interrogation process known in the USA as extraordinary rendition or are kept in U.S. custody on foreign sites" (Amnesty International 2006).

Newsweek magazine confirms the existence of a special CIA plane that is specifically used for the CIA rendition program: *Newsweek* has obtained previously unpublished flight plans indicating the agency has been operating a Boeing 737 as part of a top-secret global charter servicing clandestine interrogation facilities used in the war on terror (Hirsh, Hosenball, and Barry 2005). We argue that this practice, along with the practice of establishing U.S. secret prisons in countries like Poland and Romania (Moore 2007), all justified under the aegis of the war on terror, is just another tool by which the U.S. government can appear to be a role model on human rights and yet carry out the very types of torture it condemns in countries like Syria.

Taken together, torture inside U.S. prisons and rendition constitute the hypocrisy that the Elsner quote points out: By condemning the human rights practices of other countries and not policing itself, the United States is behaving in a manner that leads to the label rogue state. We now shift our focus to a discussion of the death penalty.

THE DEATH PENALTY

The ICCPR is clear with regard to the death penalty. As stated above, this document uses as its inspiration the Universal Declaration of Human Rights, adopted in 1948, that clearly denounces the death penalty. In this section, we argue that in addition to the question of whether the death penalty violates the Universal Declaration of Human Rights, we examine two key features of the death penalty as it is employed in the United States: (1) the execution of innocent individuals; and (2) the charge that the death penalty, as executed, often constitutes cruel and unusual punishment. We begin with the question of innocence.

Is Everyone We Execute Guilty?

One of the most important questions facing any person or institution involved in any phase of the death penalty process is the absolute assurance that people who are executed are guilty of the crimes for which they were given this sentence. There is an abundance of literature that documents the fact that the system of justice in the United States is plagued by problems, specifically racism and classism. Race and class bias lead to disparities at every stage of the criminal justice system, from the likelihood of arrest to the types of sentences that are handed down (for a lengthy discussion, see Hattery and Smith 2007; Western 2007). African Americans and the poor are more likely to be arrested, charged, convicted, and to receive more severe sentences than their white and affluent counterparts.

With specific regard to innocence and the death penalty, the Innocence Project, a national nonprofit organization that provides legal counsel and seeks exonerations for individuals who believe they were wrongly convicted, offers some estimates of innocence. The group reports that there have been 194 postconviction exonerations based on DNA evidence, and that, of these exonerees, fourteen were at one time sentenced to death or served time on death row. The Innocence Project reports that it is virtually impossible to know the number of innocent people who have been executed, primarily because DNA evidence is not always collected and because there is virtually no one willing to pay the fees necessary to investigate the cases of those already executed (as opposed to investing in determining the innocence of those serving time on death row). However, those working on these issues use the data above to speculate that many innocent people have been executed in the United States (http://www.innocenceproject.org). The Death Penalty Information Center reports: the danger that innocent people will be executed because of errors in the criminal justice system is getting worse. A total of 120 people have been released from death row since 1973 after evidence of their innocence emerged. Twenty-one condemned inmates have been released since 1993 (http://www.deathpenaltyinfo.org/article. php?scid=45anddid=292).

Based on these data we can conclude that the probability is very high that the United States has indeed executed innocent people. According to Sam Gross, professor of law at the University of Michigan Law School and author of the Larry Griffin Execution Report for the NAACP, there is specific and compelling evidence of the execution of innocent people in at least ten cases (Gross et al. 2005), one of which is the case of Ruben Cantu. According to an investigation by the *Houston Chronicle,* there is substantial evidence, with two corroborating witness—including the victim—that Ruben Cantu, a special education student with a ninth-grade education who committed a crime as a juvenile (he was seventeen), was innocent of all charges and wrongly executed on August 24, 1993 (Olsen 2006).

All of this begs the question: If we are going to retain the death penalty in the United States, is it reasonable to do so within a criminal justice system that is so terribly flawed? Recognizing this, the state of Illinois passed a moratorium on executions until flaws in the system of justice could be examined. It is also important to note that of the 194 exonerees, 112 or 57 percent have been African American (http://www.innocenceproject.org). And, though African Americans are disproportionately represented in prison (Hattery and Smith 2007; Western 2007), African American men make up 43 percent of all men incarcerated, yet they make up 57 percent of the exonerees. Thus, the data suggest that African American men are more likely than their white counterparts to be wrongly convicted. We turn now to a discussion of the death penalty as cruel and unusual punishment.

The Death Penalty as Cruel and Unusual Punishment

In addition to the question of innocence, opponents of the death penalty argue that whatever the method of execution, if not executed properly the death can amount to cruel and unusual punishment. In a visit the authors made to the Mississippi State Penitentiary at Parchman, we toured the death house and death chamber. There we saw both the gas chamber that was used for executions as recently as the 1980s and early 1990s as well as the lethal injection chamber. In talking with the guards there we heard about what it was like when a man was executed in the gas chamber. Deaths were so violent that eventually they installed a helmet at the top of the chamber to keep the man's head from banging violently against the side of the chamber while his body was spasming from the poisoned gas.

In a report by the Death Penalty Information Center, Michael Radelet details thirty-eight examples of botched executions (http://www.deathpenaltyinfo.org/article. php?scid=8anddid=478). He admits that this is not a comprehensive list; it does not include cases before the federal moratorium on the death penalty that ended with the firing squad execution of Gary Gilmore in Utah in 1977. The following are three descriptions:

> May 2, 2006. Ohio. Joseph L. Clark. Lethal injection. It took 22 minutes for the execution technicians to find a vein suitable for insertion of the catheter. But three or four minutes thereafter, as the vein collapsed and Clark's arm began to swell, he raised his head off the gurney and said five times, it don't work. It don't work. The curtains surrounding the gurney were then closed while the technicians worked for 30 minutes to find another vein. Media witnesses later reported that they heard moaning, crying out, and guttural noises. Finally, death was pronounced almost 90 minutes after the execution began. A spokeswoman for the Ohio Department of Corrections told reporters that the execution team included paramedics, but not a physician or a nurse. (Liptak 2006; Mangels 2006)

> December 13, 2006. Florida. Angel Diaz. Lethal injection. After the first injection was administered, Mr. Diaz continued to move, and was squinting and grimacing as he tried to mouth words. A second dose was then administered, and 34 minutes passed before Mr. Diaz was declared dead. At first a spokesperson for the Florida Department of Corrections claimed that this was because Mr. Diaz had some sort of liver disease. After performing an autopsy, the medical examiner, Dr. William Hamilton, stated that Mr. Diaz's liver was undamaged, but that the needle had gone through Mr. Diaz's vein and out the other side, so the deadly chemicals were injected into soft tissue, rather than the vein. Two days after the execution, Governor Jeb Bush suspended all executions in the state and appointed a commission to consider the humanity and constitutionality of lethal injections. (Liptak and Aguayo 2006)

> August 10, 1982. Virginia. Frank J. Coppola. Electrocution. Although no media representatives witnessed the execution and no details were ever released by the Virginia Department of Corrections, an attorney who was present later stated that it took two 55-second jolts of electricity to kill Coppola. The second jolt produced the odor and sizzling sound of burning flesh, and Coppola's head and leg caught on fire. Smoke filled the death chamber from floor to ceiling with a smokey haze. (Denno 1994)

In sum, these descriptions provide evidence for the argument that executions, especially when not executed properly, constitute cruel and unusual punishment. This argument has long been part of the capital punishment debate and is the driving force behind the continued adoption of new, more humane methods of execution. For example, lethal injection was adopted in large part because it was deemed more humane than either electrocution or gassing.

CONCLUSION

In conclusion, we have argued that the criminal justice system, specifically incarceration and the death penalty, meet the international standards of torture and inhumane treatment of prisoners as laid out in CAT and in the ICCPR. Furthermore, we have argued that the United States is a rogue state for four reasons: (1) Unlike the geo-political states with whom it compares itself, the United States has not ratified the UN Convention on Torture; (2) There is clear evidence of the widespread torture of inmates in U.S. prisons; (3) The United States engages in rendition practices, sending detainees to other countries (on CIA planes) with poor records on human rights so that they may be tortured off U.S. soil; and (4) The United States maintains the death penalty and executes people regularly, which is out of line with our comparison of nation-states and in line with countries with poor human rights records, namely Iran and Saudi Arabia.

Finally, we have argued that the United States is a rogue state because it views itself as the world's police officer, charging many other countries with prison practices that violate UN conventions but failing to either investigate its own system of incarceration or hold its system accountable to these UN conventions. In essence, the United States behaves in a "do as I say, not as I do" mode.

NOTES

1. *Buck* refers to the first Supreme Court decision on eugenics. Oliver Wendell Holmes wrote the decision in the 1927 *Buck v. Bell* case. The decision to allow the sterilization of seventeen-year-old Carrie Buck opened the door for nearly 9,000 sterilizations that would take place in Virginia over the next several decades.

2. By power we mean the ability to remove individuals from society for decades or for life; more than 10 percent of all inmates, or 200,000 people, are imprisoned for life. Felons are disenfranchised, many for life, and most find successful reentry an impossibility due to bans on social welfare, discrimination in hiring, and so forth.

3. Figures on incarceration vary depending on what types of institutions (jails, prisons, military prison, etc.) are included in the count. The number of Americans in prison that we cite here comes from the daily "prison incarceration clock."

4. As recently as February 2007 an immigrant detainee died while in custody at a New Jersey detention center, bringing the total to 66 since 2004 (Nina Bernstein, "Few Details on Immigrants Who Die in Custody," *New York Times,* May 5, 2008. http://www.nytimes.com/2008/05/05/nyregion/05detain.html?_r=1&hp&oref=slogin; accessed May 6, 2008).

5. In the late 1970s, in response to continued evidence of torture around the world, but particularly in Latin America, leaders in Costa Rica began work on what would become CAT.

6. We acknowledge that much like signing a UN convention, abolishing the death penalty may not carry much power. However, we argue that it does indicate movement in a specific direction. Abolishing the death penalty does mean that it cannot legally be imposed.

REFERENCES

Amnesty International. 2006. *United States of America: Below the Radar Secret Flights to Torture and Disappearance,* available at http://www.amnestyusa.org/document. php?lang=e&id=ENGAMR510512006. (Accessed March 30, 2008.)

———. 2005. *The Rest of Their Lives: Life without Parole for Child Offenders in the United States.* New York: Human Rights Watch.

Denno, Deborah W. 1994. "Is Electrocution an Unconstitutional Method of Execution? The Engineering of Death over the Century." *William and Mary Law Review* 551: 664–665.

Elsner, Alan. 2004. "If U.S. Plays Global Prison Ratings Game, It Ought to Play by Its Own Rules." *Christian Science Monitor,* March 4, available at http://www.commondreams. org/views04/0304-01.htm. (Accessed on March 30, 2008.)

Gross, Samuel, Kristen Jacoby, Daniel Matheson, Nicholas Montgomery, and Sujata Patil. 2005. "Exonerations in the United States, 1989 through 2003." *Journal of Criminal Law and Criminology* 95, no. 2.

Harrison, Paige M., and Allen J. Beck. 2005. "Prisoners in 2004." Bureau of Justice Statistics, available at http://ojp.usdoj.gov/bjs/pub/pdf/p04.pdf. (Accessed March 30, 2008.)

Hattery, Angela, and Earl Smith. 2007. *African American Families.* Thousand Oaks, CA: Sage.

Herbert, Bob. 2005. "It's Called Torture." *New York Times,* February 28, available at http:// www.nytimes.com/2005/02/28/opinion/28herbert.html?_r=1&oref=slogin. (Accessed March 30, 2008.)

Hirsch, Michael, Mark Hosenball, and John Barry. 2005. "Aboard Air CIA." *Newsweek* (February 28).

Imparto, Andrew J., and Anne C. Sommers. 2007. "Haunting Echoes of Eugenics." *Washington Post.* Sunday, May 20, B7.

Liptak, Adam. 2006. "Trouble Finding Inmate Vein Slows Lethal Injection in Ohio." *New York Times,* May 3, available at: http://www.nytimes.com/2006/05/03/us/03inmate. html. (Accessed March 30, 2008.)

Liptak, Adam, and Terry Aguayo. 2006. "After Problem Execution, Governor Bush Suspends the Death Penalty in Florida." *New York Times,* December 16.

Mangels, John. 2006. "Condemned Killer Complains Lethal Injection Isn't Working." *Plain Dealer* (Cleveland), May 3, available at http://query.nytimes.com/gst/full-page.html?res= 9A07E2D81231F935A25751C1A9609C8B63. (Accessed March 30, 2008.)

Mauer, Marc. 2003. *Comparative International Rates of Incarceration: An Examination of Causes and Trends.* Washington, DC: The Sentencing Project.

Moore, Molly. 2007. "Report Gives Detail on CIA Prisons." *Washington Post,* June 9, available at http://www.washingtonpost.com/wp-dyn/content/article/2007/06/08/ AR2007060800985.html. (Accessed March 30, 2008.)

Olsen, Lise. 2006. "The Cantu Case: Death and Doubt: Did Texas Execute an Innocent Man? Eyewitness Says He Felt Influenced by Police to ID the Teen as the Killer." *Houston Chronicle,* July 24, available at http://www.chron.com/disp/story.mpl/metropolitan/3472872. html. (Accessed March 30, 2008.)

Western, Bruce. 2007. *Punishment and Inequality in America.* New York: Russell Sage Foundation.

ADDITIONAL RESOURCES

Amnesty International:
> http://www.amnestyusa.org/abolish/worldwide.html.

Darryl Hunt Project for Freedom and Justice:
> http://www.darrylhuntproject.org.

Death Penalty Information Center:
> http://www.deathpenaltyinfo.org.

Documentary, *Torture Inc., American Brutal Prisons:*
> http://www.informationclearinghouse.info/article8451.htm.

Film, *Ghosts of Abu Ghraib:*
> http://www.hbo.com/docs/programs/ghostsofabughraib/index.html.

Innocence Project:
> http://www.innocenceproject.org.

International Covenant on Civil and Political Rights:
> http://www.hrweb.org/legal/cpr.html.

UN Convention Against Torture and Other Cruel, Inhuman or Degrading Treatment or Punishment:
> http://www.hrweb.org/legal/cat.html.

CHAPTER SIXTEEN

∽

Human Rights and International Humanitarian Law

John Hagan and
Wenona Rymond-Richmond

GLOBAL OBLIGATIONS

Should it be entirely surprising that a country, the United States, with a history of importing African slaves and killing and displacing its indigenous people would four centuries later respond in ambivalent ways to an African country, Sudan, that has enslaved, killed, and displaced its own indigenous population? Perhaps these countries are not as entirely different as they might at first seem. There may be lessons of broader relevance in the seemingly disconnected, but in some ways similar and overlapping, experiences of the United States and Sudan. We argue that although the processes and scales of social and legal exclusion in these countries clearly differ, their logics and consequences are related. They are related by the systematic exclusion of a racial group.

The lessons of this analysis will not be entirely new, but they are of more than recurring importance. They begin with elaborations of the lessons of William Gamson's (1995) presidential address to the American Sociological Association on "Hiroshima, the Holocaust, and the Politics of Exclusion." This address in turn builds on Helen Fein's (1990) classic book on genocide, *Imperial Crime and Punishment.* Gamson's gift was to add an analysis of the logics of indirect as well as direct exclusion to Fein's account of abuses and violations of human rights and international humanitarian law. We apply the ideas deriving from international law and Gamson's further conceptualization of indirect and direct exclusion in a comparative analysis of racial forms of rights abuse in the United States and Darfur. We begin with several essential introductory points about human rights and international humanitarian law.

HUMAN RIGHTS AND HUMANITARIAN LAW

International humanitarian law begins where the sovereign responsibilities of nation-states for the protection of human rights end. International humanitarian law consists of the rules of war and armed conflicts between states that seek to protect at least some of the human rights made vulnerable in these conflicts. Armed conflicts within states are more contentiously covered by many of the same provisions in additional protocols. The provisions are intended to provide protections from internment, interrogation, and torture as well as war crimes that include crimes against humanity and genocide. These laws are most often known by the Geneva Conventions of 1949, but they have numerous historical precedents and are still evolving in additional protocols, such as the 1997 Ottawa Convention on antipersonnel mines.

The most notable recent advance in international humanitarian law is the Rome Treaty (1957), which created the International Criminal Court (ICC) in The Hague. The International Criminal Tribunals for the former Yugoslavia (also located in The Hague) and Rwanda (located in Arusha) are time-and-place bound institutions that have played more specialized but clearly connected roles along with "special" and "hybrid" courts, for example, in Sierra Leone and Cambodia. The ICC intends to be more permanent.

The line is less clear between human rights and international humanitarian law than lawyers might often have us believe. The uncertainty begins with the division enshrined by two 1966 covenants—the International Covenant on Civil and Political Rights and the International Covenant on Economic, Social, and Cultural Rights. Fein's concept of universal obligation and Gamson's analysis of indirect and direct exclusion, which are discussed below, underline the intrinsic connectedness of civil and political rights with social, economic, and cultural rights. For example, we note that the indirect process of legalized exclusion leads to the disproportionate incarceration of African American males in the United States, (1) through due process abuses of civil and political rights, that (2) in turn also result in abuses of social, economic, and cultural rights through resulting collateral consequences of disproportionate family disruption, homelessness, and community incapacitation (Hagan and Dinovitzer 2000).

Louise Arbour (2006) similarly notes that in international settings, violations of social, economic, and cultural rights also are intrinsically if not reciprocally linked to violations of civil and political rights. She makes this point with specific reference to the Darfur conflict in Sudan. "In crises like the one we now witness in Darfur, the systematic burning of houses and villages, the forced displacement of the population and the starvation caused by the restrictions on the delivery of humanitarian assistance and destruction of food crops are deliberately used along with other gross human rights violations—such as murder or rape—as instruments of war" (Arbour 2006, 4). That is, the more direct genocidal acts of violence are associated both directly and indirectly with the massive imposition of family disruption, homelessness, and community incapacitation. She adds that "moreover, no transition to a just peace will be possible in Sudan without putting into place an equitable, nondiscriminatory framework of access to land and oil" (ibid.).

Arbour's point is that human rights and humanitarian law cannot and should not prevent the joint protection and restoration of civil and political rights along with social, economic, and cultural rights. As an example of the potential for addressing broader human rights issues in humanitarian law forums, the International Criminal Court has responsibilities that include decisionmaking about reparations and compensation to victims of war crimes. The UN Commission of Inquiry on Darfur recommends in its conclusions that the International Criminal Court exercise its responsibilities for reparations and compensation programs by addressing a wide range of rights violations in Darfur. These reparations and compensations extend beyond prosecutions under international humanitarian law. The goals of these prospective decisions include reestablishing human rights for group members to pursue livelihoods within reconstituted nation-states. In more sociological terms, this legal work involves restoring rightful claims for inclusion following periods of coerced exclusion, or in other words, the recreation of "universal rights of obligation" in nation-states.

OBLIGATIONS OF INCLUSION

Fein's central concept is the "universe of obligation," by which she refers to the people who "must be taken into account, to whom obligations are due, by whom we can be held responsible for our actions" (cited in Gamson 1995, 1). The concern underlying this concept is that once people are socially and legally located outside the universe of obligation, the offenses perpetrated against them are not treated as violations of the normative order and do not trigger sanctions. That is, these persons are socially and legally excluded, and they are at high risk of becoming invisible and unprotected. This, of course, is an affront to the ideal of universality inherent to the very concept of human rights.

Gamson's further insight is to insist that there are in social practice no legal bright lines to definitively distinguish human rights from humanitarian rights. First, the distinctions between inclusion/exclusion and visibility/invisibility are continuous or multidimensional. Second, these distinctions are indirectly and passively as well as directly and actively imposed—that is, by means that are cultural and institutionally dismissive as well as political and militarily coercive.

Fein's attention to the boundaries of universal obligations and Gamson's focus on the social subtleties of these boundaries are two ways of underlining major challenges to rights work in the United States as well as Sudan. Both Fein and Gamson are particularly concerned with the ways in which racism perniciously subverts the ideals of rights work. The late modern and lasting dilemma is that the universalism of a rights-based logic can so easily coexist and persist alongside racism. Immanuel Wallerstein (1979) further asserts that universalism and racism go hand in hand with capitalism, while Loic Wacquant (2001) insists that universalism—in the forms of civil rights, human rights, or humanitarian law—can serve to legitimate and obfuscate racism. Both Wacquant and Wallerstein argue that the underlying cause is class-based discrimination. The concern is that human rights and humanitarian law can facilitate as well as mitigate these possibilities.

Our first intent in this chapter is to bring the roles of human rights and international humanitarian law more clearly into a sociological analytic frame and to trace their implications in understanding current events linking the United States and Sudan. Our second intent is to highlight the restoratively inclusive possibilities as well as punitively exclusive realities identified by applications of rights laws and sociological analyses of what Fein calls the universe of obligation.

Our empirical starting point is two jarringly different images of the consequences of international responses to Sudan's recent genocidal history. The first image is the well-told story in Megan Mylan's and Jon Shenk's documentary *The Lost Boys of Sudan* (2004) and in Dave Eggers's novel *What Is What?* (2006). This is the true tale of the thousands of young boys who, when confronted with terrifying choices in the early 1990s between being child soldiers, slaves, or killed, chose to flee from southern Sudan to refugee camps in Ethiopia. When life proved desperate there too, many of these youth fled back through the still raging killing fields of southern Sudan, winding up in refugee camps in Kenya. Finally, in 2000, the U.S. government provided legal refugee status to some of these youth and brought them to the United States where they received help, often from church groups, in negotiating a challenging inclusion and reintegration into the "universe of obligation" in the Global North (Cheadle and Prendergast 2007). This outcome was an enormously important accomplishment of transitional restorative justice for the fortunate few who survived their early lives as child victims and soldiers in Sudan. The second image is a less uplifting and more sobering reflection of the punitive and exclusionary stigma that more often has confronted refugees from Sudan's genocidal policies. This second image appeared in a color photo "above the fold" on the front page of the *New York Times,* on New Year's Eve 2005 (Allan and Slackman 2005). The picture was of a Sudanese man crying out as another man tried to deliver his infant child to safety through a bus window as they were being forcibly removed by Egyptian police from a protest in Cairo. The police that day killed at least twenty-three people, including small children, when hundreds of Sudanese refugees refused to leave a public park they had occupied to protest denials of their rights to establish refugee claims by UN officials. The officials told thousands of Sudanese camped in the small park across from their offices that they were ineligible for relocation because it was safe to return to their "homes" in Sudan. "When the officers charged, women and children tried to huddle together, and to hide under blankets as some men grabbed for anything—tree limbs, metal bars—struggling to fight back, witnesses said. The police hesitated, then rushed in with full force, trampling over people and dragging the Sudanese off to waiting buses" (Allam and Slackman 2005). Those who survived were loaded onto buses and later were released on the streets of Cairo with no possessions and nowhere to go. They were yet again victims of social exclusion.

No published reports followed as to what became of the latter group of refugee claimants and their children, but it is reasonable to imagine that their fates on the streets of Cairo were far less favorable than those of the lost boys of Sudan who were allowed the legal right to sanctuary in the United States. Of course, the Global North also has its own indigenous forms of social and legal exclusion—notably including capital punishment, imprisonment, and homelessness—and there is much research on the unfavorable life course outcomes of young as well as older persons who are treated with analogously punitive (e.g., arrest and imprisonment) as opposed to reintegrative policies (e.g., shelters, alternative schools, and work programs).

We can learn from this research, and we argue in this chapter that the implications of this work are instructive for our understanding of the Global South as well as the Global North—not just because our fates are linked by the shrinking and interconnected dimensions of the joined worlds in which we live, but also because even more fundamental aspects of our geographically separate lives may be more intertwined than they ordinarily seem.

In particular, we argue that there are lessons from the experiences of penal sanctions and homelessness for youth and families in the Global North that can make the Global South, including the life prospects of the displaced and dispossessed in Darfur, more understandable. The essential lesson of this research is that exclusionary practices cause more problems than they solve (e.g., Hagan and McCarthy 1997). This chapter ultimately considers similarities as well as differences in the law-based systems and rights violations of selective exclusion found in the United States and Sudan. The concept of social exclusion helps make clear how violations of human rights through such practices and processes as capital punishment, imprisonment, and homelessness in the United States correspond to violations of international humanitarian law in Sudan.

FROM NORTH TO SOUTH

In the Global South, late modern economic policies imported from the Global North often combine with the strengths and weaknesses of local nation-states in ways that threaten family survival and intensify youth problems. Latin and South America are sites of prodigious homelessness yielding corresponding levels of family disruption and high-risk social behavior among young people. Police and private security personnel are often paid to brutalize and eliminate these youth from the commercial streets of the Global South. This is a disturbing example of underlying social and economic rights problems interacting with civil and political rights violations.

Of course, some Latin and South American as well as African nations are also sites of direct forms of social exclusion, including state-led military and paramilitary regimes that organize massive "disappearances" as well as full-fledged massacres, resulting in even more extensive family displacement and destruction. These are very explicit violations of humanitarian law, but again with social, economic, and cultural rights dimensions. Sub-Saharan Africa is the current epicenter of one-sided, state-led humanitarian law violations involving violence against civilians and families. The Middle East and North Africa are also sites of surges in multisided violence against civilians (Liu Institute for Global Issues 2006). Violent rebellion against these circumstances is a predictable result, and this also becomes an issue in humanitarian law enforcement. An influential demography of age-related social and economic rights violations often shapes the form of this rebellion. We discuss this further below using Darfur as our example.

The challenge of the remainder of this chapter is to use new evidence from selected sites in Darfur to illustrate the range of consequences that violent as well as social, economic, and cultural assaults on the lives of African youth and their families are creating for current and future generations. There are, of course, differences of kind as well as degree between the experience of genocidal victimization in Darfur and the problems of the Global North. However, life course challenges exist as a result of what can be seen as social and economic rights violations involving high-risk youth throughout the world (see Osgood et al. 2005). Our argument is that these separate but related problems of youth in the Global North and South present an urgent new research agenda and underline the need for a reconstituted and more internationally focused sociology of human rights and international humanitarian law.

To introduce as well as provoke this new research agenda, we present a comparative snapshot of similarities as well as differences in the state-based and rights-related systems of selective exclusion we argue characterize the United States and Sudan. The comparison is summarized in Table 16.1. We acknowledge that other countries should be included in this comparison. For example, China probably would occupy a place in this figure between the United States and Sudan, while Canada and many European

Table 16.1 State-Based Systems of Selective Exclusion (Institutionalized Forms of Removal and Relocation)

Example states	*U.S.*	*Sudan*
Exclusionary method	Indirect	Direct
Selection mechanism	Racial differentiation	Racial oppression
Institutional authority	Legal/juridical procedure	Political/military and paramilitary chain of command
Operational mode	Individualized	Collectivized
Putative rights and protections	Domestic constitutional, civil, and criminal law	International humanitarian and criminal law
Forms of exclusion	Police harassment, arrest, and conviction Incarceration Homelessness Disenfranchisement Death penalty	Mass killings and rapes Displacement Deportation Property loss Refugee status
Theoretical metaphors	Crime as war ("war on drugs")	War as crime (genocide)
Predictable consequences	Criminal innovation, recidivism, and mass incarceration (street crimes)	Organized attacks, armed rebellion, and counter-insurgency (war crimes)

countries are likely to be to the left of the United States. Elaborations of this figure await further research. We focus first on the United States and Sudan.

Racial selectivity is a pervasive feature of both the U.S. and Sudanese state-based systems of exclusion. Polarized racial images are prominent in both countries, resulting in practices of differentiation if not oppression. For example, *New York Times* columnist Bob Herbert recently observed that in the United States, "No one is paying much attention, but parts of New York City are like a police state for young men, women and children who happen to be black or Hispanic. They are routinely stopped, searched, harassed, intimidated, humiliated and in many cases, arrested for no good reason" (Herbert 2007, A25). Of course, Herbert qualified his observation by drawing a "likeness" and not equivalence between the United States and police states elsewhere.

Selective exclusionary practices characteristically are implemented indirectly in the United States and directly in Darfur, which is a crucial difference. Thus in the United States, racial differentiation is customarily legalized through recourse to juridical procedures designed to protect civil and political rights, but which may often prove to be discriminatory in themselves. The more punitive treatment of drug crimes involving crack compared to cocaine, in a time when the former has been more commonly used in African American communities and the latter is more often used in majority group settings and neighborhoods, is an example of such a civil and political rights issue.

The Sudanese state obviously organizes racial oppression more visibly and directly in Darfur, through the unchecked command chains of the polity and military and paramilitary forces that operate in explicit violation of international humanitarian law. This difference involves recourse to individualized punishment in the United States and collective punishment in Darfur. Although the former individualized punishment is framed in terms of rights protection, and while the latter collective punishment is a more explicit form of rights violation, the exclusionary consequences for the racial groups involved are similar in some notable ways.

Ideally, of course, there are checks on practices of racial differentiation. These due process checks and procedures explicitly depend on the enforcement of domestic constitutional, civil, and criminal law protections in the United States, while in Darfur there is (thus far) a more visibly ineffective reliance on international humanitarian law. Organizations like the American Civil Liberties Union and Human Rights Watch have limited success in delivering protection in both places, but especially via the International Criminal Court in Darfur.

Weaknesses in legal and other protective measures in both the United States and Darfur result in extensive racial disparities. These follow in the United States, for example, from discriminatory practices of police harassment, arrest, conviction, incarceration, homelessness, and disenfranchisement. The resulting racial differentiation, including wrongful convictions, leads to misapplications of the death penalty and massively disproportional incarceration of African Americans. The results of this extensive reliance on capital punishment and imprisonment also have extensive collateral consequences for the children (family disruption), families (homelessness), and communities (loss of marriageable males) of those who are punished (Hagan and Dinovitzer 2000). These are among the mechanisms by which civil and political rights abuses in the United States are both the cause and consequence of the neglect and abuse of social, economic, and cultural rights in broader family and community settings.

Racial oppression in Darfur is more visibly and directly catastrophic. The racial consequences of the use of the political and military and paramilitary command structures of the Sudanese state to organize militia attacks on African groups in Darfur are genocidal in scale. The results are hundreds of thousands of killings and rapes, displacement, deportation, property loss, and the confinement of millions of homeless Africans in internal displacement and refugee camps. And this is even more clearly a resulting mix of civil and political with social, economic, and cultural rights abuses and violations.

These similarities as well as differences in the United States and Darfur are reflected in the parallel policy metaphors describing them respectively in terms of a "war against crime" and a "war as crime." In the United States, the crime metaphor is intermittent but often explicit and expressed in such policies as the "war on drugs," which had its modern beginning in the presidential law and order politics of Barry Goldwater in the 1960s, ultimately enacted by the Nixon administration in the 1970s. Ironically, it is the Bush administration that has extended the crime metaphor to Darfur with its ambivalent labeling of this armed conflict as genocide and its abstention on the UN referral of the Darfur case to the International Criminal Court.

Our thesis is that these wars of exclusion in both the United States and Darfur have enormously harmful and predictable consequences, even if the form and scale of these consequences may differ. We have already noted the parallel problems of family disruption, homelessness, displacement for family formation and community capacity in both the United States and Darfur. We do not argue that the mass incarceration that has occurred in the United States is of one piece with the mass killing that has occurred in Darfur. Yet we do find that by drawing connections we gain insights into global processes of dislocation and devastation.

Both Loic Wacquant (2001) and Immanuel Wallerstein (1979) have similarly focused attention on families as key sites for the reproduction and destruction of group life. Wallerstein (1979, 169) specifically notes parallels and connections between the United States and Africa in the world system, noting "formal similarities" as well as "political differences." Here and elsewhere, Wallerstein (245) emphasizes that households are "the most neglected institutional pillar" in the state domination of the world system.

We have already referred to the literature on the consequences of U.S. mass incarceration on families. We now further examine the extent of problems of family dislocation in Darfur.

THE COLLECTIVE PUNISHMENT OF FAMILIES IN WEST DARFUR

Human Rights Watch (2004) uses the term "collective punishment" to aptly describe the brutality we document further below in the southwestern part of West Darfur state: "These tactics—which were replicated throughout much of Darfur—were supplemented by other particularly brutal crimes in three Wadi Saleh, Mukjar and Shattaya localities as a form of collective punishment—and total subjugation—of the civilian population for its perceived support of the rebel movement." A key to understanding the consequences of collective punishment as a counterinsurgency strategy in Darfur involves seeing its impact beyond the killings and rapes—on the surviving families. This collective punishment that is concentrated on innocent civilians is itself an obvious violation of international humanitarian law, but its larger significance includes the social, economic, and cultural costs in terms of human rights abuses of families more generally.

An important way of understanding the impact of the counterinsurgency policy of the Sudanese government in Darfur is to reconstruct the numerical changes in family composition and how they have occurred as a result of attacks on farms and villages. We have analyzed twenty-two settlements represented by 932 refugees interviewed in a 2004 State Department survey in Chad. Table 16.2 provides a before-and-after picture of the average families in these settlements, in terms of their mean size, loss of life, and experiences of rape over the eighteen months before the 2004 survey.

This table indicates that across the twenty-two settlements, the average family size before the attacks included more than ten persons (10.44). By the time these families reached the refugee camps in Chad, however, they consisted of just over six persons (6.25), having lost on average more than four family members (4.19). Nearly 70 percent of these lost family members were males (69.2 percent), while nearly 30 percent of the respondents (29.1 percent) reported that rapes occurred during the attacks. These latter numbers reflect a pervasive pattern of killing men and raping women. The averages are influenced by especially high numbers of lost family members reported in several settlements, most notably Abu Gumra, Beida, and Karnoi. For unknown reasons, these settlements that report the highest numbers of lost family members report somewhat lower rates of rape.

The best documentation of the patterns of death, disappearances, and destruction in Darfur is in the southwestern areas of West Darfur known as Wadi Salih and Mukjar. These are among the most fertile land areas of Darfur, and the Mukjar area includes the strategically important Sindu Hills where rebel forces have often sought refuge. Four settlements in this region are highlighted in Table 16.2: Bendesi, Foro Burunga, Garsila, and Habila. Although the numbers of lost family members are somewhat lower in this area than elsewhere in Darfur, we will see that the overall destruction of black African social, economic, and cultural group life, which has led to an increase in rebel recruitment and activity, is overwhelming. This area thus provides an important illustration of genocidal victimization and its human rights as well as humanitarian causes and consequences in Darfur.

The damage to family life in the shaded part of Table 16.2 shows a very consistent pattern across the four settlements. On average, the family sizes varied between six and more than eight members (6.68 to 8.63) before the attacks. Families on average lost from about one to two members (1.44 to 2.19), so that after the attacks the average family ranged in size from about four to six members (4.56 to 6.48). About 40 percent of the respondents from these families reported that rapes occurred during the attacks on their settlements (.38 to .41). Three of the four settlements reported that more than 90 percent of the lost family members were male, while the fourth settlement reported

Table 16.2 Darfur Families before and after Attacks, Atrocities Documentation Survey, Chad, 2004

Settlement	Average family size before attacks	Average number of family killed	Percent males killed	Percent reporting rape	Average family size after attacks
Abu Gumra	25.66	19.94	.56	.20	5.71
Al Genina	9.29	2.43	.87	.45	6.86
Beida	22.62	16.31	.55	.14	6.31
Bendesi	6.75	2.19	.92	.38	4.56
Foro Burunga	6.68	1.44	.78	.41	5.24
Garsila	6.81	1.44	.96	.38	5.38
Habila	8.63	2.15	.90	.41	6.48
Kabkabiyah	8.63	2.18	.95	.33	6.45
Karnoi	17.88	11.68	.64	.31	6.21
Koulbous	8.39	1.23	.94	.00	7.15
Kutum	7.51	2.44	.79	.26	5.07
Masteri	9.59	2.33	.76	.47	7.22
Seleya	7.79	1.37	.87	.27	6.43
Sirba	7.23	1.13	.89	.29	6.10
Tine	7.13	1.13	.97	.22	6.00
Umm Bourou	8.66	2.69	.77	.27	5.96
Near Karnoi	8.56	2.44	.87	.23	6.13
Adar	10.06	3.88	.76	.35	6.18
Tandubayah	6.59	.65	.72	.06	5.94
Near Tine	9.33	1.87	.86	.00	7.47
Girgira	8.44	1.06	.53	.00	7.38
Near Abu Gumra	7.76	2.12	.91	.12	5.64
Total	10.44	4.19	.69	.29	6.25

that 78 percent of those lost were male. Thus the loss of family members was pervasive, and the direct or indirect experience of rape was extensive.

Both in the United States and Darfur, disrupted families and dislocated communities generate large numbers of young males who are at high risk of enticement into crime and violence. In the United States, Blumstein (2006) further explains how the massive reliance on incarceration in a "war on drugs" against the crack epidemic in the 1980s resulted in the exclusionary imprisonment of older gang leaders and the creation of vacancy chains for new recruits to meet continuing demands for drug distribution and sales. The vacancies were filled by not only new but younger and characteristically more violence-prone recruits who set off spiraling increases in gun deaths and subsequent surges in imprisonment in the United States. This produced the worst of several possibilities: an age-based and network-fed subcultural process in which mass incarceration led to more violent forms of crime through the 1980s and into the early 1990s.

The wider-felt effects of this repressive era in American criminal justice extenuated the neglect and abuse of underlying social and economic rights in ghettoized American communities. Our interest here is in noting how this experience is paralleled in settings like Darfur. Louise Arbour (2006, 2) has called for a form of international transitional justice that speaks to a widened range and sequence of rights violations. Her point is that this kind of rights-based justice must "reach to, but also beyond the crimes and abuses committed during the conflict which led to the transition, into the human rights violations that preexisted the conflict and caused, or contributed to it. When making that search, it is likely that one would expose a great number of violations of economic, social and cultural (ESC) rights and discriminatory practices."

Thus an exclusionary process with parallels to the United States is at work in Darfur. In Darfur, the processes involve state-led and -supported violent attacks on African groups that have intensified an armed rebellion among the targeted victims. In the same sense that mass incarceration aggravated a surge in violent crime in the United States, in Darfur military and paramilitary attacks are intensifying an armed rebellion among newer and younger recruits. Again, this is an age-based and network-fed subcultural process in which exclusion is leading to more violence, in this case armed rebellion. If the past is predictive, this increasingly youth-driven rebellion will spawn war crimes in its own right. Sociological criminology is experienced in enumerating and explaining such racially differentiated processes, and in this way the sociology of crime can inform a sociology of human rights and international humanitarian law.

DESPERATION AND DEFIANCE IN DARFUR

Should it be entirely surprising that a country with a region like Darfur, where scorched-earth tactics of ethnic cleansing against African families and communities are epidemic, would produce a violent and defiant rebel movement that is especially attractive to the youth whose families are viciously victimized? We argue that this violent subcultural response is exactly what should be predicted by a tradition of labeling and conflict theory in sociological criminology, including, for example, Laurence Sherman's (1993) late modern version of defiance theory. The more uplifting alternative prospect, of course, is the fate of the Lost Boys of Sudan, with whom we started this chapter.

Yet the true tale of the Lost Boys is a restorative story of inclusive turning points that is even less likely for the boys of Darfur than are the parallel probabilities of ghetto youth on the urban playing fields of America becoming successful professional athletes. As we demonstrate below, age-related patterns of death and displacement are the far more likely outcomes in Darfur. The lesson of defiance theory is that rebellion is too often the more plausible alternative for disadvantaged youth confronted with sobering life choices in the killing fields of nations as different as the United States and Sudan. The larger lesson of defiance theory is the unanticipated self-perpetuating rage and rebellion that is the product of exclusionary policies in many social settings, especially settings that provide too few peaceful pathways to success or even survival. It is in such circumstances that Robert Merton, Richard Cloward, and Lloyd Ohlin classically predicted innovation and rebellion. The age-connected forms of this innovation and rebellion are foreshadowed in an abundance of sociological research on crime. Again, there may be lessons of broader relevance in the seemingly disconnected but in some ways similar and overlapping experiences of the United States and Sudan.

Our starting point is thus a third image, part myth and part reality, to consider in juxtaposition to the two we have already considered in this chapter. This image is of the adolescent and young adult males in Darfur referred to in the Sudanese conflict with the demonizing imagery of "Tora Bora." The Sudanese government has simultaneously identified the Tora Bora with the history of the western frontier of the United States and the American pursuit of Osama Bin Laden into the same-named mountain range on the Afghanistan border with Pakistan. The goal of the Sudanese government is to create the image of a scourge worth fighting with brutally repressive counterinsurgency tactics.

The Sudanese government in press releases by its embassies and through other news media describe the Tora Bora as armed robbers and smugglers who prey on the Arab groups in Darfur, much as in the history of the settlers in the lawless American West.

> Historically, these groups have been existent in Darfur's extreme rural areas for many centuries conducting acts of highway robbery. The situation here is reminiscent of the eighteenth and nineteenth century American robber ... in the Wild West. The highway robbery is an ancient practice in nomadic societies which are not unique to Darfur. It is to be found in communities or similar circumstances in different parts of Africa. Groups such as the Tora Bora ... emerged as new fledglings conducting the old practice of highway robbery. (El Talib 2004)

Threatening activities of the Tora Bora are thus said to be an important source of the self-defense-motivated actions of the Arab Janjaweed militias. The argument is that "the major function and the raison d'etre for this militia are to protect herds of nomadic tribes in western Sudan from attacks of looters, highway robbery and particularly, attacks of rival nomadic tribes at times of conflict on pastures and water" (El Talib 2004).

As noted, the Tora Bora are linked further in Sudanese government news releases to Islamic extremism. "Any study of the conflict in Darfur," a government source reports, "can no longer ignore the clear involvement of Islamic extremists in ferment-ing rebellion in western Sudan" (El Talib 2004). The evidence for this assertion again features the Tora Bora images, noting that "amongst the rebels there is a self-styled 'Tora Bora' militia—named after the Afghan mountain range in which Osama bin Laden, al-Qaeda and the Taliban fought one of their last battles, and from which bin Laden escaped American capture" (Ali-Dinar 2004).

Groups of young rebels who sometimes also describe themselves as Tora Bora are a small but growing part of the Darfur conflict. These youth are part of the large number of child, adolescent, and young adult soldiers in Africa. Although young males

may always have fought wars in the largest numbers, they are an increasingly important and vicious part of African armed conflicts. The reasons are likely little different
than in the Global North, where youth as well are valued in gangs for their loyalty,
fearlessness, willingness to take risks, and readily renewable availability as new recruits
(Gettleman 2007). Also like gang members in the Global North, these youth often
are recognizable by their adopted symbols. In Darfur and elsewhere in Africa, these
menacing images include dreadlocks, wraparound sunglasses, displays of weapons, and
sometimes small leather pouches worn with string around their necks and containing
good luck pieces. They often ride into conflict in rocket-equipped pickup trucks and
gun-laden land cruisers.

It is important to emphasize the nature of the polarized racial identification of
the Tora Bora in Darfur. We have recently used the U.S. State Department survey
of refugees from the Darfur conflict (introduced above) to trace the patterns of this
conflict in the western part of Sudan. The refugee reports from this survey provide
descriptions of the attacks on their villages. There is a clear linkage between the rising
racial polarization of everyday life in Darfur, represented in our analyses in the reports
of racial epithets heard during attacks on black African villagers by Arab Janjaweed
militias. Figure 16.1 presents a summary of the rise in this expression of racism in
Darfur using three-month moving averages of the reports of hearing racial epithets in
spring–summer 2003 to the same period in 2004. This was a period of rise and fall
in killings, which peaked at the beginning of 2004.

Figure 16.1 similarly shows a peak in reported racial epithets just before this
peak in killing, at the end of 2003. However, this figure also shows that when attacks
continued to occur in 2004, the level of reported racial epithets remained high, with
about 40 percent of the respondents hearing these taunts, compared to about 20
percent at the beginning of the time series. The State Department refugee interviews
indicate that the Tora Bora references were nearly always accompanied by racial epithets
when they were heard during the attacks. The racial and Tora Bora taunts are joined
expressions of a racial demonology. In classical terms of labeling and subcultural crime
theory, or Sherman's late modern defiance theory, the youth who take on the Tora
Bora role are acting as if to say, "We are everything you say we are, and worse." They
have adopted what Edwin Lemert (1967) called the "symbolic appurtenances" of the
demonized cultural frame.

The question is thus less about the existence or size of these rebel groups than
about the sources and sequences of their development in settings like Darfur. There
is no doubt that rebel groups such as the Tora Bora exist and predate the current
conflict in Darfur. The most prominent of the organized rebel groups, the Sudan
Liberation Army (SLA) and the Justice and Equality Movement (JEM), announced
their existence in February and March of 2003. The SLA and JEM rebels joined
forces in a seven-hour attack on the al Fasher air base with thirty-three land cruisers
in April 2003, destroying a number of Sudan's air-force bombers and gunships. The
rebels killed more than seventy-five Sudanese soldiers and lost only nine of their
own. This attack is usually cited as the beginning of the current conflict (Flint and
de Waal 2005).

Figure 16.1 Moving Average Percentage of Refugees from Darfur Who Reported They Heard Racial Epithets during Attacks, by Date of Departure, Atrocities Documentation Survey, Summer 2004

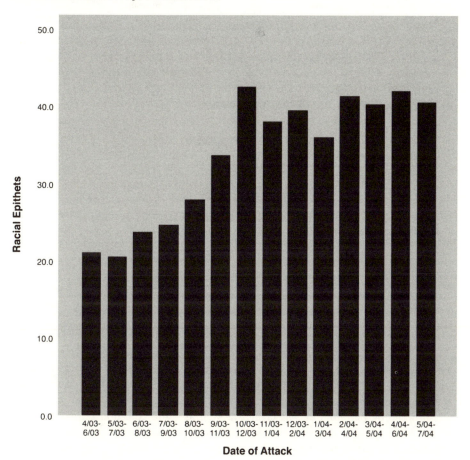

Yet the most exhaustive survey of reported attacks by both sides in Darfur reveals a very one-sided picture of this armed conflict, with few although increasing rebel attacks over time (Petersen and Tullin 2006). This survey is based on 178 witness statements/accounts and reports of attacks involving 372 sites in Darfur from January 2001 to September 2005. Although the accounting is certainly not exhaustive, it makes use of all publicly available sources.

The survey begins by revealing at least eight significant attacks on African villages before the first major rebel attack on the al Fasher air base in the spring of 2003. In total, the survey reveals only thirteen attacks by rebel forces (3 percent of the total). All of the remaining attacks (97 percent) were conducted by Janjaweed militia groups, Sudanese government forces and/or aircraft, or a combination of these groups. Perhaps of even greater interest, however, is that while three of the thirteen rebel attacks each

Figure 16.2 Age and Sex Distribution of Killed and Missing Household Members

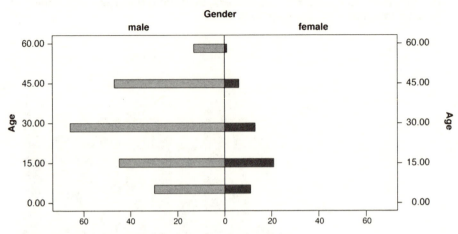

Source: Atrocities Documentation Survey, Darfur, 2004.

are reported in 2003 and 2004, the remaining seven attacks are reported in 2005. Six of these seven attacks are reported in South Darfur, with only one in North Darfur. It is very doubtful that this reporting of attacks is comprehensive, but it may well be representative of the relative distribution and sequence of the attacks, with the rebel attacks increasing over time.

The numbers of rebels seem to be growing along with the frequency of rebel actions, both against Arab targets and between rebel factions. This begs the question of who the rebels are and where they come from. Our answer is that they and their families and communities are usually the victims, and that sometimes they are also the perpetrators of war crimes as well as more common crimes of subsistence. They come from all the targeted African groups in Darfur—most notably the Zaghawa, Fur, and Masaleit tribal groups. They are mostly young and some are under eighteen. All of the rebel groups—the Sudan Liberation Army (SLA), Justice and Equality Movement (JEM), and the newer National Movement for Reform and Development (NMRD)—are predominantly made up of males in their later teens and twenties. A significant number of Fur youth under eighteen are known to have been in the ranks of the SLA and have been seen with weapons by Human Rights Watch observers (Human Rights Watch 2004b). Sudan is a ratified signatory to the Optional Protocol to the Convention on the Rights of the Child, which established eighteen as the minimum age for forced recruitment and calls on states to assist with the rehabilitation of child soldiers.

Yet any thoughts of rehabilitation or restorative transitional justice ignore the reality already described above—namely, that the Sudan government's strategy of counterinsurgency in Darfur is a policy of collective stigmatization and punishment concentrated on the families of the African farmers and villagers who are the targets of the joint government and Janjaweed militia attacks.

DEATH, SURVIVAL, AND REBELLION

The killing, abductions, and enslavement of children have long been a part of the conflict in southern Sudan, as noted in the account of the Lost Boys of Sudan above. Abductions are a smaller but still very significant part of the Darfur conflict in western Sudan. To get a further measure of the magnitude of the direct impact of these crimes on young males and females in Darfur, we developed a data file with the age and gender of every nuclear family member identified as killed or missing in the State Department refugee sample. We then constructed the population pyramids presented in Figure 16.2.

This figure makes it clear that two groups are most likely to be dead and missing from the families of refugee families: the "fighting age" population of African males between fifteen and twenty-nine years of age, and younger pubescent females between five and fourteen years of age. About a third of the former young adult males as well as the latter preadolescent girls are dead or missing. This is consistent with a policy of killing the fighting-age males while raping and killing younger females. This is also consistent with an exclusionary policy that is likely to intensify rebellion among victimized groups.

These patterns are reflected in recent prosecutorial documents setting out charges for humanitarian law violations at the International Criminal Court. Our point is that community effects of these patterns go far beyond the civil and political rights violations to include massive social, economic, and cultural rights violations that have been ongoing for some time and are now much intensified by government-supported and racially charged attacks by Arab Janjaweed militia on black African villagers. Beyond the killing and raping, these are attacks on the social, economic, and cultural survival of entire communities spread across the Darfur region of Sudan.

Note that the policy of killing fighting-age males parallels in demographic terms the earlier pattern we observed of incarcerating the young adult leaders of drug gangs in the United States. The effect of both is to create vacancy chains for the recruitment of remaining younger replacements. The potential pool of recruits is identified in the population pyramids presented in Figure 16.3 from surveys conducted in three internal displacement camps in West Darfur. This figure displays what demographers call a "population bulge" of adolescent males.

The German demographer Gunnar Heinsohn (2003) indicates that sixty-eight of the most populous nations of the world have adolescent bulges that will mature into "fighting-age" bulges, and that sixty-two of these sixty-eight nations are—or recently have been—characterized by high levels of violent mortality. As a result of its high birthrate, Sudan is already among these nations. In Darfur, this pattern is intensified by the killing of fighting-age males. Criminologists are especially sensitive to the violent potential of these population dynamics. In the Global North as well as the Global South, it is the young who are most violent and aggressive. However, they are also sensitive to further aggravating factors that we have been describing, most notably, of course, the killing of parents and siblings, and the raping of pubescent girls of approximately the same ages as the surviving males. These factors combine to make an intensified rebellion predictable, with age-graded networks of recruitment and subcultural resentments playing leading roles in focusing the group-based defiance.

Figure 16.3 Age and Sex Distribution of Surviving Household Members

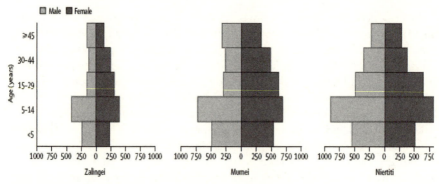

Source: www.thelancet.com. Published online October 1, 2004,
http://image.thelancet.com/extras/04art9087web.pdf.

A prosecutor's brief filed with the International Criminal Court (2007) also makes clear that the raping and killing reflected in these figures were explicitly linked to issues of rebels and the demonization of the Tora Bora. This point is illustrated by the following witness report described in the Brief:

> DFR-023 ... witnessed a separate incident of rape in which Militia/Janjaweed and members of the Armed Forces selected and led away at least ten females between fifteen and eighteen years of age. She watched as the girls were raped in a field nearby.... While carrying out the rapes, the attackers were saying "we have taken Tora Bora's wives, praise be to God." At least one woman who was raped bled in the course of the assault. When this happened the rapists shot their guns into the air and announced, "I have found a virgin woman." (Human Rights Watch 2005, 11)

Despite the references to Tora Bora, the prosecutor's brief explicitly indicates that "no defense was mounted by the residents, and there was no rebel presence in the town when it was attacked." An exception to this pattern may be the nearby town of Kudun, whose residents were apparently able to kill fifteen attackers in late August. The patterns we have described predict intensification of a more organized and youth-fueled rebellion.

Some residents of Bendesi and Mukjar and other settlements stayed in the general area for months following, hoping that they could salvage some of their crops and survive this period of violent collective punishment. A militia leader, Ali Kushayb, and a government minister, Ahmad Harun, were seen frequently with their troops in the area. In fall 2003, the Arab nomadic groups brought huge herds of their camels and other livestock into the area to graze on the newly available farmlands. This further undermined the African groups' hopes to resettle and reclaim these lands.

　　Ali Kushayb also undertook a program to systematically eliminate the leadership of the African groups in fall 2003 and winter 2004. The "educated persons" and Umdahs and Sheiks of these groups were taken into custody and executed. A refugee in Chad explained that "they were told they were being taken to Garsila but we found them in a wadi about one half hour between Mukjar and Garsila. The bodies were in long lines of twenty to fifty.... They had been shot—in the head, back, and waist."

　　The limited number of SLA rebel forces in the area had by this time withdrawn into the nearby Sindu Hills. In February 2004 the SLA were able to mount some successful attacks on government troops and installations. The government (International Criminal Court 2007) struck back with an unprecedented show of force.

> The SLA's presence and attacks prompted a massive response by Sudanese government forces and militias that targeted civilians and civilian villages. By mid-March, the government's scorched earth campaign of ground and air attacks around the Sindu Hills had removed almost all existing or perceived support base for the rebellion by forcibly displacing, looting and burning almost every Fur village near the hills and then extending "mopping up operations" to villages and towns farther away.

At this point, the villages had been destroyed and the African groups who had lived there were gone—either as a result of being killed or displaced, in large part to the refugee camps in Chad.

　　We have already presented evidence that in Bendesi and the surrounding area families lost on average one to two members. We have also seen that these losses disproportionately involved young adult men and teenage girls. This loss of life occurred in an intensely racial atmosphere that included both the shouting of racial epithets during the attacks and claims about membership and support of the Tora Bora or rebels in the area. A 2005 study of the Bendesi and surrounding area by INTERSOS (2005), for the United Humanitarian High Commissioner for Refugees, provides some final insights on the impact on families of the attacks.

　　The offensive of August 2003 destroyed about thirty villages surrounding Bendesi. The residents of these villages were predominantly either killed or displaced into Bendesi. When Bendesi came under attack, they moved on east to Mukjar and further south to Um Dukhum. After remaining in these larger towns for a period, the displaced persons tended either to stay or move further away, including to the refugee camps in Chad.

　　Of the total number of 245 villages and towns considered in this research, about 100 were found to have been destroyed, with eight more abandoned but not destroyed. Furthermore, in most of the destroyed or abandoned villages, nomad Arab groups had moved onto the sites and started to put the land to use for farming or grazing. This was especially true in the Mukjar area (Montesquiou 2007). Some of those who escaped from Bendesi to Mukjar returned to Bendesi, but this is not to say that they returned to their former ways of life. Probably for reasons of security, they tended to settle in the more central part of town.

The families and children displaced by the government offensives tend to be living in highly problematic conditions. Their lives are devastated not just in the criminal terms usually addressed in international humanitarian law prosecutions, but also in the social, economic, and cultural terms addressed in human rights law. Less than 20 percent of the children who have survived their ordeal are attending school. Girls are even less likely to be doing so than boys. It is estimated that about 10 percent of the families are very conservatively classifiable as "vulnerable" in the whole population of this region. This figure is estimated at 25 to 30 percent among the internally displaced. Single parenthood is the most common vulnerability, with the greater number of these families headed by a female caring alone for her children. Before the recent conflict in Darfur, there was a social norm known as "zaka" that fostered the reintegration of vulnerable children and families. This norm has lost much of its force and protective capacity in the current circumstances. These are among the many and most disturbing collateral consequences of the armed conflict in Darfur.

THE MEAN STREETS OF THE GLOBAL VILLAGE

Is it surprising that there are similarities as well as differences in the patterns of legal and criminal exclusion we see in the streets of the Global North and South? In the Global North there is some increasing awareness and concern that the mass incarceration of African American males is distorting the demography of ghettoized communities and creating collateral social, economic, and cultural problems, for example, for the children of incarcerated mothers and fathers. The neglect and abuse of the social, economic, and cultural rights of these children and families are implicated both as cause and effect of mass incarceration policies.

As distant and foreign as the streets of Bendesi in West Darfur may seem, they bear similarities and connections to the everyday world of the Global North. In revealing ways, they are as close as the contrasting images of the Lost Boys of Sudan and the defiant rebels of Tora Bora. It is not a coincidence that the faces of the rebel youth hiding out in the Sindu Hills nearby Bendesi—with their dreadlocks, wraparound sun glasses, and menacing weapons—look very much like the indigenous and immigrant youth increasingly seen on the streets of the Global North. In the high-speed warp of late modern electronic technology, the mean streets of the global village overlap more closely than we often imagine.

The challenge of joining late modern domestic and foreign policies is to see common themes as well as differences. Although they may often be discriminatory in their abuse of civil and political rights, the domestic policies of legal exclusion in the Global North—with their legalized forms of arrest, due process, conviction, and incarceration—are a world apart from the policies of criminal exclusion in the Global South—with their death squads, militias, disappearances, and displacements. The individualized punishments of the North offer some protection against the collective punishments of the South.

One important hope is that the institutions of international humanitarian law can narrow the distance between the worlds of the Global North and South. Yet both are based on punishment rather than restoration. They share notable features in common: the impulses to exclude and repress. Both intensify rather than reduce armed and violent conflict. The alternative impulses, to include and support, are elusive both in the Global North and the Global South. Meanwhile, mass incarceration and genocidal death and displacement display an awkward symmetry on the mean streets of the global village.

Wacquant (2001) suggests that by turning to law and its weapons of criminalization and incarceration to stigmatize African Americans, the racism of American society is made less visible. The young and impoverished black males who are the overwhelming targets are too easily dismissed as being punished for crimes committed, while at the same time insidiously making older middle-class African Americans differentiate themselves from a "dangerous" African American criminal class. Punishment and hyperincarceration are further legitimated by the "civil rights" gains of African Americans, since they now presumably enjoy the universal formal civil rights.

In the Sudan context, the existence of humanitarian law risks playing a similar role. After all, if it was genocide, then the International Criminal Court would surely prosecute it; if it was genocide, the international community could not stand by; and so on. So the irony is that as international humanitarian and criminal law gains strength, the circumstances in which it is not applied are perhaps seen as not requiring support. The reality, Wallerstein suggests, might have more to do with politics and economics, and the reality of racism, nationally in the Sudan, and internationally, notably including the United States.

Meanwhile, the fragile and disrupted families of the North parallel the destroyed and displaced families of the South. They are parallel faces of vulnerability. The mean streets of these two worlds are not the same. However, their risks and vulnerabilities are joined not only by the shrinking distances between them, but also by parallel and failed policies of punishment and exclusion. The hopeful faces of the Lost Boys of Sudan are the elusively reassuring but probably misleading alternative to the defiant faces of the rebel youth ironically known as Tora Bora in Darfur.

NOTE

Portions of this chapter were published by John Hagan and Wenona Rymond-Richmond. 2007. "The Mean Streets of the Global Village: Crimes of Exclusion in the United States and Darfur." *Journal of Scandinavian Studies in Criminology and Crime Prevention* 8 (Supplement 1), available at http://www.tandf.no/crime.

REFERENCES

Ali-Dinar, Ali. 2004. "Darfur: The Next Afghanistan?" Darfur Information, The European-Sudanese Public Affairs Council, available at http://darfurinformation.com/publications-of-interest/book17.asp. (Accessed March 30, 2008.)

Allam, Abheer, and Michael Slackman. 2005. "Egypt Disperses Migrants' Camp; 23 Sudanese Die," *New York Times,* December 31, A1.

Arbour, Louise. 2006. "Economic and Social Justice for Societies in Transition." Paper presented October 25, 2006, New York University School of Law.

Blumstein, Alfred. 2006. "The Crime Drop in America: An Exploration of Some Recent Crime Trends." *Journal of Scandinavian Studies in Criminology and Crime Prevention* 7 (Supplement 1): 17–35.

Cheadle, Don, and John Prendergast. 2007. *Not on Our Watch: The Mission to End Genocide in Darfur and Beyond.* New York: Hyperion.

Eggers, Dave. 2006. *What Is the What?* San Francisco: McSweeny's.

El Talib, Hassan. 2004. "Definition and Historical Background of the Janjaweed." Available at http://www.sudani.co.za/peace_janjaweed.htm.

Fein, Helen. 1990. *Imperial Crime and Punishment: The Jallianwala Bagh Massacre and British Judgment, 1919–1920.* Honolulu: University Press of Hawaii.

Flint, Julie, and Alex de Waal. 2005. *Darfur: A Short History of a Long War.* London: Zed Books.

Gamson, William. 1995. "Hiroshima, the Holocaust, and the Politics of Exclusion." *American Sociological Review* 60: 1–20.

Gettleman, Jeffrey. 2007. "The Perfect Weapon for the Meanest Wars." *New York Times,* April 29, Sec. 4, 1.

Hagan, John, and Bill McCarthy. 1997. *Mean Streets: Youth Crime and Homelessness.* Cambridge, UK: Cambridge University Press.

Hagan, John, and Ronit Dinovitzer. 2000. "Children of the Prison Generation: Collateral Consequences of Imprisonment for Children and Communities." *Crime and Justice* 26: 121–162.

Heinsohn, Gunnar. 2003. *Sohne und Weltmacht [Sons and World Power].* Zurich: Orell and Fussli.

Herbert, Bob. 2007. "Arrested While Grieving." *New York Times,* May 26, A25.

Human Rights Watch. 2004a. *Darfur Destroyed: Ethnic Cleansing by Government and Militia Forces in Western Sudan.* New York: Human Rights Watch.

———. 2004b. "'If We Return, We Will Be Killed': Consolidation of Ethnic Cleansing in Darfur, Sudan." Report, November 2004, available at http://www.hrw.org/backgrounder/africa/darfur1104/darfur1104.pdf. (Accessed March 30, 2008.)

———. 2005. "Targeting the Fur: Mass Killings in Darfur." A Human Rights Watch Briefing Paper, January 21.

International Criminal Court. 2007. "Situation in Darfur, the Sudan." February 27, available at http://www.icc-cpi.int/library/cases/ICC-02-05-56_English.pdf. (Accessed March 30, 2008.)

INTERSOS. 2005. "Return-Oriented Profiling in the Southern Part of West Darfur and Corresponding Chadian Border Area." UN High Commissioner for Refugees, July, available at http://www.reliefweb.int/rw/RWB.NSF/db900SID/MIRA-6GE5M7?OpenDocument. (Accessed March 30, 2008.)

Lemert, Edwin. 1967. *Human Deviance, Social Problems and Social Control.* Englewood Cliffs, NJ: Prentice-Hall.

Liu Institute for Global Issues. 2006. *Human Security Brief 2006, Human Security Centre, Liu Institute for Global Issues.* Vancouver: University of British Columbia.

Lost Boys of Sudan, The. 2004, Available at http://www.lostboysfilm.com. (Accessed March 30, 2008.)

Montesquiou, Alfred. 2007. "Darfur Graves Unearth Evidence of Atrocities." *Moscow Times,* May 28, Issue 3685.

Osgood, Wayne, E. Michael Foster, Constance Flanagan, and Gretchen Ruth. 2005. *On Your Own without a Net: The Transition to Adulthood for Vulnerable Populations.* Chicago: University of Chicago Press.

Petersen, Andreas, and Lise-Lotte Tullin. 2006. *The Scorched Earth of Darfur: Patterns in Death and Destruction Reported by the People of Darfur, January 2001–September 2005.* Copenhagen, Denmark: Bloodhound.

Sherman, Laurence. 1993. "Defiance, Deterrence, and Irrelevance: A Theory of the Criminal Sanction." *Journal of Research in Crime and Delinquency* 30: 445–473.

Sudan Embassy in South Africa, August 21, available at http://www.sudani.co.za/peace_janjaweed.htm. (Accessed March 30, 2008.)

Wacquant, Loic. 2001. "The Penalization of Poverty and the Rise of Neoliberalism." *European Journal of Criminal Policy and Research* 9: 401–412.

Wallerstein, Immanuel. 1979. *The Capitalist World Economy.* Cambridge, UK: Cambridge University Press.

ADDITIONAL RESOURCES

Protect Darfur:
www.protectdarfur.org.

Save Darfur:
www.savedarfur.org.

STAND, A Student Anti-Genocide Coalition:
www.standnow.org.

UN Judgment Report, *Prosecutor v. Jean-Paul Akayesu,* Case No. ICTR-96-4-T, 1998, International Criminal Tribunal for Rwanda, Office of the Prosecutor at 7.8, available at http://www.asil.org/ilib/ilib0102.htm#01. (Accessed March 30, 2008.)

U.S. Department of State. 2004. *Documenting Atrocities in Darfur.* Washington, D.C.: Bureau of Democracy, Human Rights and Labor and Bureau of Intelligence and Research.

U.S. Holocaust Memorial Museum:
www.ushmn.org.

CHAPTER SEVENTEEN

~

Rights to Participate in Democracy

MARK FREZZO

In this chapter, I examine attempts by social movements, nongovernmental organizations (NGOs), and the United Nations organization to reinvent the discourse of human rights to meet the challenges of the twenty-first century. Stemming from post-Fordism, or "flexible production," on a global scale and reinforced by the neoliberal policies of the International Monetary Fund (IMF), the World Bank (WB), and the World Trade Organization (WTO), these challenges include job insecurity, poverty, environmental degradation, marginalization, migration, and social unrest. In response to such issues, grassroots movements and NGOs have aligned with one another—often in the name of expanded rights or social entitlements—to pressure national governments to restrict the conduct of transnational corporations and retreat from neoliberal policies. For its part, the United Nations has formalized its relationship with the NGO sector and cooperated with NGO campaigns for alternative development, poverty alleviation, environmental justice, and the rights of indigenous peoples, peasants, and women. This raises three questions for social movement researchers, human rights scholars, political economists, and development sociologists. First, how have movements, NGOs, and UN agencies mobilized the language of rights against neoliberalism? Second, how has "rights talk" facilitated and constrained alliances among these actors? Third, how have these actors inspired debate on the potential for direct democracy?

REINVENTING HUMAN RIGHTS:
MOVEMENTS, NGOS, AND THE UNITED NATIONS

Paradoxically, the discourse of human rights—though routinely abused by great powers (from the age of revolution, through the period of British hegemony, to the period of U.S. hegemony), often ignored by transnational corporations, poorly enforced by the United Nations, and rightly questioned by Marxists, feminists, postmodernists, practitioners of postcolonial studies, and other critics of Enlightenment thought—has made a comeback in the aftermath of dramatic changes in the global system. This chapter explores the origins and ramifications of the unexpected "revolution in human rights," placing particular emphasis on the role of movements, NGOs, and UN agencies in promoting rights talk. In recent years, pushes from "below" and "above" have created a dynamic and contradictory nexus of movements, NGOs, and UN agencies—a political opportunity structure built on the highly contested discourse of human rights.

The contestation over the nature, scope, and applicability of rights discourse has three fundamental aspects. First, movements have responded to the prevailing criticisms of the discourse by highlighting the rights to clean water, arable land, livelihood, and identity; by specifying women's rights; by interrogating pretensions to universality; and by rejecting the Eurocentrism of the Enlightenment. By articulating their demands in terms of human rights and committing themselves to nonviolent tactics of resistance, movements have sought to make themselves more appealing to NGO sponsors and allies (Bob 2005). Second, in exchange for influence on objectives, strategies, and tactics, NGOs have funneled their resources into promising movements (Bob 2005). Third, in response to the proliferation of movements and the rapid growth of the NGO sector, the United Nations has distanced itself from neoliberalism and provided support for NGOs—including many entities that aspire to fill the vacuum left by the "retreating state." The resulting nexus has routinized both collaboration and competition among the movements, NGOs, and UN agencies that pressure national governments and intergovernmental organizations for new policies.

In participating in this nexus, each actor implicitly accepts certain risks. As the growing literature on the phenomenon of "NGO-ization" demonstrates, movements risk co-optation—or at least the appearance thereof—by their NGO sponsors and partners (Incite! 2007). This can lead to a narrowing of objectives, internal disputes, and antagonisms with other movements. For their part, NGOs risk losing the appearance of political neutrality in the eyes of their donors and targets alike. This can lead not only to a reduction of funding, but also to a diminished capacity to influence national governments and intergovernmental organizations. Finally, UN agencies risk tensions with one another, the permanent members of the Security Council (China, France, Russia, the United Kingdom, and the United States), and factions within the General Assembly. In short, participation in the nexus serves both to facilitate and to constrain the actions of movements, NGOs, and UN agencies.

Nevertheless, the overall trend is clear. Increasingly, movements are legitimizing their grievances, forging alliances with one another, and attracting the attention of NGOs and UN agencies by referring to the human rights canon. By invoking the master frame of human rights, groups of indigenous peoples, peasants, workers, women, gay and lesbian activists, immigrants, peace activists, environmentalists, and anticorporate activists have managed not only to build solidarity with one another, but also to appeal to the sensibilities of NGOs, UN agencies, and large segments of the world's population. In the process, they have pushed rights discourse beyond the limits of the French Declaration of the Rights of Man and the Citizen (1789), the U.S. Bill of Rights (1791), and the major UN documents in the direction of a more inclusive and expansive vision of human emancipation (Blau and Moncada 2006). Although it remains to be seen if the master frame of human rights will supplant third world developmentalism, social democracy, socialism, and other doctrines that once figured prominently among progressives, it appears that popular forces have made considerable progress in arguing for "rights bundling"—for example, tying the right to longevity to the rights to a clean environment, a livelihood, lifeways, health care, and education. In this light, it is useful to reflect on the historical roots of the cooperation and rivalry among movements, NGOs, and UN agencies.

ORIGINS OF THE MOVEMENT-NGO-UN NEXUS

Since the 1970s—a period marked by a crisis of welfare states in the Global North and development states in the Global South—five overlapping processes have contributed to the emergence of the movement-NGO-UN nexus: (1) the implementation of post-Fordism, or flexible production, on a global scale to accommodate the demands of transnational corporations for cheaper sources of labor; (2) the implementation of such neoliberal policies as fiscal austerity (cuts in spending on social programs), privatization (sale of state-owned enterprises), deregulation (loosening of labor and environmental laws), financial liberalization (loosening of controls on the flow of capital), and free trade (lifting of subsidies on exports and tariffs on imports) under the direction of the U.S. government, the IMF, the WB, and ultimately the WTO; (3) the proliferation of social movements—particularly in Latin America and other parts of the Global South—opposing neoliberalism and using new communications technologies to forge connections with one another; (4) the spread of NGOs attempting not only to fill the gaps left by retreating states, but also to assist movements in the struggle against neoliberalism; and (5) a growing gap between the IMF/WB and the United Nations, coupled with growing affinities between the United Nations and NGOs. In effect, these processes have thickened the ties among movements, NGOs, and UN agencies.

In the period between 1971 and 1974, the U.S. government elected to suspend dollar-gold convertibility, reconfigure the Bretton Woods system, and reject the proposal for a New International Economic Order (NIEO)—a call for a more inclusive development bargain that had been advanced by third world countries and ratified by the General Assembly of the United Nations. The failure of the NIEO proposal marked a watershed moment not only in U.S.-UN relations, but also in UN-NGO relations. The replacement of development policies (ostensibly designed to help the third world "catch up" with the first world) with neoliberal policies (ostensibly designed to help these countries to manage their debts and control inflation) widened the gap between the IMF/WB and the United Nations. Over time, as the IMF and WB pressured national governments to dismantle social programs and protectionist trade policies, proponents of development were channeled into the UN and the NGO sector.

Since the crisis of the 1970s, the United Nations has facilitated the growth of the NGO sector by holding conferences that bring together policymakers, academics, and activists, by cosponsoring alternative development projects with NGOs, and by providing direct assistance to such entities. The United Nations took a significant step in formalizing its relationship with the NGO sector at the World Conference on Human Rights in 1993. The resulting Vienna Declaration and Programme of Action affirmed "the need for States and international organizations, in cooperation with nongovernmental organizations, to create favorable conditions at the national, regional and international levels to ensure the full and effective enjoyment of human rights" (Office of the UN High Commissioner for Human Rights 2007). In recent years, the UN Educational, Scientific, and Cultural Organization (UNESCO) has been particularly effective in promoting cross-pollination among scholars, think tanks, and NGO representatives—especially on the intertwined issues of expanding rights and deepening democracy.

In analyzing the movement-NGO-UN nexus, I emphasize the contributions of three representative entities: the World Social Forum (WSF), which serves as a venue for a diverse array of movements and NGOs to exchange ideas, share experiences, and establish enduring alliances in the confrontation with neoliberalism (WSF 2007); the prominent NGO Amnesty International (AI), which has moved beyond its traditional purview by launching a campaign for economic, social, and cultural rights (AI 2007); and UNESCO, which has promoted the use of Information and Communications Technologies to reduce the digital divide and expand the scope of democracy in the twenty-first century (UNESCO 2007). Citing the cases of the WSF, AI, and UNESCO, I argue that a number of factors—including the post-Fordist work regime, neoliberal policies, mass migration, and new communications technologies—have created the conditions not only for new entanglements among movements, NGOs, and UN agencies, but also for the renovation of such seemingly threadbare concepts as human rights and democracy. In addition, I argue that the movement-NGO-UN nexus and concomitant shift in popular and organizational thinking about human rights, democracy, and justice harbor profound implications for the academic discipline of sociology.

Owing to differences in perspective, structure, and participation, the WSF, AI, and UNESCO maintain extremely complex relations with one another. Although the WSF's primary goals—namely, forging connections among movements that oppose neoliberalism and diffusing an organizational model of openness to smaller gatherings—fall considerably beyond the mandates of AI and UNESCO, the WSF has allowed both entities to participate in its meetings. This policy is consistent with the WSF's commitment not only to facilitating dialogue among diverse "civil society" actors across the North-South divide, but also to building a popular front that transcends the conventional divisions between "reformists" and "revolutionaries," between proponents and opponents of alternative development, between those who favor and those who reject appeals to national governments and intergovernmental organizations, and between those who advocate and those who repudiate global solutions. All of these tendencies figure prominently in the WSF. While the movements that participate in WSF events are free to issue proclamations, the WSF as a whole is precluded from adopting a political program.

The WSF, Amnesty International (AI), and UNESCO make reference—whether implicitly, in the case of the WSF, or explicitly, in the cases of AI and UNESCO—to the major documents of the postwar canon of human rights: the UN Charter (1945), the Universal Declaration of Human Rights (1948), and the International Covenant on Economic, Social, and Cultural Rights (1976). While the WSF is constrained by its charter to keep its distance from UN officials, Amnesty International enjoys consultative status at the United Nations. This has created fertile ground for the sociological study of how the doctrine of human rights circulates among different actors. Taken together, the WSF, AI, and UNESCO offer important insights into the resurgence of rights discourse in the age of globalization. However, a study of other movements or coalitions, NGOs, and UN agencies participating in the renaissance of human rights would be likely to produce comparable results. In the next three sections, I examine the cases of the WSF, AI, and UNESCO.

WORLD SOCIAL FORUM

As a meeting space for a diverse assortment of popular forces, the WSF constitutes a major player in the movement-NGO-UN nexus. In drawing prominent NGOs and UN agencies into its orbit, the WSF has contributed greatly to the debate on human rights. Based in Porto Alegre, Brazil—a stronghold of the Workers' Party and the Landless Rural Workers' Movement—the WSF serves as the hub of a transnational network of grassroots movements, NGOs, independent activists, and intellectuals resisting neoliberal policies. To date, the WSF has seen seven editions: Brazil (2001, 2002, 2003, and 2005), India (2004), Venezuela, Mali, and Pakistan (2006), and Kenya (2007), attracting as many as 150,000 participants. In the same period, the WSF model has been diffused to forums at the continental, national, and municipal levels in Africa, Asia, Australia, Europe, North America, and South America. Exemplifying what Tarrow (2005, 130) calls "downward scale shift," the organizers of smaller forums explicitly agree to respect the precepts, practices, and objectives of the WSF. As a consequence, scholars and activists alike have pointed to the diffusion of the forum model as evidence of a significant breakthrough in social movement activity.

Though grounded in a number of long-standing mobilizations in Latin America, the WSF finds its most significant precursor in the Zapatista movement in Chiapas, Mexico—an indigenous uprising that began with the implementation of the North American Free Trade Agreement in 1994 and continues to the present day. In effect, the Zapatistas paved the way for the WSF by reclaiming the discourse of human rights, by affirming nonviolent tactics of resistance, by hosting activists and intellectuals at Intercontinental Encounters in 1996 and 1997, and by making creative use of cyberactivism. In the process, the Zapatistas became the beneficiaries of a transnational solidarity network that included like-minded movements, secular and religious NGOs, and independent activists. From the outset, the founders of the WSF managed to build on the Zapatista precedent by insisting on organizational pluralism, by maintaining a critical distance from political parties and government officials, and by rejecting the idea of taking state power. These precepts are inscribed in the WSF Charter (2001), which provides the normative framework for the year-round forum process. Continental, national, and municipal gatherings that bear the name "social forum" operate in accordance with the WSF charter.

Notwithstanding its origins in the European Enlightenment and its subsequent appropriation by powerful nation-states, the modern discourse of human rights serves as the master frame of the WSF charter and, by extension, of the forum model. In concrete terms, the WSF charter articulates the demands of variegated movements in the language of human rights, thereby linking the struggles to one another and making an appeal to a broader emancipatory project. Arguably, the significance of the WSF charter derives from its *critical* engagement with such foundational documents as the Universal Declaration of Human Rights (UDHR) and the International Covenant on Economic, Social, and Cultural Rights (ICESCR). While the WSF charter implicitly recognizes the importance of these documents as monuments to past struggles (whether for national self-determination, freedom, equality, development, or other objectives), it also alludes to the *gap* between the promises of these documents—including food, housing, medical care, and education for the entirety of the world's population—and the realities of the contemporary period. Accordingly, in a theoretically and historically astute fashion, the WSF charter argues for the need to mobilize the doctrine of human rights not only in rejecting the neoliberal policies of the IMF, the WB, and the WTO, but also in denouncing the dominance of the Global North over the Global South.

Although it would be instructive to undertake a comprehensive exegesis of the WSF charter, it suffices to examine a few representative passages. Article 4 captures the central elements of the WSF's endeavor to transform rights discourse:

> The alternatives proposed at the World Social Forum stand in opposition to a process of globalization commanded by the large multinational corporations and by governments and institutions at the service of those interests, with the complicity of national governments. They are designed to ensure that globalization in solidarity will prevail as a new stage in world history. This will respect universal human rights and those of all citizens—men and women—of all nations and the environment and will rest on democratic international systems and institutions at the service of social justice, and the sovereignty of peoples. (WSF 2001)

After expressing opposition to the post-Fordist work regime and the corresponding neoliberal policies, Article 4 connects the WSF's vision of "globalization in solidarity" to respect for "universal human rights." In addition, Article 4 alludes to the push—particularly among grassroots groups in the Global South—for economic, social, cultural, gender, and environmental rights. Finally, in an effort to move beyond the UN conception of national self-determination, Article 4 affirms the "sovereignty of peoples."

In connecting the expansion of rights to the deepening of democracy, Article 10 "upholds respect for human rights, the practices of real democracy, participatory democracy, peaceful relations, in equality and solidarity, among people, ethnicities, genders and peoples, and condemns all forms of domination and all subjection of one person by another" (ibid.). In a similar fashion, Article 11 stresses the need for reflection "on the mechanisms and instruments of domination by capital, on the means and actions to resist and overcome that domination, and on the alternatives proposed to solve the problems of exclusion and social inequality that the process of capitalist globalization with its racist, sexist, and environmentally destructive dimensions is creating internationally and within countries" (ibid.). As Articles 4, 10, and 11 suggest, the WSF charter appears to have been designed to provoke debate among activists, NGO representatives, policymakers, and scholars on the accomplishments and failures of the United Nations—the institutional custodian of human rights.

Pointing to the WSF's base in the Global South, many observers and participants alike have debated whether to place the WSF in the lineage of third worldism within the United Nations—the tendency that gave rise to the Bandung Conference of Asian and African Nations in 1955, the NIEO proposal in 1974, and most significantly, fourteen summits of the Non-Aligned Movement (NAM) between 1961 and 2006. Although this analysis has its merits—especially in light of frequent references to the NIEO proposal as the last gasp of third world developmentalism—it overlooks the WSF's attempts to move beyond the limitations of the United Nations. In this light, it is instructive that both AI and UNESCO would see fit to participate in WSF gatherings.

AMNESTY INTERNATIONAL

Whereas the WSF charter argues for the extrapolation of rights discourse beyond the imaginations of the Enlightenment philosophers and the architects of the United Nations, one of AI's current campaigns adopts the rhetorical strategy of *reclaiming* lost or unrealized economic, social, and cultural rights. Long renowned for its campaigns on behalf of "prisoners of conscience"—individuals who have been incarcerated for their political beliefs, nationality, race, ethnicity, gender, or sexual orientation even though they have neither perpetrated nor advocated acts of violence—AI has, in recent years, broadened its mandate to include advocacy of poverty alleviation, alternative development, immigrants' rights, and other objectives dear to grassroots groups in the Global South and their NGO allies in the Global North. From the perspective of sociology, the sea change in AI's approach merits further elucidation—not least because it affects AI's relations with the WSF and the United Nations.

Distributed through AI's website to cyberactivists around the world, "Human Rights for Human Dignity: A Primer on Economic, Social, and Cultural Rights" (2005) explicitly builds on the legacy of the International Covenant on Economic, Social, and Cultural Rights—advanced by proponents of "second generation rights" in 1966, enacted by the UN General Assembly in 1976, signed by President Carter the next year, and rejected by the Senate. In acknowledging the devastating effects of IMF and WB-sponsored Structural Adjustment Programs on the populations of the Global South, AI's Internet campaign registers the impact of the movements against neoliberalism:

Recognition and understanding of economic, social, and cultural rights has strengthened in response to grassroots and broader civil society action. Social movements around the world increasingly mobilized from the mid-1980s against the stark impact of rapid economic reform programs, large-scale infrastructure projects, corruption and the unsustainable debt burden. Structural Adjustment Programs promoted by international financial institutions, such as the World Bank, encouraged aid recipient countries to reduce social spending in sectors such as health and education and to devote a significant portion of their budget to managing their international debt. (AI 2005, 8)

Lending credence to the framing techniques of the movements against neoliberalism, the primer continues: "Claims opposing these policies were articulated in terms of social justice and, ultimately, human rights" (ibid.).

In short, a sociological reading of the primer reveals an attempt to build a bridge between AI's traditional concerns (prisoners' rights, torture, and due process of law) and the concerns of popular forces challenging neoliberal policies. Though largely a consequence of the cross-pollination among a diverse array of NGO staff members and movement actors—a process facilitated by alternative media (including Alternet, the Independent Media Center, the Guerrilla News Network, and a proliferation of "infoshops"), think tanks, academic publications, and student clubs—AI's turn in the direction of collective rights testifies to the growing salience of rights discourse. While the shift in AI's approach attests to the cumulative effect of movement pressure, it also sheds light on the evolution of AI's allies at the United Nations.

UN EDUCATIONAL, SCIENTIFIC, AND CULTURAL ORGANIZATION

Founded in 1945, UNESCO's purview is to promote cooperation among nations and popular participation within them through education, science, and culture. Since promulgating the proposal for a "New World Information and Communication Order" in the late 1970s—the dawn of the information revolution—UNESCO has pursued six interrelated projects: access to information, capacity building, content development, freedom of expression, media development, and memory of the world (UNESCO 2007). In the process, UNESCO has worked alongside NGOs and grassroots movements in promoting participation in the information society—or what some have called the "global communications commons" or "global public sphere"—as a fundamental right. In defining the digital divide between the Global North and the Global South as a human rights issue, UNESCO has registered the influence of movement-NGO coalitions against neoliberalism.

Building on the idea of the universal right to information, as a corollary to such entitlements as livelihood and identity, UNESCO has launched a campaign for electronic democracy—the expansion of participation in decision making and deliberations on policy through the use of Information and Communications Technologies. In affirming a normative vision of e-democracy that contradicts the practices of most national governments, UNESCO emphasizes the need "to examine how digital technologies can strengthen the institutions of representative government and civil society, including parliaments and political parties, by promoting transparency and accountability in the decision-making process, effective party competition, the formation of interest groups and new social movements, and the basic conditions of human rights and civil liberties necessary for open expression of dissenting viewpoints by citizens and the media" (UNESCO 2007). Articulated in the language of human rights, UNESCO's call for transparency and accountability on the part of governments and greater popular participation in policy making resonates with the WSF charter and AI primer on economic, social, and cultural rights.

CONCLUSION

In analyzing complementary and conflicting attempts by the WSF, AI, and UNESCO to transform the doctrine of rights to address the instability, poverty, exclusion, and environmental degradation created by post-Fordism and neoliberalism, I have alluded to the relationship between sociology and human rights. In closing, I would like to make a few comments about the implications of sociological research for human rights (and vice versa). In recent years, sociologists with interests in peace studies, social movements, political economy, development, and environment have turned their attention to human rights. With the advent of the Thematic Group on Human Rights and Global Justice in the International Sociological Association and the proposal for a Human Rights Section of the American Sociological Association, this program has picked up steam.

But what is the sociology of human rights? In essence, this emerging field consists of two intertwined tendencies. The first tendency involves the analysis of how the discourse of human rights—understood as a transnational norm or "regulative idea"—is mobilized, contested, and modified by movements, NGOs, and intergovernmental organizations (Hajjar 2005; Khagram, Riker, and Sikkink 2002). In exploring how the discourse facilitates, legitimizes, and constrains the conduct of these actors, this tendency raises two enduring questions. First, how do movements and NGOs propose to extricate the doctrine of human rights from the legacy of Eurocentrism—the idea that the West is superior to the non-West? Second, how do movements and NGOs push the doctrine beyond civil and political rights into the economic, social, cultural, and environmental spheres? Arguably, in claiming and transforming the rights tradition, movements have pointed to the possibility of overcoming the rejection of human rights that characterizes many currents in social theory.

Linked to the public sociology initiative in the American Sociological Association, the second tendency involves building the advocacy of human rights into sociological research, teaching, and service (Blau and Iyall Smith 2006). This tendency challenges the idea that sociologists should be "detached" or "value-free," and argues that they should aspire not only to explain inequalities of class, gender, sexual orientation, race, and nationality, but also to mobilize their scholarly expertise—whether in publications, classrooms, or community service projects—to rectify injustices. In addition, it maintains that sociologists should attempt not only to diagnose the workings of power in large structures and personal relationships, but also to sketch sites of resistance. Finally, it contends that sociologists should endeavor not only to analyze the workings of the global economy and the interstate system, but also to intervene in solidarity with popular forces seeking more expansive rights and greater participation in democracy.

Whether by intention or accident, both currents in the sociology of human rights implicitly affirm the WSF's slogan, "Another World Is Possible"—the notion that there is nothing inevitable or permanent about a post-Fordist work regime that has unleashed transnational corporations or neoliberal policies that have tied the hands of national governments. Both currents operate from the assumption that sociologists have the capacity to assist movements and their organizational allies in constructing alternatives to post-Fordism and neoliberalism. Doubtless, it remains to be seen what form "alternative globalization" or "globalization from below" will take. But sociologists can derive inspiration from the WSF vision of prefigurative politics, with its emphasis on process, including open dialogue, decentralization, human rights, and nonviolence.

REFERENCES

Amnesty International. 2005. "Human Rights for Human Dignity: A Primer on Economic, Social, and Cultural Rights." London: Amnesty International Publications.

Amnesty International. Amnesty International Homepage. Available at http://www.amnesty. org. (Accessed July 7, 2007.)

Blau, Judith, and Keri E. Iyall Smith, eds. 2006. *Public Sociologies Reader.* Lanham, MD: Rowman and Littlefield.

Blau, Judith, and Alberto Moncada. 2006. *Human Rights: Beyond the Liberal Vision.* Lanham, MD: Rowman and Littlefield.

Bob, Clifford. 2005. *The Marketing of Rebellion: Insurgents, Media, and International Activism.* Cambridge, UK: Cambridge University Press.

Hajjar, Lisa. 2005. "Toward a Sociology of Human Rights: Critical Globalization Studies, International Law, and the Future of War." Pp. 207–216 in *Critical Globalization Studies,* edited by R. P. Appelbaum and W. I. Robinson. New York: Routledge.

Incite! ed. 2007. *The Revolution Will Not Be Funded: Beyond the Non-Profit Industrial Complex.* Cambridge, MA: South End Press.

Khagram, Sanjeev, James V. Riker, and Kathryn Sikkink, eds. 2002. *Restructuring World Politics: Transnational Social Movements, Networks, and Norms.* Minneapolis: University of Minnesota Press.

Office of the UN High Commissioner for Human Rights. Vienna Declaration and Programme of Action homepage, available at http://www.ohchr.org/english/law/vienna. htm. (Accessed July 20, 2007.)

Tarrow, Sidney. 2005. *The New Transnational Activism.* Cambridge, UK: Cambridge University Press.

UN Educational, Scientific, and Cultural Organization homepage, available at http://www. unesco.org. (Accessed July 7, 2007.)

World Social Forum. 2001. "Charter of Principles of the World Social Forum," available at http://www.forumsocialmundial.org.br/main.php?id_menu=4&cd_language=2. (Accessed February 13, 2008.)

World Social Forum homepage, available at http://www.forumsocialmundial.org.br/index.
php?cd_language=2&id_menu=. (Accessed July 7, 2007.)

ADDITIONAL RESOURCES

Amnesty International:
    http://www.amnesty.org.
Amnesty International's campaigns in the United States:
    http://www.amnestyusa.org.
UN Educational, Scientific, and Cultural Organization:
    http://www.unesco.org.
U.S. Social Forum:
    https://www.ussf2007.org.
World Social Forum:
    http://www.forumsocialmundial.org.br.

CHAPTER EIGHTEEN

~

The Social Forum Process and Human Rights

MARINA KARIDES

It is certain that, out of necessity, no less than out of realism, a palpable concern for the advancement of human rights is here to stay.
—Burns H. Weston (2006)

Another world is possible.

—www.forumsocialmundial.org

Get up, Stand up, Stand up for Your Rights
—Bob Marley and Peter Tosh (1973)

The world is being blasted with a breath of fresh air. The World Social Forum (WSF), now in its seventh year, is the major international meeting of social movement organizations, national and international nongovernmental organizations, grassroots groups, anarchist activists, feminist organizations, and indigenous rights networks that effectively support human rights and challenge the neoliberal economic model of globalization for profoundly increasing inequities and injustices throughout the globe. The WSFs, a culmination of the global justice movement, held previously in Porto Alegre, Brazil (2001–2003, 2005), Mumbai, India (2004), and Nairobi, Kenya (2007) as single events and simultaneously in Karachi, Pakistan, Bamako, Mali, and Caracas, Venezuela, in 2006 for a polycentric forum, have transformed into a worldwide process that includes regular national, regional, local, and thematic forums. There has never been a planetary effort for social justice like this before.

As a global public, the social forums provide a gathering point beyond the United Nations, academic conferences, and meetings of the political and economic elite.

Instead, the social forums are a place at which those who experience daily inequities, injustices, and abuse can formulate plans that enable human rights for all. Between one forum and another, groups build on proposals, projects, and campaigns. That the social forum process is not making headlines in major papers and mainstream media outlets does not imply that the global justice movement is not being noticed and marked as an "increasingly significant factor in international relations" (Claude and Weston 2006, 4). Indeed the media block out, as was experienced in the first U.S. Social Forum (USSF) that included more than 15,000 participants, many of whom marched through downtown Atlanta, Georgia, in the middle of a workday, may actually reflect corporate media's hesitancy to draw attention to the resounding chants for people power.

This chapter continues with a review of the expansion of human rights abuses in the era of globalization. It is this intensification of inequalities and injustices in the last thirty years that has provoked both the establishment of the social forums as well as deepening academic analyses of human rights. Two concerns in the recent human rights literature are (1) establishing respectful cross-national or cross-cultural dialogues in defining a transnational vision of human rights and (2) creating the conditions for human rights to be achieved. I consider how these two issues are being enacted in the social forum process and correspond to one of the core tensions of the WSFs—Is the social forum a space or an actor? The chapter concludes with reflections on the USSF held in the summer of 2007, a most monumental event for the United States as we join the world in the struggle against empire and more deeply embrace human rights.

GLOBALIZING HUMAN RIGHTS ABUSES: A LOSS IN CAPABILITIES

"Empire" as a term and concept reentered public and academic vocabulary to describe the external and internal actions of the U.S. government in recent decades (Hardt and Negri 2000). Once a politically unpopular position, many now openly defend U.S. hegemony—supporting the expansion of the U.S. military and bolstering the economically privileged U.S. position through the transnational reach of its corporations and as a center of consumption (Ferguson 2003). These academics and policymakers suggest that U.S. global dominance is a positive dynamic that will benefit not only the United States, but also all of humanity by extending democracy and human rights.

Critiques of ethnocentric U.S. foreign and domestic policies, including those by political leaders, scholars, and activists, have used the term "empire" most emphatically to direct people's attention to the overwhelming extension of U.S. government power throughout the world and toward its citizens (Mann 2003). Their discussions reveal the false face of democracy the United States presents, the power of U.S. weaponry deployed on poor nations, and the very weak record of the United States in defending and enabling human rights. The bold actions of U.S. political abuse as witnessed in Guatemala and other Central American nations in the 1980s and Iraq currently or the political neglect of U.S. policymakers as in Taliban-controlled Pakistan almost a decade before September 11, 2001, or in the massacres in Rwanda and the death toll in Somalia are decisive examples for appreciating the United States as a rogue state that acts as an empire.

Neoliberalism, globalization, or the project to reassert political and economic power in the hands of elites was ushered in under U.S. president Ronald Reagan in conjunction with Margaret Thatcher, England's prime minister at the time, the International Monetary Fund (IMF), and the World Bank (Harvey 2006). Under this collaborative partnership referred to as the Washington Consensus, the IMF and World Bank became the key entities to entrench the world in a global economy and political systems that rely on human rights violations.

The IMF and the WB set up in 1944 under the Breton Woods Agreements were to resuscitate Europe's shattered economy after World War II and assist newly independent nations to advance their economies that were underdeveloped due to colonialism. The structure of these agreements was shaped to a large extent by the theoretical articulation of John Maynard Keynes in *The General Theory of Employment, Interest, and Money* (1936), a very important volume that continues to influence social and economic thought. Keynes's analyses, or Keynesianism, were guided generally by an interest in bolstering government's ability to manage capitalist expansion in the interest of preserving the purchasing power of labor and improving their work conditions. Despite this influence, the international agencies established at the meeting of political and economic elites in Bretton Woods, New Hampshire, were the maintenance of U.S. or Western dominance.

For an assortment of reasons, including the revival of Europe's economy and Japan's success as an economic competitor, U.S. failure and the high death toll of U.S. citizens in Vietnam, the continuation of the cold war, the rise of the civil rights and black power movements, and the formation of the Organization of the Petroleum Exporting Countries (OPEC) in 1973, U.S. hegemony was politically threatened and economically challenged. In the late seventies, the power gained by the masses was palpable—throughout the world national governments were ready to challenge U.S. dominance, and U.S. citizens, particularly women, working folks, and people of color, were making claims to the social rights they had struggled to achieve.

In response, U.S. capitalists and political leaders with economic and political elites worldwide set out to reassert their prominence. And the reinforcement of racist, sexist, and patriarchal stereotypes paved the road to globalization (Escobar 1995). Workers are paid less and marginalized based on their nationhood or immigrant status, race, gender, and sexual orientation. In the Global North work has been restructured so that there is less pay, fewer benefits, and less security. The Global South has been subject to structural adjustment programs (SAPs). SAPs require Global South nations to drastically cut back their expenditures on social goods such as health and education, privatize government holdings and entities that often get purchased by foreign capital, typically companies from the United States and the European Union (EU), and require nations to accept trade agreements that inevitably favor large Northern nations and their corporations.

This international system of labor and profit renders the poorest and most low-income workers, usually women from the Global South, expendable (Mies 1999).

These workers are paid so little and work in dangerous health conditions for extended hours so that a larger profit can be earned from their labor. The fact that these workers can easily die or be debilitated from their work environment does not influence the corporate actor who recognizes that his customers, who must be kept alive and well, live on opposite (distant?) shores.

THE HUMAN RIGHTS REVIVAL

The empires of the past extracted foodstuffs and goods from the hard and forced labor of its peasants, occupied and ravaged lands to meet ever-growing material excesses, and mounted violent retaliations against uprisings by the exploited. Similarly, neoliberalism or the top-down globalization the world has been experiencing for almost three decades *depends* upon the inhumane treatment of people and gives scarcely a consideration for stewarding the earth's ecology to sustain life. The rights to water, housing, and living wages are systematically disparaged for the sake of corporate profit.

Like the IMF and WB, the Universal Declaration of Human Rights by the UN General Assembly in 1948 was created in the wake of World War II atrocities, marking for many the international legitimacy of human rights. And like the IMF and WB, which were retooled by political and economic elites to act more specifically in the interest of hypercapitalist accumulation, the UN Declaration of Human Rights and follow-up conventions also have been reimagined, but instead by global civil society to fight the daily injustices of neoliberalism and top-down globalization. "Victims of the global economy are using human rights politically and legally to articulate their demands" (Mertus 2006, 6).

A wide net of nations and peoples can be cast as the victims of the global economy, and the United Nations and the International Labor Organization (ILO) have emerged to articulate a broad array of human rights (Blau and Moncada 2005). To a great extent the agreements, treaties, and proposals of these nations counterpose the policies and programs of the IMF and World Bank. In addition, found in the new constitutions of many African and Latin American nations are expressions of social justice that are not even readable into the Constitution of the United States and other Northern nations. Yet, a major critique of these well-thought-out articulations of human rights is the lack of teeth these agencies and governments have had in implementing them both on the ground and in their bureaucracies.

The WSF process stands as a separate entity in the struggle for human rights and a stance against neoliberalism. We may well see that its teeth are sharklike, with sets of replacement teeth in reserve, catapulting efforts through grassroots trans-national exchanges to define these rights by enacting human rights in the forum process and by developing proposals and strategies based on action to make human rights possible. There are various factors that pushed the WSF into being. Some key precursors to the WSF are (1) the protests throughout the Global South as the IMF structural adjustment policies pressed the already poor by forcing fiscal austerity, (2) the transnational women's and feminist movements that initiated after the Beijing Conference for Women in 2005, (3) the global protests marked by the Zapatista resistance to NAFTA in 1994 and in 1999 in Seattle, Washington, against the WTO, and (4) dissatisfaction with the UN system in making lasting social change (Smith et al. 2007).

The WSFs are scheduled purposely at the end of January to counter the World Economic Forum in Davos, Switzerland, an annual set of meetings of economic and capitalist elites that has occurred for the last few decades and at which major decisions regarding the global economy are made. While anti-Davos protests had become a regular protest in Europe, it was not until 1999 that European and Brazilian groups forged an alliance. European organizations, such as the Association for the Taxation of Financial Transactions for the Aid of Citizens (ATTAC); Brazilian-based social movements, especially the Brazilian Landless Movement (MST); and the Brazilian state through the Partidos dos Trabathadores (PT), the Brazilian worker party that controlled the city government collaborated and brought the WSF into being (Glasius and Timms 2006). It was in 2002 that the social forum process extended beyond the international and burst into multiple regional, national, and local forums throughout the world, but most heavily in Latin America and Europe (Conway 2005).

DEFINING HUMAN RIGHTS

Determining a credible understanding of human rights that can be agreed upon across cultures and across nations obviously is not an easy task. Those who promote a universal set of human rights—rights that apply to all individuals regardless of characteristics— believe that this is the only strategy for assuring that "the sovereignty of humanity supersedes the sovereignty of the state" and to deter "dominant social groups from protecting their rights to the neglect of the rights of less powerful" (Weston 2006, 41). Various debates surround the foundation of human rights, yet underlying universalism is a belief in a common vision of justice that is an expression of all humanity.

While the call to a global set of rights seems honorable, there are many who criticize what they define as a human rights regime. Some of these criticisms stem from the original Western-based orientation of the Declaration of Human Rights and other UN Human Rights conventions, which as foundations for capitalist liberal democracies, preclude their applicability to wider struggles of injustices. Although the United Nations, to a considerable extent, serves as the locus for a host of treaties that have expanded human rights far beyond the Vienna conference in 1948. The institution is limited by the implementation of human rights treaties with the economic policies and programs of the IMF, WB, and WTO, led by officials with uncanny visions of human rights.

Most striking is the experience of postcolonial nations with Northern-based development agencies, the IMF, and WB that historically have prescribed solutions to local problems with very little input from those on the ground (Escobar 1994). Many international policymakers and professionals, who argue for and attempt to implement international standards, are guilty of having "Western eyes" with which they gaze upon nations of the Global South as a monolithic entity mired in economic and social problems that were created by the weakness of the society, culture, or political leaders (Mohanty 1991).

An appreciation of how colonialism shapes social systems and economic opportunities across the globe is often missing in Global North policymakers who offer solutions or prescriptions to improve the living conditions by Global South nations. Intertwined with racist and sexist stereotypes, the negative perspective of the Global South is so embedded in U.S. media outlets and educational systems that many in the United States are hardly able to accept the agency and personhood of Global South nations, limiting the opportunity for a real exchange on the meaning of something so profound as human rights.

Burns H. Weston (2006, 27), a human rights scholar, argues that for a universal human rights project to take hold "dialogue across cultures and societies is an essential component of any international project and brings to life every single major human rights convent, convention, and declaration." He offers a "methodology of respect" to support dialogue between those who support a universal vision of human rights and those who prefer a more culturally specific set of human rights.

Weston seems to miss that the WSFs are the contemporary space in which the meaning, expanse, and applicability of human rights have been discussed respectfully for the last seven years. Groups, organizations, and activists from the Global South have claimed the concept of human rights despite its rhetorical use by the U.S. government to deploy more troops and dictate nations' economic policies. They have created the space at the WSF and other national and regional forums to talk to each other and with groups and organizations from the Global North on equal footing and on specific issues of human rights. At the social forums, organizations collaborate on articulating a broad application of rights on issues such as housing, safe labor conditions, clean water, food sovereignty, immigrants, and gender equality.

The social forum space has evolved over the last several years. The Charter of Principles, thematic shifts, the relocation of the forum around the globe, and the development of self-organized events are some of the key conditions that make this space possible. The Charter of Principles stipulates that any "civil society" organization that renounces neoliberalism and imperialism, affirms the doctrine of human rights, and commits itself to nonviolent tactics of resistance may participate in a social forum. In several of the principles it is reiterated that the WSF is not a decision-making body but a space for organizations and groups from various perspectives to exchange ideas. Though written in the aftermath of the first World Social Forum in 2001, the charter serves as the blueprint for gatherings bearing the name "social forum."

The social forums are not static; they innovate in order to engage the entire globe in a discussion of human rights. They have particularly highlighted the voice of the Global South. As the first location of the WSFs, Porto Alegre, Brazil, is etched in the minds of global activists as the first space for a new world of global justice. While attendees from around the globe came to Porto Alegre, they arrived primarily from Latin America. The decision to move the forum to Mumbai, India, in 2004 was to engage South Asia and Asia and address the tremendous poverty and civil injustices that exist in these regions. After returning to Porto Alegre in 2005, a polycentric forum was held in 2006 to simultaneously engage several continents, and in 2007, the WSF relocated to Africa to engage some of the poorest nations. Purposefully engaging the most marginalized in discussions of human rights and the global future is clearly a thoughtful and provocative strategy. It permits a grounded discussion and debate on human rights and the development of a truly collective consciousness of what these rights mean in different contexts, how they overlap, and how they might be universally defined.

The nation or region in which forums are held also determines who attends and the thematic focus of the forums. For instance, the prominence of indigenous rights was central for the first Social Forum of the Americas (SFA) held in Quito, Ecuador, in 2004 and will be highlighted in the next SFA, which is scheduled for October 2008 in Guatemala City, Guatemala. Each of the six WSFs and the polycentric forums in 2005 were organized around several particular themes or thematic terrains or axes that were identified by organizing bodies as fundamental for creating global social change. The themes of the WSF show that for the first two years, economically driven or political themes organized the program (see Table 18.1).

In 2003, values, human rights, diversity, and antimilitarism were added to the four original themes, reflecting the growing participation of grassroots activists who widened the scope of the WSF. Another significant change made to the programming of the WSF in 2003 was the development of self-organized events. Rather than the WSF committees organizing the events at the forum, groups and organizations that attend organize events independently or in conjunction with other groups. For example, if a group registered to participate in the Nairobi Forum, they were allotted up to four time periods in which they could organize an event using their own formatting, invite speakers or not, and focus on the topic of their choice.

Glasius and Timms (2006, 190) explain that the social forum is not only a space that brings people together to engage in political discussion but also "a space that facilitates people coming together, either in person or virtually, to engage with each other on political issues" using participatory and democratic principles. The self-organized events continued to expand, and by 2005 all events at the World Social Forum were self-organized or organized in conjunction with organizations. In regional and national forums, the organizing and planning committees may construct events in the forum, but the majority of events are self-organized.

The Nairobi WSF in 2007 departed from other forums—thematic terrains moved to Objectives for Actions "around which all struggles, actions, and alternatives are made visible and strengthen" (WSF Program 2007, 167). Approximately ten objectives for actions organized the program of WSF 2007, and these were further broken into twenty-one "actionable themes." The fourth and last day of the forum was devoted entirely to facilitate platforms for action, permitting organizations from around the world to present and discuss openly their proposals for action in one of twenty-one miniforums—a clear example of a "methodology of respect" (see Table 18.2). A large open meeting followed in which all WSF attendees could participate and listen to the series of proposals lifted from the small meetings that preceded it. The Nairobi Forum further established the WSF process as a collective definer of human rights, one that is willing to navigate the murky waters of globalization to determine concrete actions that can foment real social change.

Table 18.1 Trajectory of Themes at the World Social Forum, 2001–2006

Themes/ Axes*	2001	2002	2003	2004	2005	2006 Caracas
Wealth production and social reproduction	X	X				X
Access to wealth and sustainability	X	X	X		X	
Civil society and media	X	X	X	X	X	X
Political power and democracy	X	X	X		X**	X
Principles and values, human rights, diversity, and equality			X	X	X**	X
Antimilitarism and promoting peace			X	X	X	
Democracy, ecological and economic security				X		
Natural resources as alternatives to commodification					X	X
Arts creation and culture					X	
Ethics, cosmovisions and spiritualities					X	
Autonomous thought, reappropriation, and socialization of knowledge and techologies					X	

Notes:
* The themes/axes as listed are based on the WSF official themes. Beginning with 2003 the wording of the themes/axes varies from year to year.
** Two themes have been collapsed into one category.

CAPABILITIES AND THE SOCIAL FORUM AS ACTOR

The social forum process has succeeded in creating a global public space for groups worldwide to come together—but how will this lead to transformative social change? Scholars engaged in the human rights debate have also asked a similar question: How can human rights actually be implemented? Emphasizing that human rights is a concept that lacks theoretical and conceptual clarity (Nussbaum 2006), scholars focus on the capabilities of a person to act upon her right as a way of concretizing the concept of human rights.

In *Development as Freedom* (2000), Amartya Sen lays out the grounds for what has evolved into the capabilities approach. His emphasis is on individuals and their

Table 18.2 Objectives for Actions and Actionable Themes at the WSF 2007

Objectives for Actions	Actionable Themes
Memory of struggles and resistance	Water National/international institutions and democracy
Housing	Peace/war Housing
Life before profits: Demystifying and defeating AIDS/HIV	Women's struggles Dignity/human diversity/discrimination
Knowledge and information	Human rights Youth
Defeating the empire for a just and peaceful world	Food sovereignty/land reform Labor
Toward a world without borders: Challenging the international apartheid—Migration and diaspora	Education Environment and energy Health Knowledge/information/communication
Global environmental and common goals	Debt Migrations
Dignified labor for a just world	Free trade Culture
Women	Transnational corporations
Living alternatives	Children Alternative economies

freedom to live a life based on their values or preferred lifestyle. In other words, a person is not free when he or she does not hold the capability to achieve a desired goal. For example, homelessness occurs because of the lack of opportunity to hold a job or have an affordable rent that keeps them from safe housing. Sen's analyses speak to neoclassical economists, who, in dictating much economic policy, fully neglect opportunities and focus solely on outcomes. The capabilities approach has been utilized by scholars to convey that human rights cannot be achieved without the conditions that will allow individuals to engage them.

Nussbaum, who has built on the capabilities approach explicitly, explains that Article 28 of the Universal Declaration of Human Rights states, "Everyone is entitled to a social and international order in which the rights and freedoms set forth in this declaration can be fully realized." But as she explains, these rights and freedoms cannot be realized "unless and until the social, economic, and political conditions prevailing domestically and internationally ensure each rights-holder the combined capability to exercise the rights he or she may desire" (Nussbaum 2006, 34). Unlike Sen who suggests that a society requires a process for distinguishing appropriate capabilities as a measurement for just and free individuals, Nussbaum (2000) emphasizes humanness and argues for a basic set of "capabilities" as a core for a dignified life.

The capabilities approach is an instructive direction for human rights debates because it may ensure that human rights is something more than what is written on paper (Nussbaum 2006). Yet while those who write on capabilities, like Nussbaum and Sen, understand the importance of implementing programs that can practically ensure human rights or freedom, they seem less clear on how the global system of oppression begun during colonization and embedded in globalization fundamentally limits the distribution of human rights. Sen, in particular, embedded in rationality and individualism, seems to overlook the history of social justice movements (Unterhalter 2003) that were privy to an understanding of capabilities or the necessity of the freedoms to pursue one's life goals (whether this be food, shelter, a family, or a professional job), before he articulated them. While recommendations for foreign aid and technical cooperation may do some good toward enabling human rights (Nussbaum 2006), ending the debt slavery of the Global South and free trade agreements, shutting down the WTO, and reducing the power of corporations to dictate global policy seem to be some of the actions necessary to develop the capabilities of human rights.

At least these are some of the suggestions made by the groups and organizations that attend the social forums and sponsor events. These groups center on corporate-led globalization, and while they experience inequality and human rights abuses daily and locally, they emphasize the larger global conditions that have created them. Like the capabilities approach to human rights, many WSFers are calling for action to make the changes necessary so that all people can lead a humane life, and they are also grappling with where and how that change will be brought about.

Some contend that the WSF needs to rise as an actor to push forth a global agenda of human rights. President Hugo Chavez made this call in 2006 at the polycentric forum in Venezuela at which he chided WSF participants for languishing in dialogue without visible action. Social forum actors resist and protest, and alter the shape of the social forum events. Participants in the first WSF, critical of elitism, marched into designated VIP rooms chanting, "We are all VIPS, We are all VIPS," ending the practice of roped-off spaces. Small grassroots groups and anarchists protested the control of large institutional NGOs at the European Social Forum by creating "autonomous spaces" that surrounded the official forum.

While change has been enacted internally at the forums, the grassroots pull toward action and change has led to the formation of the Social Movement Assemblies as a method by which to coordinate global action. The Social Movement Assembly almost serves as a compromise between those who would like to maintain the WSF as space for networking, exchange, and dialogue and those who would like to see the WSF take a more active political role. Throughout a social forum, participants are invited to submit resolutions, declarations, and demands. These are then presented at the Social Movement Assembly, scheduled as the very last event of the forum and open for all participants to present proposals. Many of the proposals request participants to engage in global, national, or regional days of action, join a campaign on an urgent political struggle, and support protests on particular trade policies or human rights abuses. The last edition of the WSF clearly embodies the push toward global action.

While many human rights researchers agree that "as the world globalizes no positive transformation of the human rights situation of ordinary people will occur without a social movement for those rights" (Howard-Hassman 2006, 56), they are unable to distinguish a method by which human rights abuses can be redressed—"the mechanisms for the enforcement of human rights are still in their infancy" (Weston 2006, 304). Yet in working out solutions, many of these researchers continue to believe that neoliberal globalization is "not only inevitable, it is the only path to long-term economic growth" (Howard-Hussman 2005, 53). Indeed, the emphasis on globalization's permanency by scholars and the mainstream media should not be overlooked as a critical factor in how they decide to pursue social justice (Smith 2007).

The movements that contribute to the social forum process are also grappling with solutions to the current state of the world and the long line of human rights abuses. At the social forums, activists, experienced in being shortchanged on rights, struggle to articulate and enact conditions that are necessary for leading a fully human life, whether this means access to education, safe drinking water, political expression, or a nice green field to plant a garden or run through. We are at a pivotal moment in humanity's struggle for justice. How do we make it happen? New ideas are needed—for new forms of governance, for new shapes of economies, and for upholding the principle of human rights—they are being discussed at social forums as "we make our path by walking."

Those engaged in the social forum process are not waiting for those in the realm of power, policymakers and legal experts, to make policies that will ensure human rights. While many of the organizations that attend the social forums are members of several networks that are part of a wider web of nesting networks with connections to major international nongovernmental organizations (INGOs) such as the Third World Institute (Blau and Moncada 2005), participation in the social forums builds a sense of grassroots global justice that grounds human rights in real-life conditions that, while not completely disconnected, often get lost in policy making. Most of those engaged in the social forum process not only believe that another world is possible beyond economic globalization; they are ready to make it happen. It may be that grassroots networks of human rights in the Global South, through their demands, have inspired the capabilities approach. Nussbaum suggests that educating "learners" on the causes of their deprivation can lead them to "tak[e] control of the transformation of that reality until they attain a higher level of capability" (Nussbaum 2006, 28). That may be good advice, but it overlooks the knowledge base of persons living in conditions of deprivation and their awareness of the contextual limitations of their personal ability to create transformation. The high attendance at the social forums attests to a global understanding that a larger or more connected body of struggles for human rights is necessary.

THE U.S. SOCIAL FORUM AND HUMAN RIGHTS

As many chapters in this volume illuminate, exceptionalism is the U.S. hallmark on human rights. Human rights are deployed to the rest of the world, while the United States maintains state sovereignty. The unwillingness of the United States to sign treaties or be judged in a world judicial body also demonstrates its self-serving understanding of international agreements and leanings toward empire. Yet while books are written on the exceptionalism of the United States, the nation's deteriorating economic conditions, its miserly stance on immigration, the loss of good jobs for college graduates, the interference with civil rights by the PATRIOT Act, and the impact of Katrina on New Orleans and Gulf Coast residents have ushered in a new appreciation of human rights and the global economy by U.S. citizens.

This was fully articulated at the first U.S. Social Forum that took place in Atlanta, Georgia, in the summer of 2007. What happened at the USSF fulfilled the hopes and long hours of labor that activists and organizers across the United States put into the social forum process. The USSF was not an elite-run event; instead the poor, low-income, immigrant, and otherwise marginalized U.S. population were in attendance and on the panels. The language of "rights" was widely used in smaller self-organized events and in the larger events organized by the National Planning Committee. Located in the center meeting point of the USSF was an "Immigration Rights Tent," a "Right to Water Tent," and a "Poor People's Economic Human Rights Tent." In fact, almost 5 percent of the listed events used the term "rights" in their titles.

The USSF is the first ever national grassroots dialogue on social justice campaigns that began to bridge the deep sectorial divisions between environment and labor, gay and trans rights, migration, indigenous rights, and Latinos/as and African Americans even as it was being organized. Underlying the USSF was the People's Movement Assembly (PMA) that, like the social movement assemblies, organized the proposals, declarations, and calls for participation to be presented to the larger group on the last day of the forum.

What was widely recognized at the forum was the depth of injustices that were occurring within the United States. The social forums are an educational space, and no matter how well read you might be, you will always learn more by attending a social forum. The Global Day of Action January 26, 2008, drove the PMA. Coordinated by planning committees of the WSF, the Global Day of Action was to replace the off year of a single WSF with events organized by groups in their local communities, nationally, or regionally to demonstrate global solidarity in the struggle for human rights and justice.

CONCLUSION

The value of dialogue and the impetus to action are beholden to human rights advocates inside and outside of the social forum process. The growth of the WSF since 2001 suggests that many social justice advocates hold a refined awareness that global solidarity over human rights is the baton passed to those of us living in the twenty-first century (Vasak 1977; Weston 2006). The social forum process is the self-conscious enactment of globally envisioned human rights in forum spaces that organizations, movements, and participants bring to the forums, broaden, and return to their local and global communities. Components of this process are both structurally and politically driven, but more important is that the social forums express a culture of human rights in practice.

Procedurally and topically, human rights prove to be the lynchpins in the social forum process. The program and happenings of social forums are reflected and critiqued by organizers, commented on and protested by participants, and then altered where needed to open the forum to a wider net of participation, whether this requires being more inclusive of particular groups, such as increasing the representation of women on panels or relocating the forum to allow greater regional diversity and provide access to those marginalized from easy international travel. The forums have been fairly fluid and provide a wonderful methodology for creating respectful dialogues across a gamut of differences.

Our current moment in history is clearly one that requires action. Advocates of the capabilities approach to human rights and those who advocate the WSF to take an active political stance especially taste the bitter immediacy of the human rights violations and abuses perpetrated by the United States that need to be reigned in now. It may be at the nexus of the legacy of human rights conventions and declarations and the social forum process that the move forward on human rights will occur. The WSFs may eventually be heralded for moving the call for human rights away from academic debates, out of the speeches of U.S. policymakers, and into the streets, fields, forests, and valleys of the world.

REFERENCES

Blau, Judith, and Alberto Moncada. 2005. *Human Rights: Beyond the Liberal Vision.* Lanham, MD: Rowman & Littlefield.

Conway, Janet. 2005. "Social Forums, Social Movements, and Social Change: A Response to Peter Marcuse on the Subject of the World Social Forum." *International Journal of Urban and Regional Research* 29:2: 425–428.

Escobar, Arturo. 1995. *Encountering Development: The Making and Unmaking of the Third World.* Princeton, NJ: Princeton University Press.

Glasius, Marlies, and Jill Timms. 2006. "The Role of Social Forums in Global Civil Society: Radical Beacon or Strategic Infrastructure?" Pp. 190–236 in *Global Civil Society,* edited by Marlies Glasius, Mary Kaldor, Helmut Anheier, and Frona Holland. London: Sage.

Hammonds, John L. 2006. "The Possible World and the Actual State: The World Social Forum in Caracas." *Latin American Perspectives* 148, no. 33: 122–131.

Hardt, Michael, and Antonio Negri. 2000. *Empire.* Cambridge, MA: Harvard University Press.

Harvey, David. 2006. *A Brief History of Neoliberalism.* London: Oxford University Press.

Howard-Hassmann, Rhoda. 2006. "The Second Great Transformation: Human Rights Leap-Frogging in the Era of Globalization." Pp. 53–62 in *Human Rights in the World Community: Issues and Action,* edited by Richard Pierre Claude and Burns H. Weston. Philadelphia: University of Pennsylvania Press.

Mann, Michael. 2003. *Incoherent Empire.* London: Verso.

Mies, Maria. 1999. *Patriarchy and Accumulation on a World Scale: Women in the International Division of Labor.* New York: Zed Books.

Mertus, Julie A. 2006. *Bait and Switch: Human Rights and U.S. Foreign Policy.* London: Routledge.

Mohanty, Chandra. 1991. "Under Western Eyes: Feminist Scholarship and Colonial Discourses." Pp. 51–79 in *Third World Women and the Politics of Feminism,* edited by Chandra Mohanty, Anna Russo, and Lourdes Torres. Bloomington: Indiana University Press.

Nussbaum, Martha. 2006. "Capabilities, Human Rights, and the Universal Declaration." Pp. 27–36 in *Human Rights in the World Community: Issues and Action,* edited by Richard Pierre Claude and Burns H. Weston. Philadelphia: University of Pennsylvania Press.

———. 2000. *Women and Human Development.* Cambridge, UK: Cambridge University Press.

Sen, Amartya. 2000. *Development as Freedom.* Oxford University Press.

———. 2002. *Rationality and Freedom.* Cambridge, MA: Harvard University Press.

Smith, Jackie. 2007. "Economic Globalization and Strategic Peacebuilding." Paper presented at the Annual Meetings of the American Sociological Association, August, New York City.

Smith, Jackie, Marina Karides, Marc Becker, Christopher Chase Dunn, Dorval Brunelle, Donnatella Della Porta, Rosalba Icaza, Jeffrey Juris, Lorenzo Mosca, Ellen Reese, Jay Smith, Rolando Vasquez. 2007. *The World Social Forums and the Challenges for Global Democracy.* Boulder, CO: Paradigm Publishers.

Unterhalter, Elaine. 2003. "Crossing Disciplinary Boundaries: The Potential of Sen's Capabilities Approach for Sociologists of Education." *British Journal of Sociology of Education* 24: 665–669.

Vasak, Karel. 1977. "Human Rights: A Thirty-Year Struggle: The Sustained Efforts to Give Force of Law to the Universal Declaration of Human Rights," in *UNESCO Courier* 30, Paris: UNESCO.

Weston, Burns H. 2006a. "Human Rights: Concept and Content." Pp. 27–36 in *Human Rights in the World Community: Issues and Action,* edited by Richard Pierre Claude and Burns H. Weston. Philadelphia: University of Pennsylvania Press.

———. 2006b. "The Universality of Human Rights in a Multicultured World." Pp. 39–51 in *Human Rights in the World Community: Issues and Action,* edited by Richard Pierre Claude and Burns H. Weston. Philadelphia: University of Pennsylvania Press.

World Social Forum. 2007. *The World Social Forum Program.* 7th ed. Nairobi, Kenya.

ADDITIONAL RESOURCES

United States Social Forum:
   www.ussf2007.org.
World Social Forum:
   http://www.forumsocialmundial.org.br.

CHAPTER NINETEEN

~

Freedom and Security

JUDITH BLAU AND ALBERTO MONCADA

Civil and political rights are often juxtaposed with economic and social rights, but that is not because they rest on different principles. Indeed, they rest on the same identical principles, and they are enshrined as mutually interdependent and reinforcing rights in the 1948 Universal Declaration of Human Rights. It was the United States that made this crisp distinction, favoring civil and political rights and dismissing economic, social, and cultural rights. This was not always the case. In fact, President Franklin Delano Roosevelt in his 1944 State of the Union Address proposed "An Economic Bill of Rights" that fully embraced economic and social rights (see Blau and Moncada 2006; Sunstein 2004). Although he died shortly afterward and his proposal never made it out of congressional committees, the fact that he could propose it to the nation suggests that Americans were favorably disposed to the idea that rights were indivisible and that people's freedoms depended on such indivisibility and coherence. The Great Depression and war years had taken a great toll on all Americans, and besides that there were strong feelings of solidarity.

The cold war changed all this, basically by politicizing human rights. The ideological message was that Americans had unique freedoms, including the freedoms of consumption, employment, competition, entrepreneurship, and capitalist freedoms, whereas the socialist system was one of tyranny, oppression, and the denial of freedom. To enforce this contrast, children had to hide under their desks at school, in closets at home, and to pray for agnostic Russian souls. The House Committee on Un-American Activities, chaired by Senator Joseph McCarthy, embarked on a fierce witch-hunt, accusing authors, filmmakers, artists, teachers, and others of being communists, and finally broadening its net to accuse government bureaucrats and military officers. McCarthy was finally forced to resign in infamy, but the lasting legacy of this period—the cold war—was the sharp break between, on the one hand, freedoms—civil and political rights—and on the other hand, security—economic and social rights. Capitalism was a "moral" system for "moral" Americans, and it rested on assumptions about freedoms, eschewing assumptions about rights.

The Europeans, our practical, but hardly our ideological, allies, did not see the world exactly in these same terms. Beginning in the postwar decade, they started implementing varieties of welfare plans ("social democracies"), providing their citizens with economic security, codetermination in the workplace, housing rights, pension plans, assistance with education, health care, and labor protections. Whereas Americans were led to believe that market freedoms and political freedoms were cut of one cloth, Europeans felt that personal freedoms were best achieved when people were buffered from the excesses and rawness of capitalism.

THE INDIVISIBILITY OF RIGHTS

The human rights perspective does not abstract people according to their functional roles in the polity and economy, but rather grants persons freedoms and self-determination and recognizes their integral social, economic, and cultural needs and their social, economic, and collective responsibilities. Thus, among the consequences of acting in terms of rights it enlarges the spaces for cooperation and collaboration, encourages new projects that enhance popular democracy and economic fairness, and allows people and groups to contribute in ways that are consistent with their distinctive interests, capabilities, and strengths.

Economic and social rights, political and civil rights, environmental rights, and cultural rights are thus indivisible and interdependent, making up an integral set of rights that ensures full equality and underscores each person's self-determining agency and the responsibilities they have to others. Aside from the responsibilities that people have in their communities to ensure equality of rights, human rights accompany the obligation, often met by states, to protect vulnerable groups and individuals. There is, for example, an emphasis on the rights of children, the elderly, and the disabled. In principle there is no distinction either between human rights provisions and humanitarian laws, but because crimes against humanity, war crimes, apartheid, and genocide are such atrocious violations they are handled within their own distinct legal framework. The point to be made here is that human rights compose a coherent and unified logic, and because human rights advance human security they also advance human freedom, which no competitive economic system possibly can do.

THE ICCPR AND THE ICESCR

The stated goal in 1948 when the UN General Assembly proclaimed the Universal Declaration of Human Rights was to redraft the declaration as a single treaty, a legal standard that could help to clarify worldwide norms regarding state responsibilities to their citizens, standards for employment and social security, and common standards for legal protections. The United States signed the UDHR, and indeed, Eleanor Roosevelt chaired the committee that drafted it. Yet within a few short years the United States became adamantly opposed to its provisions for economic, social, and cultural rights. The United States held its ground until it got its way and the declaration was divided into two treaties: the International Covenant on Civil and Political Rights (ICCPR) and the International Covenant on Economic, Social and Cultural Rights (ICESCR). Most countries in the world have ratified both, whereas the United States (conditionally) ratified only the ICCPR. Here we must emphasize that U.S. opposition to the ICESCR is not simply legalistic, as is its ambivalence to the ICCPR, but deep and profound, as we will clarify below. First, we describe the similarities and differences between the two covenants. The ICESCR embraces the rights of women, labor, and children, and the rights to housing, health care, and education.

First, it is important to mention that the preambles of the two charters as well as Articles 1, 3, and 5 are virtually identical. The preambles recall the foundation of freedom, justice, and peace, and they recall the inherent dignity and the equal and inalienable rights of all members of the human family. Article 1 of each covenant states that all people have the right to self-determination and calls upon states to promote the realization of that right and to respect it. Article 3 is also identical and affirms the equal rights of men and women. Article 5, in both cases, provides safeguards against the destruction or undue limitation of any human right or fundamental freedom.

The ICCPR includes all the protections that the U.S. Constitution does, including freedom of association, equality before the law, right to speech and conscience, protections from arbitrary arrest, and protections in criminal and civil proceedings. Yet the ICCPR goes further than the U.S. Constitution in several respects, including prohibition of torture and other cruel or degrading punishment; prohibition of the death penalty; eliminating contract violation as grounds for imprisonment; prohibition of propaganda for war; recognition of the rights of children; and protection of the rights of ethnic, religious, and linguistic minorities.

A total of 160 countries have ratified the ICCPR, including the United States, but there is a hitch with the U.S. ratification. Whenever the United States ratifies a UN Treaty, an ILO Convention, or any other international instrument, it adds as a reservation that "it is not self-executing." In other words, until the United States passes enabling legislation, which it never does in the case of human rights treaties including labor conventions, it does not recognize them. The United States recognizes no international human rights treaty whatsoever. This is unconscionable. Because the United States has not ratified the ICESCR and has exempted itself from the ICCPR and from all other treaties, the United States can play no legitimate role in human rights discussions in the United Nations and, sadly, Americans have become isolated from international discussions related to human rights.

AMERICAN FREEDOM AS CREATION MYTH

Almost all societies have creation myths. The Aztecs believe that Coatlique was first impregnated by an obsidian knife and gave birth to Coyolxanuhqui, goddess of the moon, and to a group of male offspring, who became the stars. In the Navaho creation myth, First Man ('Altsé Hastiin) and First Woman ('Altsé 'Asdzáá) were two of the beings from the First or Black World. First Man was made in the east from the meeting of the white and black clouds. First Woman was made in the west from the joining of the yellow and blue clouds. It might be said that the functional equivalent of a creation myth for the white settlers in America and for subsequent generations was the story about freedom and liberty. Americans return to it time after time, when recounting their war of independence from Great Britain, conquering the frontier, stories about the struggles of immigrants, landing a man on the moon, America's entrepreneurial spirit, the American inventor, and the embodiment of individual courage and personal initiative. It is a tradition to be proud of, and people around the world admire Americans, partly because this love of freedom accompanies equalitarian and anti-authoritarian attitudes.

When cold war politicians, like McCarthy, pitched an appeal to Americans, they used two code words—freedom and liberty. When one of his fiercest opponents, Senator Margaret Chase Smith, drafted a declaration, dated June 1, 1950, she used the strongest language one could use in America, and fighting fire with fire, she said, "basic principles of Americanism—are the right to criticize, the right to hold unpopular beliefs, the right to protest, and the right of independent thought." For our purposes, the American creation myth that embraces freedom and other virtues is drawn upon by all sides—left, center, right, prowar, antiwar, procapitalism, and anticapitalism. This freedom myth mobilizes as nothing else possibly can in America.

When Americans are stressed, as they were after September 11, recalling the creation myth is comforting, as George W. Bush instinctively knew, and what he told Americans was, "They want to take our freedom away from us. Americans love freedom. They don't have freedom. Oh, and by the way, Go shopping." Bush's statements put down on paper look ludicrous, but his oral argument after September 11 seemed to have made a lot of sense to Americans. The air was aflutter with American flags—cars, houses, highway overpasses, buildings, fishing boats, and bicycles. As if to say, "No, they can't take my freedoms away from me."

FREEDOM AND SECURITY

When it became known that the U.S.-led invasion of Iraq was carried out under false pretenses and that Saddam Hussein did not have weapons of mass destruction (as Bush had known all along), Bush's high ratings in opinion polls began to drop. But none so far in the Senate has been brave enough to issue a declaration against him as Margaret Chase Smith did in 1950 against Joseph McCarthy. But then, it still might happen. We suspect that the case would have to be made on the basis of America's Creation Myth that Bush is threatening the freedoms of Americans. This was the heart of Chase's message to the Senate.

We have argued that freedom and independence are so salient that for Americans to support virtually anything, it needs to be consistent with their creation myth. Smith knew this. So did Franklin Delano Roosevelt, who, when proposing the Second Bill of

Rights, stated that "necessitous men are not free." He knew that his audience cherished freedom, and he also knew that in 1944 they would be thinking of the difficult years of the Great Depression. But we can update this because we live in different times. Globalization threatens the security of everyone on the planet. Multinationals close operations without warning, leaving massive numbers of unemployed behind, and free trade practices have created huge inequalities around the world. These days America's bridges collapse because there are precious few funds for infrastructural maintenance and repair. There is virtually no housing aid for the homeless in America, and when the homeless become ill, they often do not get medical treatment. Bit by bit, Americans are losing their security, and the loss of security is also the loss of freedom

Countries around the world are revising their constitutions to ensure greater security for their populations, and as the accompanying discussions and documents make clear, these revisions are largely in response to globalization and to some extent, to the threats posed by pending environmental catastrophes. These constitutional reforms go far to advance the welfare and security of citizens, and none impairs the freedoms of citizens. When a state constitution is revised, most typically the revision includes provisions for human rights (including labor rights, health care rights, protections against discrimination, and so forth), provisions that will promote greater democracy, and often provisions that will bolster cultural social pluralism. The U.S. Constitution is the oldest in the world—nothing to be proud of. Were the U.S. Constitution revised to encompass the full complement of rights, Americans would newly discover they have their freedoms.

REFERENCES

Blau, Judith, and Alberto Moncada 2006. *Justice in the U.S.: Human Rights and the U.S. Constitution.* Lanham, MD: Rowman and Littlefield.

Sunstein, Cass R, 2004. *The Second Bill of Rights: FDR's Unfinished Revolution and Why We Need It More Than Ever.* New York: Basic Books.

Postscript

JACK DONNELLY

The Leading Rogue State: The United States and Human Rights is an important book for a number of reasons that go well beyond the substance of the problems in the world and in American policy that it documents. At least three virtues merit special mention.

First, it is a book by and for sociologists. The scholarly and popular literatures on human rights have over the past three decades been dominated by legal and international perspectives. International lawyers make up the largest group of professional practitioners and academic analysts. Only in the subfields of international law and international relations is human rights a well-established mainstream perspective. Even in political science, relatively few specialists in comparative politics focus centrally and explicitly on human rights—even when they deal explicitly with issues that are appropriately understood as involving respect for or violation of internationally recognized human rights. This is even more true of sociology. Although one can point to exceptions—for example, Rhoda Howard Hassmann has been working primarily and explicitly on human rights since the early 1980s, and Bryan Turner has dealt recurrently with human rights since the early 1990s—human rights have been largely outside of the mainstream of the discipline. The engagement of sociology with human rights can only be a good thing for both.

For example, social stratification, a central, taken-for granted theme in Sociology, is oddly absent in much of the literature on human rights, which focuses excessively on the elaboration and implementation of international legal norms and national and international legal processes. As a result, human rights violations are too often presented as the unfortunate consequences of the actions of evil men, or the result of readily remedied institutional or legal problems, rather than a predictable consequence of social structures of inequality and domination. Human rights, as a subject of analysis and a matter of practice, can only benefit from the active engagement of a discipline that sees their fate as a matter of *social,* not merely legal and political, systems and practices.

As for the benefits to sociology, it is hard to see how the discipline cannot be invigorated by direct engagement with one of the hegemonic ideas of our time. Especially because sociology has long been dealing with the substance of the protection and violations of human rights, it is time for the discipline to do so directly. This book represents an exciting effort to do so across a wide range of topics.

Second, *The Leading Rogue State* is particular notable for Americans because it brings human rights home. Too many Americans think of human rights violations as problems that only occur in places that they have to fly over large bodies of salt water to reach. Other countries torture people. We have a problem with police brutality. And if it is done to the proper people, it is not a problem at all—as long as we observe the legal niceties of making sure that it is not done on American soil. Another common American attitude is that we "invented" human rights and thus whatever goes on in the United States simply is what human rights means. But as this book documents, over and over, there are real and important human rights issues, problems, and violations in all domains of American life. And the United States not merely violates but flouts human rights norms accepted throughout the rest of the world.

The American reluctance to use the language of human rights goes well beyond the refusal to recognize many internationally recognized economic, social, and cultural rights. As I was writing this postscript, the country was offered the spectacle of an ulti-mately successful nominee for attorney general who claimed to believe that it required extensive and apparently arcane legal research to determine whether it amounts to torture to tie suspects to an inclined board and pour water over them until it is forced into their lungs and they began to drown. He would not even say that whatever we call it, it is and ought to be illegal for Americans to do it to any human being anywhere.

The United States government applies international human rights standards freely, and at times even forcefully, to other countries. For example, for thirty years the State Department, by congressional mandate, has produced annual human rights country reports on the practices of all states that receive foreign assistance. And since the end of the Cold War, human rights diplomacy has become not merely a concern of "liberal" administrations but a nonpartisan element of American foreign policy. Yet international human rights norms are treated as if somehow not relevant to the domes-tic practices of the United States. This book loudly, repeatedly, and with considerable impact challenges these comfortable self-understandings.

Third, the book is critical, engaged, and intentionally provocative. It seeks out problems, not successes, and insists that this country should be judged as one specially committed to human rights. *The Leading Rogue State* does not provide a bal-anced account of successes and failures—because it does not try to do that. Rather, it laments the all too frequent failures of the United States, primarily domestically, but also internationally. And it cries out for a renewed commitment to the slogan, first popularized by the UN High Commissioner for Human Rights during the celebration of the fiftieth anniversary of the Universal Declaration of Human Rights, "all human rights for all"—even Americans.

As one would expect in a self-consciously critical volume that breaks new ground, there are problems. Rather than settle for demonstrating that American performance is grossly inadequate, individual authors often make indefensible claims that the United States is the worst in the world. In addition, too much attention is focused on introduc-ing international norms to sociologists rather than engaging in sociological analysis of the state of American human rights practice. Although understandable, given the unfamiliarity of many sociologists with a human rights perspective on their issue of substantive expertise, this means that many of the chapters do not provide the sort of model of sociological analysis that we should aspire to, and expect to see, in the next generation of work. And by largely passing over the failures of the United States with respect to civil and political rights, the volume misses an opportunity to document the full range of America's roguish behavior.

But despite occasional missteps, *The Leading Rogue State* represents a large and significant stride in a direction that can only benefit both sociology and the national and international struggles for human rights. In issue after issue, the contributors to this volume recap the relevant international standards and show the *systematic,* not merely accidental, failure of the United States to comply with these norms. And they admirably insist not only that international human rights norms apply to the United States but that this country in particular must be held to the highest level of performance.

Index

About the Editors
and Contributors

Damayanti Banerjee is an assistant professor of sociology at the University of Tennessee-Knoxville. She previously taught at Western Kentucky University. Damayanti received a PhD in sociology from the University of Wisconsin–Madison in 2006. She is interested in issues of human rights, environment, and social movements and has published multiple papers on these issues in leading journals in sociology.

John Barnshaw is research projects coordinator at Disaster Research Center and a doctoral student in the Department of Sociology and Criminal Justice at the University of Delaware. As projects coordinator, Barnshaw works with colleagues on a variety of research projects ranging from the evacuation of lower Manhattan during the September 11, 2001, World Trade Center attacks to the more recent evacuation of New Orleans in the aftermath of Hurricane Katrina. His research interests include stratification and inequality in a variety of social contexts ranging from disasters to educational tracking to infectious epidemiology. In addition to his research interests, Barnshaw has been involved in assisting local villagers in sustainable development projects in Mbita and Mfangano, Kenya, ranging from environmental improvement to microenterprise.

Judith Blau is coauthor, with Alberto Moncada, of *Human Rights: Beyond the Liberal Vision* (2005), *Justice in the United States* (2006), *Freedoms and Solidarities* (2006), and *Two Logics: Globalization and Human Rights* (2008). With Keri Iyall Smith, she is coeditor of *Public Sociologies Reader.* She also coedits *Societies without Borders* and is president of the U.S. chapter of Sociologists Without Borders. She is professor at the University of North Carolina–Chapel Hill.

David L. Brunsma is associate professor of sociology and black studies at the University of Missouri–Columbia. He is the author or editor of several books, including *The Sociology of Katrina: Perspectives on a Modern Catastrophe* (2007), *Beyond Black: Biracial Identity in America,* 2d. ed. (2007), *Mixed Messages: Multiracial Identity in the "Color-Blind" Era* (2006), and *The School Uniform Movement and What It Tells Us About American Education* (2004). He is a member of Sociologists Without Borders and is currently working on critical autoethnographies and a book on whites who have historically resisted white supremacy. He, his wife Rachel, and their three children live and love in Columbia, Missouri.

Rodney D. Coates was born in East St. Louis, Illinois, received his BA from Southern Illinois University, an MA in sociology and anthropology from the University of Illinois, and a second MA and PhD in sociology from the University of Chicago. He holds the rank of professor in the Department of Sociology and Gerontology, and for fifteen years directed the Black World Studies Program at Miami University. Dr. Coates specializes in the study of race and ethnic relations, inequality, critical race theory, and social justice. He has published dozens of articles; several edited books; and frequently writes on issues of race and ethnicity, education and public policy, and civil rights and social justice. In the summer of 2007 Coates received the Joseph Himes Career Award in Scholarship and Activism from the Association of Black Sociologists. He is currently finalizing an edited volume on *Covert Racism* for Oxford University Press.

Jack Donnelly has written several books in the area of human rights, including *The Concept of Human Rights, Universal Human Rights in Theory and Practice, International Human Rights,* and more than fifty articles and book chapters, which have been translated into nine languages. He is best known for a series of articles on human rights and cultural relativism, which advance a strong argument for a relatively universalistic approach to implementing internationally recognized human rights. He has also written on the theory of human rights, the development and functioning of international human rights regimes, human rights and development, group rights, humanitarian intervention, and democracy and human rights.

Mark Frezzo is assistant professor of sociology and associate director of peace studies (undergraduate program) at Florida Atlantic University. He publishes and teaches in the areas of social movements, political economy, development sociology, and the sociology of human rights. He is particularly interested in the role of post-Fordism and neoliberalism in provoking both collaboration and competition among movements, NGOs, and UN agencies in the quest for economic, social, and cultural rights. He is a member of Sociologists Without Borders.

Tanya Golash-Boza (PhD, University of North Carolina–Chapel Hill, 2005) is assistant professor of sociology and American studies at the University of Kansas. She has conducted ethnographic research in Peru on national discourses of blackness, racial identity, collective memory, and social whitening among Peruvians of African descent. She is currently working on a book-length manuscript, tentatively titled "Yo Soy Negro: Locating Afro-Peruvians in Local and Global Discourses of Blackness," based on that research. She has also published work on the racialization of Latinos and Latinas, bilingualism, and the dehumanization of immigrants in the United States.

Brian K. Gran teaches at Case Western Reserve University and is a research affiliate of the Joint Center for Poverty Research of Northwestern University and the University of Chicago. He earned a law degree from Indiana University (Bloomington) and a doctorate in sociology from Northwestern University. Gran was a Robert Wood Johnson Foundation scholar in health policy research at Yale University. His interests include comparative social policy, political sociology, sociology of law, and methodology. Gran's most recent work appears in the *Sociological Quarterly, Social Science Quarterly, Journal of Aging Studies, Buffalo Public Interest Law Journal,* and *International Journal of Health Services.* Gran's current research focuses on comparative social policy as it is formed in the intersection of the public and private sectors.

John Hagan is John D. MacArthur Professor of Sociology and Law at Northwestern University and a senior research fellow at the American Bar Foundation. His most recent books are *Justice in the Balkans: Prosecuting War Crimes in The Hague Tribunal* (2003) and *Northern Passage: American Vietnam War Resisters in Canada* (2001), which received the 2004 Albert J. Reiss Award from the Crime, Law and Deviance Section of the American Sociological Association. His most recent paper is with Alberto Palloni on "Death in Darfur" in *Science,* September 2006.

Angela Hattery holds the Zachary Smith Reynolds Associate Professorship in Sociology and Women's & Gender Studies at Wake Forest University. Her research focuses on race, class, gender, stratification, and violence. Along with Earl Smith she is the author of *African American Families* (2007) and *Race, Human Rights and Inequality* (2008). Her first book was *Women, Work and Family: Balancing and Weaving* (2001).

Núria Homedes is a physician and holds a doctoral degree in public health. She is an associate professor at the School of Public Health, University of Texas–Houston, and is responsible for the Global Health Program. Her areas of expertise include comparative health systems and pharmaceutical policies, and she has researched and published on Latin American health reforms and on U.S.-Mexico border health problems. She is coeditor of *Boletín Fármacos,* an electronic journal to promote the appropriate use of pharmaceuticals among Spanish-speaking populations.

Keri E. Iyall Smith is assistant professor of sociology at Stonehill College in Easton, Massachusetts. She is the author of *The State and Indigenous Movements* (2007) and is coeditor with Judith R. Blau of *Public Sociologies Reader* (2006). She has published articles on hybridity and world society, human rights, and teaching sociology. She teaches courses on globalization, indigenous peoples, and sociological theory.

Marina Karides is associate professor of sociology at Florida Atlantic University. She has published multiple works on autonomous employment strategies, gender inequalities, and economic development ideologies. She is one of eleven coauthors of *Global Democracies and the World Social Forums* (2007), and has coedited a book on the World Social Forum and the U.S. Social Forum with Judith Blau (2008). She serves as the representative of Sociologists Without Borders on the National Planning Committee of the USSF. Marina Karides mkarides@fau.edu.

Gerald F. Lackey is a PhD candidate in sociology and an NIMH predoctoral fellow at the University of North Carolina–Chapel Hill. His research involves political coalition building among African Americans and Latinos, mental health trends and social network changes among Hispanic immigrants, and the contextual factors influencing the formation of political trust. His research has involved both quantitative and qualitative studies. He has reviewed papers for *Social Forces, The Journal of Politics,* and *Demography.*

Jean M. Lynch, PhD, is a professor in the Department of Sociology and Gerontology and an affiliate in Women's Studies at Miami University in Oxford, Ohio. For the past twenty years, she has published extensively on lesbian/gay issues, with her most recent work centering on the lesbian/gay stepfamily. Her newest interest is in disability issues, focusing on the identity formation of persons with disabilities and on the development of ally behaviors. She teaches honors courses in disability issues in which students are encouraged to translate acquired classroom content into practical activism. She is currently working on a paper investigating images of disability in popular films and a paper demonstrating some of the issues and challenges involved in teaching courses on disability issues.

Andrew W. Martin is an assistant professor of sociology at Ohio State University. His primary research interests focus on the organizational dynamics of social protest. He is currently analyzing how American labor unions have recently begun to employ social movement–style tactics to overcome fifty years of membership decline and organize new workers. Additionally, he is interested in U.S. strike activity, particularly how this form of collective action has changed over time. He is also currently involved in a project that analyzes the growing number of— disturbances that have occurred on college and university campuses over the past twenty years.

Cecilia Menjívar is associate professor of sociology in the School of Social and Family Dynamics at Arizona State. Her research focuses on the social aspects of migration—social networks, gender relations, family dynamics, and religious communities—and on contexts of violence in women's lives. She has conducted qualitative field research in several U.S. cities and in Guatemala. Her publications include *Fragmented Ties: Salvadoran Immigrant Networks in America* (2000); *Through the Eyes of Women: Gender, Social Networks, Family and Structural Change in Latin America and the Caribbean* (edited) (2003); and *When States Kill: Latin America, the U.S. and Technologies of Terror,* coedited with Nestor Rodriguez (2005).

Alberto Moncada is vice president of UNESCO's Valencia Center and president of Sociólogos sin Fronteras—Internacional. Moncada has a PhD in public law from Madrid University, and studies in sociology and education from London University. He has taught at several universities: Madrid, Stanford, Florida International, Lima, and Alcalá, and was the first rector of the University of Piura, Peru. Besides his collaborative books with Judith Blau on human rights, Moncada is the author of articles in academic and general journals and thirty books, the most recent of which is *Para Entender la Globalización* (2006). Moncada is regularly consulted by Spanish media.

Dave Overfelt is a doctoral student at the University of Missouri–Columbia. Most of his work focuses on space and place. In this, he is interested in the ways that we can reconstruct spaces of injustice to create spaces of justice. As a radical public sociologist, he focuses his work on the everyday lived spaces that need the greatest change sociology can contribute. In pushing to apply sociology to real life, Dave's work challenges sociologists to be careful with their own practices and to give as much to the community as possible.

Douglas Parker (BA, English-language arts, San Francisco State University; MA, PhD, sociology, University of California–Berkeley) is a professor of sociology at California State University–Long Beach. Previously he taught at Queen's University in Kingston, Ontario, and Colorado College in Colorado Springs, and was employed in the epidemiology division of the National Institute on Alcohol Abuse and Alcoholism, where he was the principal investigator for a study of occupational conditions, drinking patterns, and psychological functioning among 1,367 full-time employed men and women in metropolitan Detroit. He has published papers in sociological, public health, and substance abuse journals and chapters in books and research monographs.

Tola Olu Pearce obtained her PhD in sociology from Brown University, Providence. She is a professor at the University of Missouri–Columbia, with a joint appointment in sociology and women's and gender studies. Her research interests include Africa, women and health, globalization and development issues, and social inequalities. Publications include "Globalization and the Cycle of Violence in Africa" (forthcoming), "Contextual Impact of Development and Globalization on African Women" (2005), "Human Rights and Sociology: Some Observations from Africa" (2001), "Death and Maternity in Nigeria" (2000), and "Gender and Governance in Africa: A Conceptual Framework for Research, Policy, and Monitoring" (2000).

Frances Fox Piven is distinguished professor of sociology and political science at the Graduate Center of the City University of New York, and the immediate past president of the American Sociological Association. She is the author or coauthor of many books, including *Regulating the Poor, Poor People's Movements, Why Americans Still Don't Vote,* and most recently *Challenging Authority: How Ordinary People Change America.*

Vincent J. Roscigno is a professor of sociology at Ohio State University. His main fields of interest are theory, stratification, education, work, social movements, and labor. Much of his current research is analyzing race, sex, and age discrimination in employment, as well as workplace incivility and supervisory bullying and the ways they are enacted in contemporary American employment settings. He also coedits the *American Sociological Review* with Randy Hodson.

Rubén G. Rumbaut is professor of sociology at the University of California–Irvine. He is the founding chair of the Section on International Migration of the American Sociological Association and an elected member of the ASA's Council, the Sociological Research Association, and the Committee on Population of the National Academy of Sciences. Among other books, he is the coauthor (with Alejandro Portes) of *Immigrant America: A Portrait* and *Legacies: The Story of the Immigrant Second Generation.* A native of Havana, Cuba, he received his PhD from Brandeis University.

Wenona Rymond-Richmond is assistant professor at the University of Massachusetts–Amherst. Her areas of interest include criminology, race/ethnicity, human rights, urban sociology, qualitative methods, and law. For her dissertation, she conducted qualitative research in a public housing development undergoing transformation to better understand how geographic space matters for individuals in violent neighborhoods. Publications include "Transforming Communities: Formal and Informal Mechanisms of Social Control" in *The Many Colors of Crime* (editors Peterson, Krivo, and Hagan) and "The Criminology of Genocide: The Death and Rape of Darfur" (2005) in *Criminology.*

Jenniffer M. Santos-Hernández is a doctoral student in the Department of Sociology and Criminal Justice and a lead graduate research assistant for the Disaster Research Center at the University of Delaware. Her interests include demography, development, risk communication, disasters, geographic information systems (GIS), social change, collective behavior, and environmental inequality.

Earl Smith holds the Rubin Distinguished Professorship in American Ethnic Studies at Wake Forest University. He is also professor of sociology. Smith specializes in the areas of urban sociology, and sociology of sport and social stratification. His most recent books are *Race, Sport and the American Dream* (2007), and he is coauthor with Dr. Angela J. Hattery of *African American Families* (2007).

Bryan S. Turner is currently professor of sociology in the Asia Research Institute, National University of Singapore. He is the research leader of the cluster on religion and globalization, and he is a research associate of GEMAS (Centre National de la Recherche Scientifique, Paris). Currently writing a three-volume study of the sociology of religion for Cambridge University Press, he edited the *Cambridge Dictionary of Sociology* (2006) and published *Vulnerability and Human Rights* (2006) with Pennsylvania State University Press. With Patrick Baert he edited *Pragmatism in European Social Theory* (2007). His *Rights and Virtues* will be published with Bardwell Press. Turner was the founding editor of *Citizenship Studies.*

Antonio Ugalde is professor emeritus, Department of Sociology, University of Texas–Austin. His research interests include international health policies, the pharmaceutical industry, and access to medication among low-income groups. Currently he is studying the purchase of medicines in Mexico by U.S. border residents. He is coeditor of *Boletín Fármacos,* an electronic journal to promote the appropriate use of pharmaceuticals among Spanish-speaking populations.

Catherine Zimmer is the senior research consultant at the Odum Institute and is adjunct professor of sociology at the University of North Carolina–Chapel Hill. Her main fields of interest are work and workplaces, corporations, inequality, and quantitative sociology. For much of her recent research, she has served as the quantitative methodologist while learning a great deal about a variety of substantive areas. Catherine is currently the treasurer of Sociologists Without Borders.